THE MIDDLE EAST IN THE

Also by Haifaa A. Jawad

EURO-ARAB RELATIONS: A Study in Collective Diplomacy

The Middle East in the New World Order

Second Edition

Edited by
Haifaa A. Jawad
*Senior Lecturer in Middle East
and Islamic Studies
Westhill College, Birmingham*

First edition 1994
Second edition 1997

Published by
MACMILLAN PRESS LTD
Houndmills, Basingstoke, Hampshire RG21 6XS
and London
Companies and representatives
throughout the world

ISBN 0-333-67747-1 hardcover
ISBN 0-333-66993-2 paperback

A catalogue record for this book is available
from the British Library.

10   9   8   7   6   5   4   3   2   1
05   04   03   02   01   00   99   98   97   96

Printed and bound in Great Britain by
Antony Rowe Ltd, Chippenham, Wiltshire

Contents

Preface and Acknowledgements

This volume is the outcome of a sustained collaborative effort over several years, beginning with a conference at New England College, Arundel, in 1992, and subsequent additional work by the authors represented in the book. Following the publication of the first edition, developments in the Middle East continued to stimulate discussion and reinterpretation among the contributors. The Arab–Israeli peace process unfolded with all its attendant pitfalls and setbacks; the regional situation in the Gulf festered; socio-political tensions in Bahrain and Saudi Arabia became more prominent; and the democratizing experiment in Yemen as well as unification itself came under tremendous strain.

For this edition many of the chapters were substantially rewritten and expanded; in some ways, therefore, this is a new book. It retains, however, its nature as a coherent and up-to-date overview of the key contemporary trends and issues in the Middle East, providing both information and authoritative analysis.

I would like to thank again my former colleagues at New England College – in particular Dr Paul Latawski, Dr Tamar March, Dudley Woodall and Fran Hewitt. Warm thanks also go to the contributors of this book, for their continued part in the project, and the thoroughness with which they addressed the task of producing this new edition.

HAIFAA A. JAWAD

Notes on the Contributors

Heather Deegan is Lecturer in Comparative Politics at Middlesex University. She has published *The Middle East and Problems of Democracy* (1993).

Anoushiravan Ehteshami is Reader in Middle East Politics at the University of Durham. His publications include *Nuclearisation of the Middle East* (1989); *Iran and the International Community* (co-editor) (1991); *(with G. Nonneman) War and Peace in the Gulf: Domestic Politics and Regional Relations into the 1990s* (1991); *After Khomeini: the Second Iranian Revolution*; and numerous articles on Gulf security and strategic affairs in the Middle East.

Raymond A. Hinnesbusch is Professor of Political Science at the College of St Catherine in St Paul, Minnesota. He is the author of numerous articles on Syria and of a book on Egyptian politics under Sadat (1985); he is the co-author, with Alistair Drysdale, of *Syria and the Middle East Peace Process* (1992).

Haifaa A. Jawad is Senior Lecturer in Middle East and Islamic Studies at Westhill College, and has taught Middle East politics at Al-Mustansriey University, Exeter University and New England College. Her publications include *The Euro-Arab Dialogue* (in Arabic, 1980) and *Euro-Arab Relations: A Study in Collective Diplomacy* (1992), as well as numbers of articles on Middle East and Islamic affairs.

George Joffé is Deputy Director at the Geopolitics and International Boundaries Research Centre, School of Oriental and African Studies, University of London; research fellow at the University of Exeter; teaching fellow at the University of Southampton; and consultant editor for the Economist Intelligence Unit. In addition to a large number of articles on the Middle East, and on the Gulf and North Africa in particular, his published works include *North Africa: Nation, State and Region* (1993); *The Gulf War: A Survey of Political and Economic Consequences* (with K. McLachlan) (1984) and *The Gulf War: Building on the Stalemate* (1988).

Emma C. Murphy is Lecturer in Middle East politics at the Centre for Middle Eastern and Islamic Studies at the University of Durham. She has specialized in Palestinian/Israeli political economy and in the phenomenon of economic liberalization in the Middle East. Among her publications is *Political and Economic Liberalisation in the Middle East* (co-editor with Tim Niblock), (1993).

Tim Niblock is Professor of Middle East Studies, and Director of the Centre for Middle Eastern and Islamic Studies at the University of Durham. His publications include *Social and Economic Development in the Arab Gulf* (editor) (1980); *State, Society and Economy in Saudi Arabia* (1982); *Iraq: the Contemporary State* (editor), (1982); *Class and Power in Sudan* (1987); and *Political and Economic Liberalization in the Middle East* (co-editor, with Emma C. Murphy) (1993).

Gerd Nonneman is Lecturer in International Relations at Lancaster University, England, and has taught Middle East politics at the Universities of Manchester and Exeter and the International University of Japan. His publications include *Iraq, the Gulf States and the War, 1980–86 and Beyond* (1986); *Development, Administration and Aid in the Middle East* (1988); *War and Peace in the Gulf: Domestic Politics and Regional Relations into the 1990s* (with A. Ehteshami) (1991); and *The Middle East and Europe: The Search for Stability and Integration* (editor, 1993).

Rodney Wilson is Reader in Economics at Durham University, with particular expertise on the economics of the Middle East. He has written widely on issues of investment and trade in the Middle East, as well as on Islamic banking. Among his publications are *Banking in the Arab Gulf* (with J. R. Presley) (1991); *Politics and Economics in Jordan* (1991) and *Islamic Financial Markets* (co-editor) (1990).

1 A Framework for Renewal in the Middle East?*

Tim Niblock

THE DIMENSIONS OF CHANGE

This book is intended to provide insight into the overall situation in the Middle East today. The particular need for such analysis arises from two major developments which occurred at the turn of the 1990s, and which have changed some of the parameters within which the politics of the region have moved. The first of these developments was external to the region itself: the transformation in the global system which occurred with the break-up of the Soviet Union. Middle Eastern states now found themselves in a world where the superpower which was most overtly supportive of Arab regional ambitions (albeit suspected by many Arab governments of harbouring subversive intentions) had effectively disappeared. The transformation in the global system has forced regional states to review and restructure their relationship to the outside world – responding to a new balance of strategic power, taking cognizance of a range of new international actors (especially the new Caucasian and Central Asian republics), finding themselves engulfed by new sources of instability, and forging new patterns of alliance and cooperation.

The second development was internal to the region, but came to have strong international repercussions: the Gulf crisis of 1990–1. The character of the issues raised by the crisis, the intensity of the feelings provoked, and the importance of the interests which were at stake led Middle Eastern states into lines of action which would have been barely conceivable before Iraqi troops moved into Kuwait. The policies pursued by external states in their relations with Middle Eastern states underwent a similarly radical change. Syria and Iran moved quickly from being international pariahs to valued partners in the Western-orchestrated coalition; Saudi Arabia played host to the largest

1

foreign armed force to have been present on Arab soil since the Second World War; and Israel was restrained by the United States from retaliating against Iraqi missile attacks.

The short-term significance of these two developments for the policies pursued by Middle Eastern governments is clear. The concern of this introductory chapter, however, is to assess whether they are likely to give rise to a longer-term re-structuring of Middle Eastern politics.

To set the scene for this assessment, it is worth recalling the predictions of fundamental and far-reaching change which were made while the Gulf crisis was unfolding. This writer, for example, committed himself rashly to the statement that 'the politics of the region will never be the same again'.[1] Some of the perspectives which observers put forward envisaged change of a negative character: the bitter divisions spawned by the war would destroy once and for all the hopes for Arab unity; the countries of the region would lose any leverage in international relations, becoming openly and explicitly dependent on external powers (especially the United States) militarily and economically; and hopes for the resolution of the Palestine problem would be frustrated by the sharpened dichotomy between Israeli strength (buttressed by support from the only remaining superpower) and Arab weakness.

Some of the perspectives were of a more positive nature, and often directly contradicted the assertions put forward on the negative side. It was argued that the severity of the crisis would deliver a shock to the politics of the area, leading the peoples of the region to seek and to achieve substantive political and policy changes. The proven dangers stemming from dictatorial governments (both as regards the treatment of domestic populations and as regards external aggression) would encourage local populations to press for democratization; the ironies of the Western powers raising the slogan of opposition to dictatorship in confronting Saddam Husain, yet maintaining in power regimes which themselves lacked democratic pretensions, would ensure that regional governments conceded to such pressures; the renewed international awareness of how the Palestine problem encumbered Arab attitudes towards any Western involvement in the area, would impel outside powers to approach the resolution of the Palestine problem with a new resolve (which, indeed, was specifically promised by a number of Western politicians during the crisis);

and the extent of the damage caused by inter-Arab conflict would lead to more substantial frameworks of cooperation and coordination being created.

Looking back on these issues five years after the Gulf War, it is clear that while changes have occurred, predictions of fundamental change have been realized only partially. One is struck by the extent to which the structure of Middle Eastern politics has retained much the same character as it had before Iraqi troops moved into Kuwait. This is particularly apparent at the level of domestic politics. There have been no major regime changes. Despite some institutional innovations, regimes have continued to balance the various forces which confront them in much the same way as before. Nor have there even been many significant changes in political leadership. In the Arab world, the only two political leaders to fall from power between August 1990 and the time of writing were Algeria's Chadli ben Jedid and Qatar's Shaikh Khalifa al-Thani. In neither case did the demise of the leader have any direct connection with developments outside the state. Even the regimes and political leaderships of Iraq and Kuwait have so far survived with little change.

At the regional and international levels, also, there has been a measure of continuity. There has been no substantial move towards strengthening the cooperation and coordination between Arab countries, but Arab governments still give attention to the pan-Arab dimension in their external policies. The pattern of regional alliances has been characterized by the same pliability as it had before. The possibility that the coalition of Arab states which supported the military action against Iraq might form a continuing and perhaps dominant alliance in the region soon vanished – the idea outlived the war by little more than two months. The leverage which Arab states can exert at the international level, never very substantial in recent years, has not been substantially lessened. Such leverage as there is, moreover, often stems from the weakness of regimes: Western powers are reluctant to exert their influence too strongly in case they bring about the demise of regimes (i.e. lead to an Islamic fundamentalist backlash; open the way for Iran to strengthen its influence; etc.).

Nevertheless, some significant changes in the structure of Middle Eastern politics did occur. Two such changes are worthy of particular emphasis. The first has occurred openly and in the

light of considerable publicity: the movement towards an Arab–
Israeli peace settlement. The second is perhaps masked by the
continuity of regimes and political leaderships: there is a growing
restiveness in the domestic politics of the states of the region,
characterized by the growth of political opposition and the
attempts by regimes to find new bases on which they can lay
claim to political legitimacy.

To understand the significance of such changes in the dynamics
of Middle Eastern politics as have occurred, some analysis is
needed of the nature of these changes and the factors which have
shaped them. To what extent are they the product of the
transformation of the global system, the effects of the Gulf crisis,
or the outcome of quite different factors?

ARAB–ISRAELI RELATIONS: SETTLEMENT AND BEYOND

As the Arab–Israeli conflict has dominated the politics of the
Middle East for the whole period since the end of the Second
World War, a peaceful settlement would be of immense importance to the region's political dynamics. Whether the Gaza–Jericho plan agreed in September 1993, and the agreement on
further Israeli withdrawal concluded in September 1995, constitute the basis on which the conflict can be brought to an end
is not certain.

What is clear, however, is that the parameters within which
Arab–Israeli relations have been shaped and developed have
begun to change. The key elements in this are an Israeli
government which recognizes the opportunity to limit the costs
(material and moral) imposed by Palestinian discontent and to
find an accepted place for Israel within the region (and which
believes that it can attain this without weakening Israel's security
or abandoning traditionally held Israeli interests); a Palestinian
leadership which considers that time may not be on its side, and
that an agreement which establishes a measure of autonomy on
the West Bank and Gaza (however far this may fall short of full
self-government) may be better than none; the determination of
Hafez al-Assad to secure the return of the Golan Heights to Syria
before he leaves the scene (and al-Assad's recognition that
Syria has no means of attaining this objective through the use of

force); and the preparedness of external powers to take an active role in bringing about a settlement.

These 'changed parameters' are not incidental. They reflect, at least in part, changes in global international relations. The disintegration of the Soviet Union deprived Syria of the super-power ally which could have enabled it to pose a military challenge to Israel; gave Israel more leeway to experiment with policies it might have deemed too risky before; narrowed the range of strategies open to the PLO; created new opportunities for Israel to benefit from cooperation with states in the wider region (e.g. the new states of Transcaucasia and Central Asia), provided it could purvey a less discriminatory and oppressive image; and left the United States free to pursue its own preferred strategy on Arab–Israeli matters, uninhibited by fears that a superpower rival would exploit any initiative by undermining United States influence.

The Gulf War brought in a dynamic of its own, but equally crucially it helped to highlight the changes wrought by a trans-formed global order. It revealed the dilemmas inherent in Syria's new international position, the advantages which Israel might draw from finding an accepted place within the region, the vulnerability of the PLO, and the ability of the United States to shape events in the area.

The changes at the global level affected the domestic politics of regional states, *inter alia* contributing to the defeat of Shamir's Likud party in the 1992 Israeli elections. The changing regional and international environments gave the Labour Party's pro-gramme more coherence as a strategy for the country's future, and the emergence of the Labour government in turn streng-thened the potential for an Arab–Israeli initiative.

Changes in the international order thus created opportunities for Israel. Without the continued resistance on the West Bank and in Gaza, however, Israeli governments might not have sought to grasp the opportunities. The damage the Palestinian uprising inflicted on Israel's image in the world, and on Israel's image of itself, was of crucial importance.

To attach significance to the opening up of the Arab–Israeli question is not intended to suggest that the issue has been resolved. The likelihood is that Arab–Israeli contacts will, at some levels, remain fraught. Settlement agreements between Israel, the PLO and neighbouring Arab states will not necessarily enable

Israel to integrate itself fully into the region. Substantial sectors of Arab public opinion may reject the agreements – especially if it is perceived that the Palestinians retain justified grievances.

With or without a lasting settlement, however, the relationship between Israel and the Arab states in the 1990s seems likely to be rather more fluid – less constricted by rigid divisions and absolute prohibitions – than in the past. This will affect the foreign policies of all states in the Middle East, with Israel becoming a more overt and active factor in the shifting patchwork of alliances, cooperation and confrontation which has characterized intra-regional relations.

The system may be even less stable than before, given that the range within which foreign policies can move will be greater (and less circumscribed by accepted principles). It may, however, be less prone to actual conflict: the rigidity of the lines of confrontation in earlier years provided a powerful dynamic towards war.

GROWING RESTIVENESS IN DOMESTIC POLITICS: ISLAMIST OPPOSITION

The second important change in regional politics since the late 1980s, the growing restiveness in domestic politics, has manifested itself both in the strengthening of Islamist opposition movements and in the attempts by governments to find new bases of legitimacy. An assessment of the likely stability of the Middle Eastern region in the 1990s of course depends on where one considers that these developments may lead.

The strengthening of Islamist movements in the area could be seen as simply the continuation of a process which has been under way ever since the late 1970s. Yet the period since the end of the 1980s has witnessed the emergence, or the growth in strength, of some particularly militant Islamist organisations – sometimes in countries which had previously been little touched by the phenomenon. Four very different cases will be used here to provide evidence for this contention: Saudi Arabia, Algeria, Palestine and Egypt. It is precisely the diversity of the factors which have shaped the four cases which makes clear the importance of the overall development.

First, Saudi Arabia. The Wahhabi creed espoused by the Al Sa'ud has itself often been seen as a brand of 'Islamic fundamentalism', and perhaps for this reason militant oppositional varieties of Islamism have previously attracted little support in the kingdom. Since the end of the 1980s, however, it has become clear that Islamist militancy is beginning to pose a threat to the Saudi regime. The threat is of particular significance in so far as its inspiration has come primarily from clerics living in what is usually regarded as the heartland of the Al Sa'ud: the Qasim region. An article in *The Guardian* described the situation as follows:

> Like Khomeini and his mullahs who descended out of nowhere to be met by millions of supporters, the preachers of Saudi Arabia are unknown in the West, but their names are familiar to all Saudis. They include young radicals like Sheikh Salman al-Odeh, who is just in his thirties, Awad al-Garni, who comes from the poor southern province of Asir, and Safar Hawali, a young preacher in Mecca. Their message is relayed on audio cassettes sold in every town in Saudi Arabia.[2]

The oppositional ideology is articulated by the younger Islamic preachers and clergy, draws its strength from the large numbers of students who graduate from the Islamic universities every year, and is antipathetic to the older religious leaders, who are deemed as having 'sold out' to the Al Sa'ud. Its social base lies in the marginalized elements of Saudi society. The Islamic universities attract students from poorer backgrounds, providing substantial financial support for students with limited means. The academic records of entrants to the Islamic universities are often weak, and the courses provided are deficient in the technical training which would enable graduates to gain employment. A pool of unemployable and strongly religiously motivated graduates has thus been brought into being. The message which is imparted by the oppositional Islamist movement is that the Al Sa'ud have become corrupt, that the links with the United States are unacceptable, and that the regime has departed from the tenets of Islam.

Increasingly the militants are employing direct action to expose what they see as 'corrupt elements': raiding houses where they suspect that people have been drinking alcohol, publicly denouncing members of the government and royal family who they suspect of corruption, circulating cassettes criticizing the government and most recently launching a campaign of terror by planting a bomb in the capital city of Riyadh. The Gulf crisis, bringing with it a very public United States military presence in Saudi Arabia and emphasizing the alignment of the two countries' regional policies, may have provided a new twist to the Islamists' discontent. The roots of the discontent, however, lie deeper – in the character of the country's recent social, economic and educational development.

The confrontation between the radical Islamist movement and the state in Algeria has attracted rather more attention than have developments in Saudi Arabia. The years since 1990 have seen the transformation of the Front Islamique de Salut (FIS) from a political party, competing in elections, to an underground organization seeking the violent overthrow of the regime. The scale of the threat which the FIS has posed to the regime is indicated by European and American assessments, reported in November 1992, that the regime might be swept away within eighteen months;[3] the deployment in April 1993 of some 15 000 troops in Algiers to try to bring the insurgency under control;[4] Algerian government estimates that 6388 civilians were killed by militants during 1994;[5] Amnesty International's estimate in August 1995 that a total of some 40 000 people had lost their lives since the conflict began in 1992;[6] and by the upsurge of violence leading up to the presidential elections of November 1995.[7] Diplomats in Algiers have estimated that there are some 10 000 to 15 000 'armed militants' in the country.[8] It is worth stressing that the transformation in the FIS's role was brought about primarily by changes within the Algerian state: the resignation of Chadli ben Jedid from the presidency and the cancellation of the parliamentary elections by the military had closed the electoral route to power.

The increasing following which the Islamist HAMAS movement has attracted in the Occupied Territories perhaps fits rather uneasily within the category of 'growing restiveness in domestic politics'. The Palestinian *Intifada* (an extreme expression of 'restiveness'), after all, first began in 1987; the high morale which powered it in the early years has ebbed. Yet the shift of support away from the PLO-affiliated groups to HAMAS in the early 1990s was significant; it weakened and indeed threatened to undermine what had been a strong and established political structure in the region.

No doubt the Gulf crisis was partially responsible for the situation in which the PLO found itself. Yasser Arafat's embrace of Saddam, interpreted however wrongly as expressing support, cut off much of the Gulf funding which underlay the organization's activities. The loss of international credibility gave encouragement and sometimes external backing to those who were intent on challenging the PLO. Yet the mainsprings of the growing support for HAMAS (whose members were themselves largely pro-Iraqi during the Gulf crisis) lay in the political and economic situation on the West Bank and Gaza. The PLO needed to present itself as a respectable partner for the negotiation of a peaceful settlement. The image and the approach required by this role were increasingly at variance with the anger and frustration felt at the popular level.

HAMAS's preparedness to use arms to prosecute the struggle against Israeli occupation, moreover, did seem to achieve results. The Israeli government's move towards negotiations, as pointed out above, was in part impelled by the continued resistance on the West Bank and Gaza. In the final stages before the Gaza–Jericho plan was accepted, a significant element in this resistance was the HAMAS-orchestrated random and organized attacks carried out against Israeli soldiers and citizens. Indeed, the very willingness of the government of Israel to treat the PLO in a more conciliatory manner appears to have been shaped by the belief that the Islamists posed a more violent and therefore more serious challenge. If the PLO is not successful in developing the Gaza–Jericho agreement in a manner which most Palestinians deem favourable, HAMAS stands to gain further support.

While Islamist oppositional activity in Egypt has on occasions in the more distant past employed violent means (as with the assassination of Sadat in 1981), it is only since 1991 that an organized campaign of violence has been undertaken. The scale of the confrontation between the government and the Islamists was indicated by the arrest in late May of 822 members of a group which called itself the Vanguards of the New Holy Struggle; the group was alleged to have organized itself on a pyramid cell structure and to have recruited among students and workers. Its objectives were to overthrow the government and to establish a purist Islamic state.[9] The organization had not achieved mention previously, with attention having focused on the more widely known Jama' at and Jamiyat groupings. The scale of Islamist militancy in Egypt is considerably smaller than in Algeria, and there is evidence that the government is achieving some success in containing the phenomenon. Nevertheless, Egyptian government statistics (almost certainly an underestimate) indicate that, up to mid-1995, a total of 780 persons had died in the political violence which was initiated in 1991.[10] According to the Egyptian Human Rights Organization, 87 of these died in January 1995 in the vicinity of the town of Mallawi (25 policemen, 50 terrorists or 'suspects', and 12 civilians).[11] The attempted assassination of President Mubarak on a visit to Ethiopia in June 1995, apparently by the Jama'at group, emphasized that the Islamist problem was not resolved.[12]

The growth of this Islamist oppositional activity has clear economic roots, complemented by a cultural dimension. It is linked to the IMF-inspired removal of some of the safety nets which had previously safeguarded the standard of living of the poorest elements of the population.[13] It is fuelled by the perception that those close to the government are benefiting while the mass of the population suffers, and that this is the natural outcome of the élite's abandonment of Islamic values. The comment of a Cairo intellectual reported in a recent newspaper article illustrates how the behaviour of the governmental élite has sapped the confidence even of those who could be its allies against rising Islamism: 'We are confronted with an impossible choice between corruption and terrorism, between a rotten regime and the Islamic fanatics.'[14]

THE GROWING RESTIVENESS IN DOMESTIC POLITICS: ATTEMPTS BY REGIMES TO FIND NEW BASES OF LEGITIMACY

The second manifestation of political restiveness, the attempts by regimes to find new bases of legitimacy, has taken as many diverse forms as has the growth of Islamist oppositional activity.

Some regimes have sought to introduce a full parliamentary democracy, with all the major political forces in the country able to participate on a reasonably equal basis – and with the intention that the government formed would reflect the views of the majority in parliament. Three regimes have started out on this path: those of Jordan, Yemen and Algeria.

The Gulf crisis neither inspired the initiation of the undertaking nor determined its outcome in any of the three cases. The opening up of the political systems predated Iraq's entry into Kuwait. The process was set in train in Jordan and Algeria (in 1989 and 1990 respectively) by the economic difficulties which the two countries faced, and by the desire of the governments to broaden responsibility for the adoption of unpopular economic measures. The latter were required by international financial and banking institutions. In Yemen, the democratization followed from the union between North and South in 1989, which itself stemmed from the changing international role (and ultimately disintegration) of the Soviet Union. South Yemen had lost the material and diplomatic support which it needed to guarantee its survival as a viable independent state.

The democratization experiments in Jordan and Yemen have moved ahead despite the Gulf War. A freely contested general election was held in Yemen at the end of April 1993, although the democratic significance of this was severely undermined by the brief but intense civil war which broke out in the middle of 1994. In October 1992 the Jordanian government made it possible for political groupings to register formally as political parties – in preparation for the general election which was held in November 1993. The democratic trend in Algeria was brought to an end in January 1992, for reasons which related purely to Algerian domestic politics.

Elsewhere, there are regimes which have worked towards forms of 'managed democracy': where power remains firmly in the hands of a ruling group, but where a limited and contained electoral framework is maintained, with some restrictions on the political parties which can be formed (often the restrictions are on precisely those political organizations which may prove most popular). Tunisia, Egypt, Lebanon, Kuwait and Morocco all fit within this category.

In Tunisia, the parameters of the managed democracy, and the dimensions of the conflict which followed from this, were set in 1988 and 1989. The regime of Zain al-Abdin bin Ali needed to find a new base of legitimacy after the overthrow of Bourguiba. The tough austerity measures which the government was having to implement (as part of an IMF-sponsored package agreed in 1986) also required a political framework where responsibility was more widely shared than before.[15] The denial of a legitimate political role to the Islamist al-Nahdah party led the latter into direct confrontation with the government in late 1989 and early 1990. The edge was taken off the confrontation during the Gulf War, as both sides were focusing their attention elsewhere, but the pattern reasserted itself immediately thereafter.

Egypt and Morocco both maintained, and continued to develop, the limited and managed measures of liberalization which they had practised before the Gulf crisis. The measures drew much of their inspiration from the need to project a liberal image to the United States and the European Community, whose political and economic support they needed. Neither political system was greatly affected by the events in the Gulf. It is significant that an election for the Egyptian National Assembly was held in October 1990, two months after Iraqi troops had entered Kuwait, and that the Gulf crisis figured little in the electoral contest. The election was boycotted by two of the main political parties (the Wafd Party and the Labour–Islamic alliance), but this was for domestic political reasons.

Lebanon held its first election for some twenty years in August/September 1992. This stemmed from the conclusion of the Taif agreement in 1989, which did have a link with the changing international order. With the withering of Soviet power, the United States had become more willing to see the Lebanese conflict end on terms which left the former ally of the Soviet Union, Syria, in a strong position to influence events in Lebanon.

Only in the case of Kuwait did the re-emergence of an electoral arrangement come about specifically as a result of the Gulf crisis. Following the ejection of Iraqi troops from Kuwait, the 1962 constitution was reinstated and the intention announced to resurrect the Kuwaiti national assembly (which had been suspended indefinitely in 1986). Pressure from United States diplomats was important in ensuring that this intention was given effect. Elections were held, on a non-party basis, in October 1992. Of the 50 candidates elected, 32 were deemed to belong to various shades of the opposition.

A further group of states, all of them Gulf monarchies, have instituted – or have discussed the institution of – new governing arrangements which involve more formalized consultation. The most important case is that of Saudi Arabia. The political reforms announced by King Fahd on 1 March 1992 envisaged the formalization of the basic system of governance in the kingdom; a system of local government in the provinces; and the introduction of a national consultative council (the *majlis al-shura*). The consultative council was to be made up to 60 members to be chosen by the king and would perform many of the discussive and investigative activities undertaken by parliaments elsewhere. It would not, however, enact legislation. This development was clearly linked to the criticism of the Saudi system which was unleashed by the Gulf War (it was announced exactly one year after the end of the Gulf War). It is questionable, however, whether the development carries any long-term significance. As was correctly pointed out by King Fahd when he announced the reforms, they constitute a formalization of the existing system rather than a substantive political change.

IMPLICATIONS FOR THE FUTURE

The expectation that the Gulf War would lead to important political changes in the region was perhaps misguided from the outset. The termination of Iraq's occupation of Kuwait by Western-orchestrated military force, little more than seven months after it had first been imposed, left few opportunities for new political dynamics to impinge on the region's politics.

Yet there are significant changes occurring in the political landscape of the Middle East. At the level of intra-regional relations, these stem primarily from the transformation which has occurred in the global system. At the level of domestic politics, they stem from a growing popular awareness of the bankruptcy of some of the political and economic formulae on which regimes have based themselves.

The regimes of the area have in the past shown some skill in adapting to changed circumstances. By adapting policies and buying off or containing discontent they survived the impact of the Iranian revolution. The challenge which will confront them through the decade of the 1990s, and therefore the adaptation which will be necessary, may be more substantial. It could be that what comes out of this adaptation may be a 'framework for renewal'.

NOTES

*   This introduction has been developed from a chapter entitled 'Emerging Patterns of Conflict and Order in the Middle East', which the writer contributed to R. Müller-Syring and H. Fürtig (eds), *Ursachen gewaltförmiger Konflikte in der Golfregion* (Peter Lang, Frankfurt am Main, 1993). The writer wishes to thank Drs Müller-Syring and Fürtig for permission to reprint some of the material.

1   Tim Niblock, 'The Gulf Crisis (1990–91) and the Comprehension of Middle Eastern Politics', in T. and J. Ismael, *Politics and Government in the Middle East and North Africa* (Florida: Florida International University Press, 1991), p. ix.

2   *The Guardian*, 15 May 1993.

3   *The Guardian*, 24 November 1993.

4   *The Guardian*, 20 May 1993.

5   *The Guardian*, 7 March 1995.

6   *The Observer*, 22 October 1995.

7   *The Guardian*, 24 October 1995.

8   *The Guardian*, 20 May 1993.

9   *Al-Ahram*, 20 May 1993.

10 *The Guardian*, 8 August 1995.

11 *The Guardian*, 18 February 1995.

12 *The Guardian*, 5 July 1995.

13 Tim Niblock, 'International and Domestic Factors in the Economic Liberalisation Process in Arab Countries', in T. Niblock and E. Murphy (eds.), *Economic and Political Liberalisation in the Middle East* (London: British Academic Press, 1993), pp. 58–71.

14 *The Guardian*, 20 May 1993.

15 John Marks, 'Tunisia', in Niblock and Murphy, pp. 167–73.

2 Democratization in the Middle East
Heather Deegan

INTRODUCTION

In recent years attention has focused on moves towards demo-cratization in various regions of the world. The shift away from single-party, authoritarian state structures and the tentative steps towards multi-party politics and pluralistic forms of government have been carefully monitored. Yet there has been little discussion of democratization in the Middle East. In the study by Diamond *et al.* of twenty-six countries in Latin America, Africa and Asia, the states of the Middle East, Islamic and otherwise, were omitted, on the grounds that 'they generally lack much previous democratic experience, and most appear to have little prospect of a transition even to semi-democracy.'[1] Similarly, though from a different perspective, Giacomo Luciani writing in the late 1980s of the notion of a 'rentier state' also implied that democratization in the Middle East was unviable. The rentier state analysis rests on the hypothesis that external sources of income resulting from the export of oil, in other words, oil revenue, is in fact a form of rent. The state, in such a system, does not raise income through the more traditional route of domestic taxation and economic strategy (which are often seen to be associated with popular demands for political reform and legitimacy), but externally through the sale of oil. This situation leads to a paradox: while a number of Middle Eastern states are wealthy in terms of gross national product, which might present a prima facie case for political development, this wealth is not the result of industrialization and societal differentiation – factors once seen as necessary for political change – but simply the result of enormous oil revenues. In non-rentier states, governments have an interest in economic development and good governance in order to increase the chances of being able to raise revenue. Without such an interest, it is inevitable that 'rentier states will display little tendency to evolve towards democratic institutions.'[2]

In a sense, then, there has tended to exist a feeling that the Middle East is something of a 'lost cause', a view which largely rests on the assumption that 'tremendous barriers' exist to the establishment of 'fully functioning democratic political systems' in the region.[3] Divided ethnically, lacking strong political institutions, tethered to authoritarian structures of government, lacking in unity, political legitimacy and tolerance for opposition, exploited by the external factor of the cold war and, recently, in thrall to fundamentalist religion, the countries of the Middle East have been regarded as possessing characteristics inimical to any form of democratization.

In this chapter, that view is disputed, and attention is drawn to a number of points. First, the situation in the Middle East is changing, particularly after the 1991 Gulf War, and the implication of these changes for democracy should be discussed. Second, in this discussion the notion of democracy should not solely be confined to Western-style liberal democracy. Third (the previous point notwithstanding), some new developments within a number of Middle Eastern states – for example in terms of the reintroduction of elections, the removal of bans on political parties and more generally in the sphere of participation – may be viewed as steps paving the way for a fuller democratization in a liberal-democratic sense. Certainly, there has been considerable discussion of democracy in the Middle East recently, coming from previously perhaps unlikely quarters. President Assad of Syria announced at a ceremony in March 1992 marking his new seven-year term of office: 'Democracy does not mean political chaos. It means making available the best circumstances that enable the citizen to make a free choice.'[4] A few months earlier King Hussein of Jordan declared in favour of democratization and political pluralism, with due care and attention to be paid to freedom of expression and human rights.[5] The Lebanese prime minister proclaimed the government's commitment to 'parliamentary and municipal elections, held within a framework of freedom', and the Iraqi oppositionist group, the Supreme Assembly of the Islamic Revolution in Iraq (SAIRI), has reiterated its respect for 'freedom of opinion, the multi-party system and free elections'.[6] These developments in the political arena have begun to attract academic attention, for instance in the work of Hudson, Piscatori and Owen.[7]

A necessary caveat, in any inquiry into the phenomenon, is that the region must not be seen as politically homogeneous.

Important differences exist between the various states, such that a move towards democratization in one country may be symbolized by the removal of the ban on the formation of political parties, while in another it might be characterized by the establishment of a more equitable parliamentary system. The political systems of Kuwait and Lebanon, for instance, are very dissimilar. Nevertheless, the commonalities shared by virtue of their 'Arabness' (and all that may imply) are important factors in understanding political reform.

In discussing democracy in the Middle East, this chapter will address three issues of particular relevance. First, there is that of citizenship, and the implications which this concept and its embodiment have had in the Middle East, in a context characterized by high population mobility. Second, the impact of socio-economic change must be discussed; and finally, there is the role of Islam.

CITIZENSHIP

Over a decade ago the Dutch academic Herman van Gunsteren lamented the demise of the concept of citizenship, which he claimed had 'gone out of fashion among political thinkers'.[8] Today the concept is very much in intellectual fashion, and in any analysis of democratization processes within the Middle Eastern countries the role of citizenship is absolutely crucial. Indeed, in liberal democratic theory with its emphasis on the place of the individual's rights and responsibilities set within a legal framework, the citizen must assume a primary position.

Citizenship clearly constitutes the most basic conduit for integration into the state and defines a person's relationship with the political environment.[9] Van Gunsteren, however, sees the 'notions and practices of citizenship' to be 'variable and conflicting', containing ambiguities which truly reveal the 'conflicts and problems between a plurality of people who history has brought together in relations of interdependence and dominance'.[10] Citizenship, then, is an area of 'contestation and struggle' centred on the inclusion or exclusion of persons within a nation state. Historically, of course, there always existed certain qualifying conditions associated with citizenship, e.g. gender, residence, property/land ownership, etc.; indeed, this still remains the case.

Citizenship implies the bestowal of certain rights and duties upon the individual and as such the good citizen will acknowledge and abide by the conventions and expectations of his or her society. Accordingly, there must a procedure by which 'citizens exert control over government and make it aware of their demands, but correspondingly, there must also be a readiness to allow the government to enforce policies'.[11]

In other words, citizens are enfranchised and may participate in the political process, but equally are under a duty to accept being ruled; otherwise there might be a drift towards mass politics, characterized by unruly, large-scale activities of the citizenry outside the structure and rules instituted by society to govern political action. Mass politics is to be avoided at all costs, because it involves violence against opposition; a lack of respect for minorities; the rejection of peaceful solutions to conflicts; and the pursuit of short-term objectives. It results, therefore, in either anarchy or dictatorship.[12] The only way to counter this development is through the establishment of a pluralistic social structure which will enable the citizenry to form independent and limited pressure groups and facilitate the 'free and open competition for leadership, widespread participation in the selection of leaders and restraint in the application of pressures of leaders'.[13]

The role of citizenry, then, can be both stable and responsible given certain circumstances, but what is the situation in a region which witnesses a high degree of population mobility, for either political or economic reasons? The Arab states, particularly Lebanon, Syria, Jordan, Egypt and Kuwait, utilize two basic principles in their definition of citizenship: *jus sanguinis* and *jus soli*. The principle of *jus sanguinis* recognizes an individual's citizenship as determined by the citizenship of his/her parents. *Jus soli*, on the other hand, holds that citizenship is based on the individual's place of birth. These two principles constitute the framework of Arab citizenship laws.[14] Citizenship carries political rights which vary depending on which country is under examination.

Where there is a high degree of population mobility, or migration, naturalization processes become significant. Bahrain, Egypt, Iraq, Jordan, Kuwait, Syria and the United Arab Emirates all have naturalization laws which stipulate conditions such as the length of residency along with an individual's personal characteristics which must be fulfilled in order to become a naturalized citizen of a given state. In Kuwait, with a population estimated around 2.2 million on 1 August 1990, of which approximately 70 per cent was non-Kuwaiti, the question of citizenship and naturalization raises other important issues: the extent to which democratization can take place in a country where nationals represent only 30 per cent of the population.[15]

The residency requirement in Kuwait is between 10 and 30 years before an applicant can apply for naturalization – without any guarantee that it will be granted. The decision to impose very severe controls on naturalization procedures, together with the institution of restrictions on the rights of naturalized citizens, must be viewed against a background of spiralling immigration and the state's fairly recent acquisition of independence (1961).[16] A large heterogeneous and changing population was clearly at odds with the preservation of nation-state identity; political rights were therefore strictly controlled. While naturalized Kuwaitis are granted citizenship rights such as civil service employment, property ownership and access to welfare benefits in the form of education and retirement allowances, they are not permitted the 'right to vote for any representative body until twenty years after the acquisition of citizenship and are ineligible for nomination or appointment to a representative body or ministerial position'.[17] It is quite apparent that within a given set of procedures citizenship can be graduated and controlled; it is, in fact, the usual practice for countries to engage in this form of exercise. It is also clear, however, that in nations where most of the population falls into the non-citizen or semi-citizen categories, democratization is a problematic issue, because political participation will usually be confined to the minority comprised of full citizens.

The lessons from history suggest that only when the issue of citizenship is approached can the questions of participation and democratization be fully embraced. According to S. S. Russell, 'States differ in the extent to which naturalization has been used as a means to involve immigrants in the process of solidifying their own sense of identity as a state.'[18] The corollary of this statement is the assumption that nation-statehood demands a loyal citizenry enjoined with that particular state, and no other. The demands on the citizen are absolute. This concept is not just the subject of abstract discourse, as becomes obvious when it is applied to the position of the Palestinians and, more especially, their role within Jordan.

The displacement of the Palestinians during the 1948–49 Arab–Israeli War, Jordan's subsequent annexation of the West Bank, and the 1967 conflict during which Israel's seizure of the West Bank resulted in the exodus of an estimated 300 000 Palestinians, have all been important factors in Jordan's responses to naturalization and citizenship.[19] Following the first influx of Palestinians into Jordan and the annexation of 1950, Jordan extended full citizenship to Palestinians. In 1954 naturalization laws were passed in which a four-year residency requirement was established together with a declaration affirming that full citizenship rights would be extended to all naturalized persons. Palestinians represented around 60 per cent of Jordan's population, and for strategic reasons it seemed appropriate to adopt a more liberal naturalization procedure. However, the difficulties which Jordan faced centred on the issue of citizen loyalty; that is, where precisely did the affinities of former Palestinian, newly Jordanian citizens lie? With most of the members of the Palestine National Council (the executive body of the Palestine Liberation Organization) holding Jordanian citizenship, the spectre of 'double allegiances', and the suspicion that a significant proportion of the population were indifferent or, indeed, antipathetic to the 'host' country, were inevitable.[20]

The charge was made that Palestinians, irrespective of their citizenship in other countries, would always cling to their own political interest; in other words, their focus of attention would centre on the restitution of their own homeland. As such, they would suffer a conflict of loyalties in their citizenship and this would be reflected in their political behaviour. The contradiction of being a citizen of one country while identifying with another would have a deleterious effect and would result in instability, conflict and political regression in the 'host' state. In addition, the nature of the Palestinian quest for nation statehood has sometimes been used as a reason for denying Palestinian migrants citizenship with or without political rights. There also exists the fear that the granting of such rights would destabilize the precarious balance which often exists among the indigenous citizenry within a country, as for instance in Lebanon. The Palestinian situation displays some similarity to that of other groups of people within the Middle East – the Kurdish community comes to mind. However, doubt surrounds the extent to which the Kurds' demand for self-determination within an autonomous region of say, Iraq, actually implies the break-up of Iraq. In short, citizenship can contain and encompass a community's desire for regionalism, federalism or autonomous status within a state, but it cannot allow for a group's affiliation to another state, be the state actual or notional. In J. S. Mill's opinion, the permanence of representative institutions depended upon 'the readiness of the people to fight for them in case of their being endangered'.[21] If the citizenry of a country are not committed to the nation they may well undermine democratic development and retard any reforming process.

SOCIO-ECONOMIC CHANGE

As Table 2.1 indicates, Iran, Kuwait, Syria, Jordan and Lebanon made considerable advances in the spheres of educational and health improvements over the past fifteen to thirty years, and their economies have witnessed a shift from the agricultural sector into the service sector. In all countries, the breakdowns of labour figures for 1985–87 indicate a higher percentage employed within the service sector than in either agricultural or industrial sectors. In Iran the labour force of 11 million is more evenly divided between the three sectors. Literacy rates have improved in all countries between 1970 and 1990. According to

Social and Economic Data

Table 2.1   GNP, life expectancy and adult literacy

	GNP per capita (US$)		Life expectancy (years)			Adult literacy (% population)	
	1976	*1992*	*1960*	*1975*	*1990*	*1970*	*1990*
Israel	3 920	1 3230	69	72	76	88	95
Jordan	610	1 120	47	59	67	47	80
Lebanon	—	—	60	65	66	69	80
Syria	780	1 640	50	59	66	40	65
Bahrain	—	8 510	—	—	71	—	72
Iran	1 930	2 190	50	57	66	29	54
Iraq	1 390	—	48	59	65	34	60
Kuwait	15 480	14 610	60	68	73	54	73

data from the Iranian Republic's national census of population and housing, released in 1989, 65 per cent of urban women and 80 per cent of urban men were literate, although rural rates were

Table 2.2 Health statistics

% population with access to safe water 1988–90	Under-5 mortality (per 1000) 1960	1990	Daily calorie-supply (% of requirements) 1964	1988–90
Israel	—	40	14	10	118
Jordan	99	218	52	93	110
Lebanon	98	92	56	99	127
Syria	79	218	59	89	140
Bahrain	100	17	17	—	—
Iran	89	254	59	87	125
Iraq	93	222	86	89	128
Kuwait	—	128	19	—	130

Table 2.3 GDP, GNP and expenditure as percentage of GNP

	GDP ($bn) 1987	GNP ($bn) 1987	Expenditure as % GNP Health 1960	1986	Education 1960	1986	Military 1960	1986
Israel	35.0	29.8	1.0	2.1	8.0	7.3	2.9	19.2
Jordan	4.3	4.4	0.6	1.9	3.0	5.1	16.7	13.8
Syria	24.0	20.4	0.4	0.8	2.0	5.7	7.9	14.7
Iran	—	—	0.8	1.8	2.4	3.5	4.5	20.0
Iraq	—	—	1.0	0.8	5.8	3.7	8.7	32.0
Kuwait	17.9	27.3	—	2.9	—	4.6	—	5.8

Table 2.4 Debt service, annual inflation and urban population

	Debt service (% exports) 1987	Annual inflation (%) 1990–87	Urban population (%) 1991
Israel	25	159.0	92
Jordan	22	2.8	68
Lebanon	—	—	84
Syria	17	11.0	51
Iran	—	—	57
Iraq	—	—	71
Kuwait	—	4.6	96

Heather Deegan

Table 2.5 Breakdown of labour force (percentages)

	Agriculture		Industry		Services	
	1965	1989–91	1965	1989–91	1965	1989–91
Israel	12	3	35	24	53	73
Jordan	37	10	26	26	37	64
Lebanon	29	14	24	27	47	59
Syria	52	22	20	36	28	42
Iran	49	25	26	28	25	47
Iraq	50	13	20	8	30	79
Kuwait	2	—	34	—	64	—

Source for Tables 2.1–2.5: *Keesing's Contemporary Archives*, February 1991 and 1994.

lower at 60 per cent and 36 per cent for men and women respectively.[22]

The under-five mortality rate dropped significantly across the region between 1960 and 1990. Health and education expenditure did not reach the heights of military expenditure throughout the period, but in basic economic trends the figures suggest a modernizing tendency: a differentiated labour market, invariably reflected in a changing class structure and an increasingly literate population with access to education and health care.

However, it would be unwise to link democratization too closely with socio-economic determinants. In fact, several scholars have cautioned that the process of economic modernization may actually produce destabilizing consequences. As Diamond *et al.* maintain:

New interests are generated, new consciousness is kindled and new political and organizational capacities are acquired at the individual and group level. Demands multiply both for the right to participate and for tangible and symbolic benefits.[23]

If these are not met, institutions run the risk of breaking down, with society lapsing into chaos.

Many analysts have pointed to the rapid and uneven economic development witnessed in the Middle East as being responsible for the societal disorientation and disenchantment which underpinned the rise of an adherence to the ethics and values of Islam.[24] Education has been viewed ambivalently, either feared because it exposes people to alternative ideas, or supported on the grounds that it assists in socializing certain values supportive of the state. Islam has proved a powerful attraction for both the educated and the ill-educated, although a study conducted in Jordan in 1991 proposed the establishment of a stronger link between democratization and education. The *Education in the Arab World in the 21st Century* report looks forward to economic development and political participation taking place based on the premiss that education would become standardized to include the principal freedoms of speech and association.[25] King Hussein has announced that courses of democracy will be taught in educational and cultural institutions.

Interestingly, recent debate within a number of countries in the region has linked the issues of economic and political reform. In June 1991, Jordan lifted the ban on political parties and simultaneously emphasized the desire for economic reform and the adoption of policies which would provide 'an appropriate climate to activate the private sector'. The Amir of Kuwait spoke of the need to 'transfer some activities and services to the private sector' and President Assad commented on Syria operating 'within a framework of economic pluralism', which would secure the 'widest possible participation of citizens in the nation's economic development'. President Hirawi of Lebanon looked forward to an 'economy that encourages private initiative and a free market'.[26]

These statements suggest that economic development would take a more liberalized form. Economic reform, then, would seem to imply a diminishing role for the state and possibly for the present political leaderships. The corollary of such a move would be some form of political change or readjustment. It is quite conceivable that the generally acknowledged incompetence and inefficiency of the command economy has been recognized in the Middle East. The rentier state analysis of the 'allocative state' may become inadequate as state structures no longer control a monopoly of economic functions, and therefore need to accommodate different economic interests. As Rodney Wilson pointed out, 'State-owned and run industries were established at huge expense in Syria and Iraq and none of the ventures has achieved commercial viability.'[27]

To take the rentier state argument one step further, and analyse this sophisticated interpretation of the relationship between economic forces and political reform, one may consider the example of Kuwait. The image of the paternalistic ruler, dispensing welfare in a benevolent state and thus buying off demands for political liberalization, seemed an apt picture of Kuwait's political system. Some analysts have supported such a view. Michael Hudson wrote in the late 1970s that, apart from 'occasional stirrings of resentment at the family's monopoly of power, there has been no serious challenge'. The reason for this rested with the Amir's 'competence and custom'.[28] However, events in the early 1990s present a rather different view of political behaviour in Kuwait: the dissolution of the National Assembly and the Amir's rule by decree, the shift away from constitutional modes of conduct, the recourse to imprisonment for leading opposition figures, the secret petitions calling for a return to representative government, and the demonstrations in the streets raising pleas for greater democratisation and accountability all point to an increasingly uneasy domestic political environment, unpacified by welfare packages. Add to this the threat of regional tension and belligerency, and a picture emerges of a ruling family which is anything but secure in its traditional politics of charitable dispensation of oil wealth.[29] The new, if limited, elections following the 1990–91 Gulf war, and the modest shift towards political participation, are in recognition of this changed reality.

ISLAM

Islam is a major force within the spectrum of political advancement in the Middle East. In recent years a debate has developed over the role played by Islamic organizations, and the extent to which Islam is compatible with pluralist democracy. One strand of Islamic thought associates democracy with secularism, with the consequence that democracy becomes a deliberate violation of God's law and 'usurps God's role'. Democracy is seen as a foolish, absurd notion in that there can only be one relationship: that between God and man.[30] Islam, it is argued, has a totality of view, exclusive of other beliefs, which militate against full participation in multi-party politics. Other writers suggest, on the contrary, that in traditional Islamic discourse 'tolerance, justice, fair play and universal brotherhood' were prominent features.[31] If Islam is regarded as opposed to the main elements of Western democratic tradition, and as based on 'violence and intolerance', then, so goes the argument, this is a view founded on misunderstanding and misinterpretation: it is possible to be both a Muslim and a democrat.[32] In this interpretation, the institution of the *shura* is a central component of the Islamic political system. *Shura* can refer both to 'consultation' and to a 'consultative council', elected by the people. As Choudhury elaborates:

> The 'Shura' will assist and guide the Amir (leader). It is obligatory for the Amir to administer the country with the advice of the Shura. The Amir can retain office only so long as he enjoys the confidence of the people, and must resign when he loses this confidence. Every citizen has the right to criticise the Amir and his government, and all reasonable means for the expression of public opinion should be available.[33]

If Islamic states appear not to construct their political structures in precisely this manner, then this, Choudhury maintains, is not the fault of Islam and its ideals, just as the 'limitations and shortcomings' which may be found in some democratic states 'should not be attributed to democracy and its ideals'.[34]

The notion of consultation, then, is an important component within Islam. Ayalon cautions against identifying *shura* in a *majlis* (council) as parliamentary democracy. He argues that it would be misleading to 'mistake fully sovereign Western parliaments for councils with limited advisory power'. While the term *majlis* is used in the Middle East to denote a national assembly, Ayalon asserts it is a word 'with no traditional political connotations' and must be qualified, as in *al-majlis al-ali* (a cabinet or senate), *majlis al-umma*, (a national assembly), *majlis shura al-madaris* (a council of education), and so on.[35] Yet it is as well to remember that many a Western parliament has been dismissed as simply a 'talking shop' with little authority but to deliberate and advise a recalcitrant executive. The central issue here is accountability and the degree to which deputies in the *majlis al-umma* represent the interests of a particular constituency, or the extent to which their role is instructed by Islam.

Islamic organizations contest elections, perform political functions and, more recently, have produced political programmes committed to freedom and pluralism. Indeed, the Muslim Brotherhood has contested elections since 1941. On the other hand, King Fahd of Saudi Arabia has proclaimed that the existence of the Qur'an precludes the need for a separate constitution. He argues that Islam is a social, political and economic system with *Sharia* (Islamic law) providing a comprehensive constitution, which comprises social and economic justice with a judicial structure.[36] The Islamic Republic of Iran relies less on the Qur'an and more on the principles it has enshrined within its constitution. Key articles of the latter support voter participation through national and regular elections to be conducted within the framework of an Islamic state. In the Iranian elections to the *majlis* in April 1992, over 2000 candidates, including 56 female candidates, stood for 270 seats. If electoral participation is important in the Shi'a Islamic Republic of Iran, so too, at the time of Ayatollah Khomeini's rise to power, was the use of the referendum. Clearly, then, certain political features identified as democratic have been and still are employed in Islamic states.

Some commentators, both academic and other, contend that inevitable differences between the political dynamics of East and West are rooted in their wholly different cultures. Thus, for instance, Akbar Ahmed asserts that the central difference between the West and Islam lies in their two 'opposed philosophies: one based in secular materialism, the other in faith'.[37] The implication then appears to be that it is futile and perhaps misguided to hope for, or wish to impose, democracy in the Middle East, as it is, presumably, alien to the region's culture.

Admittedly, the debate is a complex one. Yet it is argued here that if the question of democratization in the Middle East were not considered to be so important, this very debate would most likely never have begun. In other words, were democracy considered to be so trivial a concept, associated with Western imperialism and holding little meaning in an Islamic society, there would exist no imperative to attempt to connect the two 'opposing philosophies'. That the issue of democracy – whatever its exact formal embodiment might be – is being so widely discussed in the region today is precisely because the idea is attractive to the peoples of the Middle East: peoples who wish to form political parties, vote in elections for a variety of different candidates, hold their representatives accountable – in short, to avail themselves of political rights and responsibilities.

Certainly, a discussion is taking place within Islamic organizations and societies, and in some cases a reorientation of policy has been evident. In January 1992 Sheikh Fadlallah, spiritual guide to Lebanon's Shiite community, announced: 'A turning point has been reached in political practice. Certain currents used to call for revolution as the shortest path to power. Now the tendency among Islamic movements in the world is to take advantage of all democratic means available, which will mean participation in elections and politics.'[38] Paradoxically, it is precisely this shift in policy which has kindled fears that Islamic groups are not truly committed to a pluralist structure and democratic government. In short, the apprehension exists that Islamic parties might use the so-called 'fascist card', playing democratic politics only to gain power, then to subsequently undermine democracy. This, of course, would deny the basic principle in multi-party competitions for power, that the party which is voted into power may, in due course and through the same procedural arrangements, be voted out of office. Liberal democratic government is not only dependent on participation but also on a 'competitive struggle for the people's vote'.[39]

Yet these principles seem to have been recognized by the Iraqi oppositionist Shia organizations, the Supreme Assembly of the Islamic Revolution in Iraq (SAIRI), who, in 1992, outlined their programme:

1. Respect for Islamic doctrine, law and education.
2. Respect for ideological freedom, political pluralism and popular opinion.
3. Insistence on the unity of Iraqi territory and political unity.
4. Respect for national and social pluralism.
5. Commitment to the new internal trend to set up systems based on human freedom.[40]

A senior official in the US State Department, Edward Djerejian, has acknowledged that the United States had been in contact with the Iraqi opposition before SAIRI issued the programme in February 1992. According to one analyst, 'The readiness of Shiite fundamentalist movements to form a united front with non-Islamic organizations and to adopt the principle of liberal democracy is largely the result of the invasion of Kuwait.'[41] Why Islamic groups in the post-cold-war–post-Gulf-War international environment may feel the necessity to mouth liberal democratic sentiments is unclear. Certainly, SAIRI's publication in Arabic contain ambivalent messages: 'Rather than suggestions of a liberal democratic future', statements assert 'a clear commitment to the establishment of Islamic rule in a liberated Iraq, without any qualifications.'[42]

There is, of course, no basic touchstone on which to judge the democratic intent of Islamic groups other than to encourage participation and then adopt a policy of 'wait and see'. In Baram's view,

> since the relations between Islamic and non-Islamic oppositional forces in Iraq thawed in 1990 further cooperation may be expected . . . the longer such cooperation takes place, the more established it becomes and one may expect tolerance to grow. In its turn it may bring about a more democratic outlook.[43]

But Baram cautions that while the willingness of Shiite fundamentalist movements to form a united front with non-Islamic organizations may suggest 'a step towards a less sectarian, less totalitarian political approach', all these changes are 'still reversable'.[44]

Nevertheless, should a coalition of Islamic and non-Islamic groups decide to act in concert with one another then it may be possible for a democratic consociational model of government to develop which could be embraced as both legitimate and representative. Such a political system would operate on a fixed proportional representation basis, thus offering a process of controlled democratic participation which might preserve stability and encourage further political reforms. G. H. Jansen argues that it is possible to have 'pluralism without democracy'.[45] This view is, of course, quite correct; it is also possible to have participation without democracy. But although procedures may not fully correspond with the characteristics of liberal democracy, pluralism and participation are important moves towards a measure of democratization in the Middle East. The next move must surely be in the direction of accountability. Jordan's first multi-party parliamentary elections since 1956 were held in November 1993. The parties competing included the Muslim Brotherhood and the Islamic Action Front, who collectively won 16 of the 70 seats. The 69 per cent turnout was hailed as a sign of Jordan's growing political maturity and democratic development. Yet the elections must be viewed in the light of developments which took place before they were held. The amendment to the electoral law, introducing one person, one vote, ended the block voting system and meant that a voter could only vote for one candidate. What the new electoral system effectively meant was, for the most part, that voters would only vote for candidates with whom they identified ideologically, or on the basis of religion, kinship or clan affiliation. Nevertheless, the Jordanian elections have resulted in a form of shared democracy which might be a more appropriate way forward.

CONCLUSION

So what may we conclude about moves towards democratisation in the Middle East? The signs for reform may seem propitious but is talk of democratization misleading? It is obviously too premature to judge definitively. Diamond *et al.*, in their comparative study of democracy in developing nations, found that one common thread which consistently reappeared was 'the crucial importance of effective and democratically committed leadership'.[46] Although any emphasis on the role of leadership tends to stress the importance of elite groups, they argue that corrupt, opportunistic and undemocratic practice of leaders can seep down the hierarchical structure and inflict damage: 'When a prolonged period of undemocratic or inept leadership is experienced, the system itself may begin to decay.'[47] Undoubtedly, the role of the leadership is important in the Middle Eastern states, simply on the grounds of their political structures and their general authoritarian frameworks. In the traditional monarchies/dynasties 'the powers of rule-making, rule application and even central adjudication are merged in the head of the state.'[48] Even the Ba'ath Party has 'radically changed its nature' over the past twenty to thirty years of power in Iraq and Syria. From a party with an overt military presence in the early years of rule it has become a party very much linked to a 'cult of personality', in the forms of President Assad and Saddam Hussein.[49]

In the Middle East, some leaders have, ostensibly, raised the question of democracy. When President Assad states that 'the democratic form is not a commodity that is imported from this or that country but it is the framework through which the citizens practise their rights and duties,' he is quite correct, but unless the dominant role of the Ba'ath Party is minimized through constitutional amendment, his words appear vacuous.[50] There are few ways of assessing the *vox populi* of countries within the region except through the conduit of demonstrations and riots. Still, one could arguably interpret the discernible shift away from the Ba'ath Party in favour of the Independents at the latest Syrian elections as indicating a strong disenchantment with the party and, indeed, the leadership. However, any such moves will remain largely futile unless the disparities between the parties competing in elections is changed. If King Hussein's dictum that 'one-party rule, political armies, dictatorships and autocracies are all things of the past' is to have any real meaning then words will have to be turned into action.[51]

The leadership in the Middle East may, of course, feel obliged to make democratic statements because of international pressure and structural adjustment programmes of the World Bank. The argument can be made that this is what brought about King Hussein's decision to reintroduce elections. However, there had been demonstrations and demands for the establishment of democratic government in Jordan for some considerable time: while there may be external pressure to democratize, domestic pressures can, and have been, equally at play.

This brings us back to the question of whether liberal democracy is desired in the Middle East. According to one analyst, the Arab states reject the democratic option 'because of where it comes from rather than what it contains'.[52] It is perhaps inevitable that the Arab states should resent the West and not wish to emulate liberal democratic political structures, but this ambivalence to liberal democracy has not inhibited the current discussion of democratization. As Esposito and Piscatori point out, modes of political expression are not static:

It is difficult to ascertain or to predict whether the evolution of Muslim thinking about democracy will lead them to convert their views into action and what particular form democratization might take in diverse Muslim cultures. It is clear, however, that in the new Muslim world order, Muslim political traditions and institutions are evolving, just as social conditions and class structures are changing. Both are important for the future of democracy in the Middle East.[53]

The ending of the cold war has created a new environment in which states in the Middle East may enjoy not only new possibilities of political autonomy, but also – and perhaps more significantly – greater demands for responsibility and accountability. In a sense, the onus is now on the states of the region to define and determine their political progress in a democratic direction. Through discussion, the acknowledgement of the importance of citizenship, the reintroduction of elections and greater political participation, the first tentative steps have been taken on the road to a fuller and more expressive form of democracy. As history reminds us, those first moves towards democratization are often the hardest.

NOTES

1. L. Diamond, J. L. Linz and Seymour M. Lipset (eds), *Democracy in Developing Countries – Asia* (Adamantino Press, London, 1989), p. xx.
2. G. Luciani (ed.), *The Arab State* (Routledge, London, 1990), p. xxiv.
3. *Middle East International*, 13 September 1991.
4. BBC, *Summary of World Broadcasts* (SWB), ME/1329 A/4, 14 March 1992.
5. SWB ME/1213 A/6, 26 October 1991; SWB ME/1346 A/9, 3 April 1992.
6. SWB ME/1323 A/9, 7 March 1992; SWB ME/1317 A/9, 29 February 1992.
7. M. Hudson, 'After the Gulf War: Prospects for Democratisation in the Arab World', and J. Esposito and J. Piscatori, 'Democratisation and Islam', *Middle East Journal*, vol. 45, no. 3, 1991; Roger Owen, *State, Power and Politics in the Making of the Modern Middle East* (Routledge, London, 1992).
8. H. van Gunsteren, 'Notes on a Theory of Citizenship' in P. Birnbaum, J. Lively, G. Parry (eds), *Democracy, Consensus and Social Contract* (Sage, London, 1978), p. 10.
9. S. Russell, 'Migration and Political Integration in the Arab World', in G. Luciani, op. cit., pp. 373–93, 377.
10. Van Gunsteren, op. cit., p. 10.
11. G. Parry, 'Citizenship and Knowledge', ibid., p. 40.
12. W. Kornhauser, *The Politics of Mass Society* (Free Press, New York, 1957), p. 45.
13. Ibid., p. 55.
14. Russell, op. cit., p. 378.
15. M. Al-Rumaihi, speaking at the Royal Institute of International Affairs, London, 10 May 1991.
16. Russell, op. cit., p. 381.
17. Ibid., p. 380.
18. Ibid.

19. SWB ME/1213 A/7, 26 October 1991.
20. For further details of political reform in Jordan see Heather Deegan, *The Middle East and Problems of Democracy* (Open University Press, London, 1993).
21. J. S. Mill, *Considerations of Representative Government* (London, no date available), p. 126.
22. V. Moghadam, 'Women, Work and Ideology in the Islamic Republic', *International Journal of Middle East Studies*, vol. 20, 1988.
23. Diamond *et al.*, op. cit., p. 34.
24. See F. Halliday and H. Alavi (eds), *State and Ideology in the Middle East and Pakistan* (Macmillan, London, 1988), pp. 39–41; A. Cudsi and A. Dessouki, *Islam and Power* (Croom Helm, London, 1981), p. 193.
25. Georges Zouain (of UNESCO), 'Education and Democracy', paper delivered at St Hugh's, Oxford, 14 June 1991.
26. SWB ME/1343 A/1, 31 March 1992; SWB ME/1104 A/3, 21 June 1991; SWB ME/1233 A/12, 19 November 1991; SWB ME/1341 A/6, 28 March 1992.
27. See Chapter 9.
28. M. Hudson, *Arab Politics* (Yale University Press, New Haven, 1977), p. 185.
29. H. Deegan, op. cit.
30. Y. Choueiri, *Islamic Fundamentalism* (Pinter, London, 1990).
31. G. Choudhury, *Islam and the Contemporary World* (Thames, London, 1990), p. iii.
32. Ibid.
33. Ibid.
34. Ibid.
35. A. Ayalon, *Language and Change in the Arab Middle East* (Oxford University Press, 1987).
36. *Middle East International*, 29 May 1992.
37. A. Ahmed, *Postmodernism and Islam: Predicament and Promise* (Routledge, London 1992), p. 264.
38. SWB ME/1274 A/6, 10 January 1992.
39. J. Schumpeter, 'Democracy as Elite Competition', in H. Kariel (ed.), *Frontiers of Democratic Theory* (Syracuse University Press, New York 1970), p. 40.
40. SWB ME/1274 A/6, 10 January 1992.
41. SWB ME/1314 A/10, 26 February 1992; A. Baram, 'From Radicalism to Radical Pragmatism: The Shi' ite Fundamentalist Opposition Movements of Iraq', in J. Piscatori (ed.), *Islamic Fundamentalism and the Gulf Crisis*, (American Academy of Arts and Sciences, Chicago, 1990), p. 48.
42. Baram, op. cit., p. 43.
43. Ibid., p. 48.
44. Ibid., pp. 48–9.
45. *Middle East International*, 29 May 1992.
46. Diamond *et al.*, op. cit., p. 49.
47. Ibid.
48. D. Rustow, cited in G. Almond and J. Coleman (eds), *The Politics of the Developing Areas* (Princeton University Press, New Jersey, 1960), p. 447.

49.   M. Farouk-Sluglett and P. Sluglett, 'The Iraqi Ba'ath Party', in V. Randall
      (ed.), *Political Parties in the Third World* (Sage, London, 1988), p. 72.
50.   SWB ME/1329 A/3, 14 March 1992.
51.   SWB ME/1314 A/11, 26 February 1992.
52.   See Chapter 3.
53.   Esposito and Piscatori, op. cit., p. 440.

3 Democracy in the Maghreb

George Joffé

The concept of democracy has one meaning – I believe the true and original meaning – for which I hold a high value well worth fighting for. Democracy has not proved to be a certain protection against tyranny and oppression, as once it was hoped. Nevertheless, as a convention which enables any majority to rid itself of government it does not like, democracy is of inestimable value.[1]

I accord institutions only secondary influence over the destiny of men. I am thoroughly convinced that political societies are not what their laws make them but what they are prepared in advance to be by the feelings, the beliefs, the ideas, the habits of heart and mind of the men who compose them.[2]

At the height of their civilization, the Arabs translated all Greek philosophical and scientific books. They translated Aristotle and Plato, yet neglected the concept of democracy, that is to say, the concept of democratic organization. They had no need for it because it is alien to the Arab/Muslim mentality. The citizen himself does not feel the need for choice, whereas he has a keen sense of justice. He needs justice with regard to the police, judges and rulers. These are elements of Arab/Muslim mentality, from God's word to Ibn Khaldun, who never spoke about freedom, but laid the stress on justice, which he considered one of the pillars of a thriving society.[3]

The last statement above, by a senior Tunisian official, highlights one of the major problems that exists in discussing the role of democracy in North Africa. Many people there do not see the issue of democracy as such as the core problem they face in the national or regional political arena. Instead, they are more concerned over issues of justice and legitimacy, in the sense that government should not be seen as an alien imposition on a

35

resentful population and that the arbitrary nature of state power should be tamed by the subjugation of government to accepted legal precept.

Yet, the current atmosphere of the 'end of history',[4] with its promise of a New World Order with universal political and economic structures based on Western views of liberal representative democracy and universal integration into an economic order based on the operations of the free market, also seems to many to be a threat. North Africans, along with many others in the developing world, feel that they have increasingly little choice over the political system they must now adopt, whatever national preferences may be. Western triumphalism, in the aftermath of the war against the Saddam Hussain regime because of the annexation of Kuwait by Iraq in 1990, leaves little room for dissent, particularly when it is backed up by the threat of economic sanction, as expressed through the concept of 'conditionality' and a belief in an inevitable 'clash of civilizations'.[5]

This is a great pity, however, for it discredits democratic political systems irrespective of their relevance to or suitability for the current political scene there. There is, therefore, a growing prejudice against the democratic option – at least in those terms in which it is conceived in the developed world – whatever its innate value may be for the growth of more satisfactory and legitimate political systems inside North Africa. There is also growing resentment that indigenous Islamic, Arab and even North African political traditions are automatically thrust aside by policymakers in the developed world when they come to evaluate the political situation there. The danger of such an approach is that, ultimately, North Africans may simply reject the democratic option, however it is presented, on the grounds that it is simply alien and therefore undesirable, whatever its real utility may be, despite the widespread yearning for responsible, legitimate and representative government throughout the region.

THE NINETEENTH-CENTURY TRADITION

We tend to forget, however, that democracy was also not the automatic political option in the Anglo-Saxon world – where its modern forms were developed – when new systems of government were sought at the end of the eighteenth century and during

the nineteenth. It is appropriate, therefore, to recall the scepticism and uncertainty often felt towards the democratic ideal in
those societies which first created durable democratic systems –
Britain and the United States of America – because many of the
problems highlighted then are replicated in the North African
political discourse. The key concerns in North Africa, as was the
case in Britain and the United States two hundred years ago, are,
essentially, the issues of the rule of law, the role of the majority
and the conflict between individual liberty and communal
equality.

In Britain, a democratic system was originally seen as a means
of guaranteeing the tripartite nature of the constitutional order
between monarchy, aristocracy and democracy, particularly at
the time of the 1832 Reform Act. This was typified by the
notional separation of powers between the institutions of the
monarchy, the House of Lords and the Commons, in order to
preserve the social hierarchy or, after 1832 at least, to allow for
its slow evolution.[6] In America, democracy was a moral system
designed to guarantee individual rights through the civilizing
influence of 'republican virtue' – political and civic altruism as
expressed through an individual commitment to prior community
interests. This mediated individual freedom for the sake of the
communal ideal.[7]

Both ideals were, in the end, techniques for reconciling the
potentially conflicting demands of equality and liberty within
society. Both visions, in the end, depended on an accepted
culture of communal interdependence, together with communal
and legal limitations of the power of government and thus of the
untrammelled will of the majority.[8] Both versions of democratic
principles originally reflected their perpetrators' suspicions of the
role and purpose of political parties in democratic systems[9] and
were, to that extent, pragmatic social and political visions which
were also tinged with a healthy scepticism relieved by communal
and political compromise.

Indeed, the early concept of democracy was very unlike its
modern counterpart, nor did it openly espouse, as do supporters
of the Western vision of the New World Order and their
mentors,[10] the idea that liberal democracy had to be linked to
liberal economic structures. This new attitude is exemplified in
the concept of 'conditionality' now beloved of creditor states in
the developed world. Under this rubric, aid and other forms of

financial support are only made available to developing countries if the latter adjust their social and political systems in accordance with the conventional views of democracy held in the developed world. It has only been in the past twenty years in Europe, and since the end of the Second World War in the United States, that social democratic tradition has been progressively weakened and has now been displaced from Western views of the democratic agenda – even in those parts of Europe where, ostensibly, social democratic views still hold sway.

In fact, the original democratic vision did not make a clear link between the political and economic spheres in this way. To that extent, it also approximated far more to the situation that still exists in North Africa. During the nineteenth century in the United States, for example, there was a divergence among early theoreticians of the problem between associating the concept of the 'Gospel of Wealth' with democracy – the assumption of the individual's absolute moral right to parallel political liberties with individual economic freedom of action – on the one hand, or replacing it by the concept of the 'Social Gospel' – the communal moral obligation to treat equality of economic access as part of personal liberty – as an integral part of the democratic ideal on the other.[11] The counterpart in Britain was the development of the socialist critique started by Carlyle, Ruskin and William Morris which eventually became the British 'moralistic libertarian socialist tradition',[12] and which emphasized the egalitarian elements of the democratic tradition, rather than its libertarian components. It was this tradition, after all, which led to the egalitarianism of the Liberal Party in the early twentieth century, the socialism of the Labour Party and, after the Second World War, the development of the welfare state. This, however, was a specific European response to the problem of economic redistribution as a communal good, not to the issue of the relationship between the individual, the community and government, even though the two issues had become interrelated by their common communal concerns.

DEMOCRATIC EXPERIENCE IN THE MAGHREB

This discrepancy between early concepts of democracy in the Anglo-Saxon world and their modern counterparts is of acute relevence to the situation of democracy inside the Arab world. Here, too, although there is certainly an acute socio-economic problem of egalitarian economic redistribution, this is formally separate from the issue of mechanisms for the restraint and accountability of government in relationship to both the individuals and the community over which it rules. The former could, in large part, be solved without reference to the latter and, in reality, the process of economic development in the past has been predicated on this assumption. The various ramifications of this issue are particularly clearly demonstrated in the three countries of the Maghreb – Tunisia, Algeria and Morocco. The basic problems they face in trying to create democratic political systems are very similar to those faced in the United States and Britain during the nineteenth century.

There is, for example, the potential conflict between societal equality and personal liberty; and the confrontation between consensual communal decision and conflictual party-based democratic systems, as well as the legitimization of political power within limits defined by an impartial legal system. In addition, these countries face quite specific problems, related to the role of cultural and ethnic minorities within the body politic, as well as to the innate conflict between Islamic constitutional imperatives and secularist democratic traditions imparted through contact with the West, either during the colonial period or during the past thirty years of national independence. These two factors are intensified by the economic problems that the Maghribi states face, in which pressure for democratization runs counter to demands for economic reform and where, too, prescriptions for economic restructuring further undermine the viability of the democratic option, whatever form it may take.

In North Africa – as, indeed, throughout the Arab world and much of the developing world – there are additional and specific problems that hinder democratization. The first is the issue of the nature of the state, for, in the European and American context, the state is essentially the *nation-state* in which government, the institution controlling the state,[13] is legitimized by being the expression of the general will (in the explicit Rousseauian sense of the term) of the community over which it rules because that community is a *nation*. And a nation, in turn, is a community which shares common cultural attributes, by which its members may be identified, but which is different in that respect from any other community – it is surrounded by an ethnic boundary, in short.[14] In North Africa, however, nations in the European sense do not traditionally exist, and the states concerned have not yet completed the process of creating a sense of nationhood among their populations.

Indeed, and this is the second problem, there are competing loyalties available to individuals within the various states that make up the region (for the same argument could easily be extended to Libya and the Middle East itself, although not to Egypt, where the sense of nationhood still evokes a pharaonic response). The first is more localized than the state and reflects regional and social loyalties best typified by the issue of Berberism, in which Berbers, who are linguistically and often culturally distinct from the Arabophone populations among whom they live, often feel – for quite specific political reasons – a greater loyalty within their own minority groupings than to the state which they inhabit. This has been a particular problem in Algeria. Similar to the concept of 'Berberism', or 'Berbérité', as it is commonly known, are loyalties to regions and tribal formations, although these have been largely dissipated by the processes of modernization, nation-building and state formation.

A more serious problem is the issue of wider loyalties than those due to the state. Although Arab nationalism has never been as strong a sentiment in North Africa as in the Middle East, its local variant, a sense of Maghribi 'nationalism' – the belief that all North Africans share a common cultural and linguistic inheritance and thus should be governed by a single political institution – has been powerful. It found its ideological expression in the argument put forward by the Algerian leader, Houari Boumedienne, that North Africa should form the 'Maghreb des Peuples', rather than the 'Maghreb des Etats'. Its practical expression has been enshrined in a series of federal and confederal institutions, from the Permanent Maghreb Consultative Committee, formed in the 1960s with the encouragement of the United Nations Economic Commissions for Africa, to the Treaty of Concord and Fraternity, initiated by Algeria in March 1983 with Tunisia and later with Mauritania, which was countered by the Arab–African Union between Morocco and Libya, and culminating in the Maghreb Arab Union, better known under its evocative acronym of the UMA. Admittedly, these were political and diplomatic devices designed to neutralize one or other of the two states with hegemonic aspirations in North Africa: Morocco and Algeria. Nevertheless, they also corresponded to widespread and deeply felt popular aspirations.

Maghrebi nationalism, admittedly, hardly formed a forum for democratic political organization, although its egalitarian and cultural assumptions could have provided a basis for political legitimacy, given the growing disappointment with the national political structures bequeathed to North Africa by the colonial experience. In the event, however, the major competitor has been political Islam, particularly during the 1980s. Since Islam is both an individual doctrinal prescription for dealing with the metaphysical world and a framework for organizing communal life, in its political manifestation as reinterpreted by the various revivalist movements that have characterized the twentieth century Muslim world, it is also an authentic means of political legitimization.

This is not the place to discuss the implications of the doctrinal innovation implicit in restoring – as its supporters would claim – Islam to its rightful role as the instrument of political and social organization. Yet it must be recognized that the vision of the Islamic state, which is the ultimate goal, does contain structures for popular participation within the concept of *shura* – consultation. Admittedly, this traditionally required consultation by a ruler of appointed experts in religious law. However, in its modern form, consultation is far closer to popular participation, whether expressed through a Gadaffian vision of 'direct popular democracy' or through the electoral process for the *majlis* in Iran. In theory, too, political Islam satisfies another of the popular aspirations of the Muslim world – social justice – since it is explicitly based on revealed religious law, the *Sharia*. Once again, this is not the place to discuss whether or not, in practice, these aspirations are realized. Yet it must be recognized that, in normative terms, political Islam does satisfy popular aspirations and thus offers a culturally authentic alternative to the democratic process.[15]

The fifth competitor to the democratic process in North Africa is the indigeneous political culture which pervades the region. This, of course, is in part an amalgam of the four alternatives mentioned above. It is also, however, the direct product of an historical process in which central power, while authenticated by Islamic constitutional tradition, developed its own pattern of consultation, mediation and arbitration among the various focii of power and influence within North African political structures. Indeed, it could be argued that central authority only survived because of its mediatory function, and that this function was only acceptable because its own ability to articulate power was traditionally weak. Of course, if it had sufficient power then it would apply it in as despotic a way as possible. This, however, was usually extremely localized and, when not, was an extremely rare occurrence which prompted competitors to seek to undermine and destroy it, as Ibn Khaldun so acutely described. It was also an extremely conservative system and, in the modern world, has resulted in the complex systems of patronage–clientage which underlie all the states of North Africa[16] and, thereby, militate against the democratic option.

Nevertheless, despite these current antagonisms towards Western concepts of democracy, the Maghribi states have paid some attention towards democratic ideals ever since they achieved independence – Morocco and Tunisia in 1956 and Algeria in 1962. Each state has approached the problem of political legitimacy and the modern democratic diad of equality and liberty in its own way. To a large extent, their approaches have been conditioned the methods by which they gained independence and it has been this legacy of national liberation that has most profoundly hampered moves towards more democratic institutions and cultures in at least two of them, Tunisia and Algeria. In both countries, there was a profound discontinuity between their precolonial/colonial and postcolonial political dispensations. In Morocco, on the other hand, the continuity of the political tradition has made the apparent transformation towards a system of limited political democracy far easier to achieve.

(1) Tunisia

Tunisia achieved independence in 1956 under the charismatic leadership of Habib Bourguiba who, in 1930, successfully reorganized the Destour, the nationalist movement formed in 1920, into a new mass movement, the Néo-Destour.[17] The Destour itself had been formed by a group of politically aware young Tunisians to demand the restoration of the constitution – the first in the Arab world – granted in 1861 by Bey Muhammad as-Sadiq.[18] In effect, the demands made by the Destour were really designed to force concessions from the protecting power, France, which had unilaterally established a protectorate over Tunisia in 1881. The Néo-Destour, however, was concerned with forcing France to grant independence and, as part of this process, created a movement in which the dominant personality of the leader ensured unified and coherent mass action.

After independence this tradition was continued, so that Tunisia was effectively ruled by a single political party, the Néo-Destour, renamed as the Parti Socialist Destourian (PSD) in 1969, under the dominant personality of President Habib Bourguiba, who became president-for-life in 1975 as the result of a constitutional amendment. The system was, effectively, that of an authoritarian single party dedicated to achieving development and socio-economic equality rather than guarantees of individual liberty or democratic political control. Although, in theory, other political parties were permitted, in practice – particularly after the Parti Communist Tunisien was banned in early 1963 – there was no political alternative until the ban was removed in 1981 and until two other political parties – the Mouvement des Démocrates Socialistes founded by a former minister, Ahmed Mestiri, in 1980, and the Mouvement de l'Unité Populaire, founded in the same year by opponents of the original founder of the movement, the discredited planning minister, Ahmed Ben Salah, who had been disgraced in 1969 – were legalized in 1983.

In fact, all three parties were allowed to participate in the national legislative elections in November 1981, but, since they could only participate in the National Assembly if they obtained more than a threshold of 8 per cent of the total vote and since, furthermore, there was plenty of evidence of electoral fraud by the ruling PSD, none of them did so. The same was true of legislative elections in February 1989 and of municipal elections in 1990. Interestingly enough, the latter two elections took place after President Bourguiba had been deposed by his prime minister, Zaine el-Abidin Bin Ali, on 7 November 1987 on the grounds of his mental and physical incapacity. The new president had begun his period of office by promising a more open political system. The PSD was renamed the Rassemblement Constitutionnel Démocratique (RCD) in February 1988; the new president persuaded all legalized political currents in Tunisia to sign a National Pact, which was meant to express an consensual ideal over Tunisia's future political process, in November 1988; and non-RCD personalities became ministers in a cabinet reshuffle in April 1989.

However, despite these dramatic improvements in the political climate in Tunisia, the basic problems of democratic expression which had developed during the Bourguiba era still remain. Government, through its control of the process of legalization of political parties and through the threshold requirement for National Assembly elections, still controls an effective single-party political system. Even though the March 1994 legislative elections were run under a modified electoral law, which guaranteed nineteen seats to opposition parties, whatever percentage of the vote they obtained – in the event only 2.27 – the ruling RCD swept the board of the remaining seats, thus continuing the presidential party monopoly of legislative power. The political system, after all, was originally conceived to be the ideal modernizing system for a country in the throes of development, as Tunisia perceived itself to be in the 1950s and 1960s. It is certainly true that it allowed the Tunisian government to make dramatic changes in social and economic policy, as the shift from a planned collectivist economic system to a liberal, free-market one in 1969–70 demonstrated.

However, the Tunisian system, in common with the other political systems of North Africa, suffered from a set of structural defects that prevented it acting even as a 'substantive' democratic system.[19] These are the aspirations of the mass of the population, which may not coincide with democratic assumptions; the nature of the leadership, which is authoritarian and cannot tolerate the concept of popular validation; and the division between the population and the leadership élites.[20] This division is of vital importance, both in terms of the sense of alienation felt by the mass of the population from the leadership and in terms of the lack of a popular consensus over the nature of the Tunisian state and its legitimation by a generalized consciousness of Tunisian nationism among the population at large. Although the purpose of a single state system is to overcome these obstacles to national unity – since it is what Zartman describes as a 'tutelary system'[21] – the fact is that Tunisia is still a 'defective state' in which the political process is increasingly characterized by the political isolation of the ruling élite.[22]

These factors explain the dilemma now facing Tunisia. The Bin Ali regime has not been able to achieve the consensus it sought, nor can it incorporate oppositional political currents within its tutelary system any better than its predecessor. Not only did the Tunisian system fail, before the removal of President Bourguiba, to contain economic tensions arising from a failing developmental process since the mid-1970s and the consequences of IMF-enforced economic restructuring since 1984 – hence the constant confrontations between the government and the PDS on the one hand and the Union Générale des Travailleurs Tunisiens (UGTT) between January 1978 and 1987–but it has also continued to fail to incorporate popular political strands of opinion within its scope both before and since Bin Ali came to power. This failure is manifest in the growth of Islamic fundamentalism in Tunisia since 1973 and in the increasingly violent confrontation between it and government since 1980.

The growth of Islamic fundamentalism throughout North Africa relates to the ideological failure of Arab nationalism in the wake of the 1967 war and the failures, during the 1970s, of the various modes of economic development.[23] Arab nationalism was, in large measure, the adaption of European-style political nationalism to the specific conditions of the Arab world, both over the issue of the Arab–Israeli conflict and over the need for a unifying principle based on the concept of a secular common culture specific to the Arab world rather than to Islam.[24] Political Islam was, therefore, an appropriate indigenous alternative, once Arab nationalism was perceived to have failed and when Western political alternatives had been discredited by economic failure. Essentially secular political systems, such as that in Tunisia, were thereby particularly prone to Islamist criticism, and it has been political Islam that has accumulated and canalized the popular resentment that has developed towards the Tunisian government during the past two decades.

This was first manifest in an attempted Islamic rebellion, based on the southern Tunisian town of Gafsa in 1980, although there had been growing Islamist sentiment throughout the country since 1973. Shortly after the Gafsa incident, a fully fledged Islamic movement appeared, focused around the personalities of Rachid Ghannouchi and Sheikh Abdelfattah Mourou: the Mouvement de Tendence Islamiste (MTI). It was treated with great and growing suspicion by the Bourguiba regime, which considered it to be a cover for Islamic terrorism, funded by Iran.[25] Indeed, the tensions caused within the Tunisian government by the issue of what attitude to adopt towards the Islamist movement eventually played a major role in persuading Zain el-Abidin Bin Ali to remove President Bourguiba from power.

The Bin Ali regime has, however, found it no easier to incorporate the Islamist movements – there are two major strands, the MTI and the 15/21 movement, of which the MTI is by far the more significant – into the political system.[26] The basic problem is that, since the current Tunisian political system is defined as illegitimate by the Islamists, there cannot be a participatory political system in which both political visions can coexist. Even though Islamist leaders have claimed that they are prepared to coexist with a secular political system, the Bin Ali regime has not been prepared to take their assurances at face value.

The result has been that, although it has indicated that it is prepared to accept Islamist parties, provided that they do not express specifically Islamist policies in their mastheads (or, presumably, in their public statements), it has not, so far, actually been prepared to legalize them. The MTI, for example, attempted to satisfy government regulations that no party could proclaim a religious objective in its party name by renaming itself the An-Nahda (the Renaissance). This has not mitigated government hostility, however, and the Bin Ali regime has followed the path of outright rejectionism of the Islamist alternative that characterized its predecessor. Such an approach seems to vitiate any possibility of creating a genuine democratic system through political evolution in Tunisia. Instead, it suggests that increasingly violent confrontation between a large and alienated segment of the Tunisian population which supports the Islamist movements and the government may eventually become inevitable. At the very least, the Bin Ali regime will take over an intelligensia which is disaffected, and a disgruntled and cowed population in which repression has replaced substantive democracy.

(2) Algeria

Algeria, indeed, faces the same problem of governmental legitimacy and Islamist threat as Tunisia, except that the Algerian situation is far more acute. This is both because of the assumptions behind the Algerian one-party system after 1962 and because the economic failure in Algeria has been far more serious than elsewhere in North Africa. The most important consequence of the Algerian war for independence between 1954 and 1962 was that it legitimized the claim of the FLN to be the embodiment of the Algerian nation and its struggle for freedom. At the same time, the FLN was marginalized by a military élite which captured control of power, first because of its support for President Ahmed Ben Bella in 1962 and then by its assumption of power under Houari Boumedienne in 1964. The result was a complete fissure between the Algerian population at large and its leadership because of the failure of the FLN to act as a mediating institution. The depth of the gap grew with the passage of time and as Algerians themselves increasingly rejected the claims of the ruling group within the FLN and the government to the legitimacy acquired during the war of independence.[27]

The death of Houari Boumedienne in 1978 and his replacement by Algeria's senior army officer, Chadli ben Jedid, as president marked the beginning of the final collapse of the FLN and Algeria's tutelary political system. Initially, however, the Chadli regime attempted to exploit the FLN as it had been originally intended to operate – as a means for mediating government policy and linking together population and government. It thereby inverted the relationship which President Boumedienne had sought, whereby there was a more direct contact between government and population. It also exposed the basic hollowness of the FLN's claim to represent Algerian public opinion.

The real damage, however, was done by the worsening economic situation. Algeria had depended on its export revenues from oil and gas sales to cover its development costs and was, by the standards of the oil producers of the Middle East and North Africa, a high capital absorber. This meant that variations in oil and gas prices would have profound effects on its ability to import and, since up to 70 per cent of its food requirements were imported, as were much of its other consumer goods, its ability to satisfy consumer demand would also be severely affected. This is not the place to examine the detailed causes of Algeria's economic collapse during the 1980s. Suffice it to say that the decline in world oil prices after 1980, which became a collapse in 1986, had a disastrous effect on the Algerian consumer. The position was worsened by a government decision not to reschedule Algeria's massive foreign debt, but instead to compress imports to ensure that debt repayment schedules were met. The situation was also worsened by the short-term effects of an economic liberalization programme, designed to increase private-sector activity and, thereby, domestic output. This incidently had the additional effect of further alienating Algeria's new techno-cratic middle class, which should have been the natural ally of government but which had long harboured an interest in the private sector and now saw its opportunity to escape from the straitjacket of the public sector and government control.

The inevitable result occurred in October 1988, when there were serious countrywide riots. In their wake, the Algerian government, under Chadli ben Jedid, announced a wholesale liberalization of the political system and economic reforms, which, in 1991, meant that Algeria became a free-market eco-nomy rather than a command one (this decision was reversed in late 1992, however, and restored in 1993). Although such reforms may produce considerable benefits in the medium-to-long term, they have caused further economic chaos in the short term. The result has been massive speculation and growing recourse to the black market and the informal economy – known in Algeria as *trabando*, from 'contraband'. This, in turn, only further under-mined public confidence in the government.

In the political sphere, the economic collapse meant that the effects of political liberalization were precisely the opposite of those intended. Whereas the authorities had hoped that the growth of a large number of political parties might generate growing political and social consensus, particularly after the FLN had lost its political hegemony, there was, in fact, a growing fragmentation of the Algerian political scene. First, the gulf between Arab and Berber – long a basic cleavage in political life – intensified as specifically Berberist parties appeared among the forty-odd parties that emerged after 1988. This destroyed the normative assumption that independent Algeria, despite all its problems and failures, had at least been able to construct a nationalist consensus. This was bolstered by clear evidence of class division within the new political system.

Second, and more important, a powerful Islamic fundamental-ist movement suddenly surfaced throughout the country, with particular emphasis in the major towns along the coast. In fact, the movement had been growing throughout the 1980s and had been camouflaged by the claims of the regime to have incorpor-ated Islamic principles within its own austere socialist ideology.

However, by October 1988, its strength was evident. Although Islamists did not instigate the riots in October of that year, they certainly exploited them to achieve a high profile in the ensuing period of political liberalization. Although the movement overall was complex,[28] it soon became evident that one strand was to dominate – the Front Islamique du Salut (FIS), founded in early 1989 by Dr Abbassi Madani and Sheikh Ali Bel Hadj.

In fact, the FIS was, in reality, a coalition between Islamic nationalists who sought an Islamic solution for Algeria's problems, the traditional Islamic universalists, seeking a restoration of the Islamic *umma* as the only means of confronting the Algerian situation, and the so-called *Afghanistes*, violent, nihilistic radicals, some of whom had trained with the Afghani *mujahidin* in Pakistan and believed that only violent confrontation with the government would have any meaning. The last group took their inspiration from the activities in the mid-1980s of the Bouyali Group, Islamic guerillas who confronted the Algerian army and gendarmarie around the town of Blida.

The new strength of the Islamists was first noted in June 1990, when against all predictions they won the first multi-party municipal elections. They took control of 853 communes out of a total of 1501, particularly in urban areas along the coast. The government, alarmed by this sudden growth in Islamist power, sought to contain the threat by gerrymandering electoral boundaries, by altering voting rules (traditionally, in Algeria, husbands have been able to vote for their wives, for example), and by requiring, as in Tunisia, that no legalized political party should be permitted to publicise a specifically religious or ethnic platform. FIS protests, over what it perceived to be a deliberate attempt to ensure that its candidates would not win in the legislative and presidential elections set for 1990 and 1991, led to a major confrontation in June 1991, after which the FIS leadership was arrested.

Legislative elections were eventually held .on 26 December 1991 and, up to two weeks before, it was not certain that the FIS would field a full list of candidates. In the event and to everybody's amazement, including that of the FIS itself, it won 60 per cent of the votes cast, obtaining outright 188 seats of the 415 seats available, with the expectation of winning an outright majority in the run-off elections due in mid-January 1992. The size of the FIS success was underlined by the extremely poor showing of other parties, with the FLN only winning 15 seats, the FFS (Front des Forces Socialistes) 25 seats in its stronghold of Kabylia and the RCD (Ralliement pour la Culture et la Démocratie) winning none at all.[29]

In fact, the underlying picture was not so bleak. Although the FIS obtained 3.2 million votes, the FLN had, in fact, obtained 1.6 million and the FFS 0.5 million. Furthermore, only around 40 per cent of the 13.2 million-strong electorate had actually bothered to vote, and the FIS could not, therefore, claim a genuine popular mandate. Nevertheless, the FIS leadership, torn from within by its disparate factions and threatened from without by growing tensions on the political scene, soon made it clear that it would use its victory to force an alteration in the Algerian constitution in order to convert Algeria into an Islamic state in which there would no longer be a democratic option.[30] In effect, the Islamists warned that their definitive victory would call into question the fundamental nature of the Algerian state which had been defined by the Algerian war of independence. As a result, the Algerian army mounted a *coup d'état* and Algeria's brief flirtation with democracy was brought to a halt. The new leadership promised that it would be reintroduced in a year or two, but few Algerians believed such promises.

The new leadership revealed the complexities of Algerian politics, however, for it was headed by Mohamed Boudiaf, who had been a founder of the FLN but who, after the war of independence, had gone into exile in Morocco until recalled by the junta which had taken over power. His role was to legitimize a regime which had been jockeyed into power by the army, which had recovered its role of preserving the Algerian state and constitution but which did not want the formal obligations of direct political control. Its chosen representatives, in the Higher State Council, reflected the traditional balance of power within the Algerian state which had been largely discredited by events since 1988. To this extent, they were in direct competition with the FIS, by now banned, which also really sought to compete with the FLN for recognition as the true inheritor of the Algerian tradition of popular revolutionary sovereignty created by the war of independence, even if it used an Islamic rhetoric. Mohamed Boudiaf, as the authentic inheritor of the Algerian revolutionary tradition, was seen as a vehicle by which popular support for such a military-backed regime could be recovered and thus counter the fundamentalist onslaught.

Mr Boudiaf, however, was not prepared to be a simple figure-head; by attempting to create his own power base through the formation of an 'Assemblée Patriotique', and by starting to uncover the extent of corruption under the previous regime, both began the process of legitimization the regime had sought and also began to distance himself from it. His assassination, in late June 1992, was a reflection of the determination of those elements within the power structure which had benefited from the arbitrary and uncontrolled abuses of power during the Chadli regime – popularly known as the Mafia – to maintain their position. The army was still determined to avoid direct responsibility for power, however, and introduced Belaid Abdesslam as a new premier, while Mr Boudiaf was replaced by Ali Kafi. The Belaid Abdesslam government was meant to restore the economy, and maintain public order so that a restricted democratic regime could eventually be restored.

As a first step, the new regime sought to destroy the guerilla campaigns being waged against it both, it was believed, by the *Afghanistes* of the FIS and by disaffected elements within the regime associated with the Mafia. However, the new regime, although it was relatively successful at achieving this, failed to ensure concomitant economic reform and a solution to the pressing economic problems faced by the Algerian state. Furthermore, the external environment was unsympathetic, with France in particular refusing to aid the Algerian authorities, on the grounds that the democratic experiment had been unnecessarily aborted but in reality in order to improve its own position of influence within the armed forces and the government. By mid-1993 it had become clear that the Belaid Abdesslam government's attempt to reintroduce the austere values of the Boumedienne period and thereby recover the original FLN project for Algeria was likely to fail and that a new 'Third Way' would have to be attempted. After a period of several months, during which the extremist *eradicateurs* of the army sought to destroy urban and rural guerilla groups which had seized the initiative in the armed struggle between government and Islamic opposition, a new president – the defence minister, Lamine Zevonal – was appointed in February 1994. His chosen policy – the 'Third Way' – was one of negotiation with the Islamist movement. This was hampered, however, first by disagreements between *eradicateurs* and 'conciliateurs' in the regime, and second by disputes within the armed Islamic movement over whether negotiation and compromise was the proper course. The Groupe Islamique Armé which was close to the *Afghanistes*, operating in and around the capital, where it carried out a series of spectacular assassinations and was heavily infiltrated by Algerian military security, opposed compromise. The FIS leadership, now largely in prison but able to consult its colleagues, and the FIS's own armed wing – the Mouvement Islamique Armé, later absorbed into the Armée Islamique du Salut – did not.

The negotiating process was stalemated throughout 1994, while both army and guerillas tried to win on the battlefield. At the end of the year, a new attempt at compromise, via the FIS and the legal political parties (the FLN, the FFS, Ahmed Ben Bella's MDA and Islamist movements such as An-Nahda) took place in Rome. Its programme for an end to violence, the Sant'Egidio Accords, was accepted by all the political parties, including the outlawed FIS, but rejected by government, which riposted with its own proposal for presidential elections, which took place in November 1995. In reality the destruction continued, although it had become increasingly obvious that only a negotiated compromise could bring the violence to an end, as neither the army nor its opposition could crush the other. Such a solution, however, seemed impossibly far off and, in the continued struggle, the true losers were the mass of the Algerian population who rejected the extremism of either side, seeking only to obtain legitimate, representative government operating within the rule of law.

(3) Morocco

If the political crises and the apparent failure of a democratic option in Algeria and Tunisia were the consequence of popular alienation with government and the failure of regimes to build a modernist national consensus to support them, the Moroccan case is quite different. First of all, there was a long tradition of cohesive political culture in Morocco, stretching back to the early Idrissids in the tenth century. Second, the end of the colonial period did not mark a rupture with the past, as had been the case in Algeria and Tunisia. Indeed, the colonial period itself was one of evolution of a political system, albeit under extreme pressure, rather than its destruction by the colonial experience. In fact, the Moroccan monarchy emerged in charge of independent Morocco in 1956 with its prestige enhanced and its political control universalized in ways that had never existed in the precolonial Moroccan state.

At the same time, the state itself was about to undergo a process of modernization and development, and the tensions that ensued did much to damage the postcolonial legacy. Under King Hassan II, Morocco has experienced two attempted *coups d'état*, a rural rebellion, a major war in the Western Sahara and several significant constitutional changes. Under his father, King Mohammed V, there were also two major rural rebellions. All this has occurred within the context of a fundamental constitutional assumption that the Moroccan political system is one of a limited democratic constitutional monarchy. Indeed, today, Morocco can claim to have an operating national assembly – the Chamber of Deputies – with seven political parties represented within it.

In fact, the underlying nature of the Moroccan political scene is far more complex. The fundamental political dynamic in Morocco is to preserve political stasis and balance. Thus, the political system has traditionally been based on the process of balancing patron–client groups off against each other in a situation of political metastability. The essential component in this process has been the sultanate, traditionally weak and thereby obliged to arbitrate between such groups, particularly in the bilad as-siba, the lands of dissidence, where the sultan lacked the military power to enforce his writ. Indeed, its very weakness has, to a large extent, been its guarantee of a political role, for, although it could not threaten any established patron–client group in the bilad as-siba, it offered each of them the vital function of diffusing tensions between them.

At a normative level, however, the sultanate[31] was legitimized by the status of its occupant as amir al-muminin – one of the traditional titles of the caliphate. Indeed, the Moroccan sultanate considers itself to be sharifian and caliphical and is so considered by the Moroccan population at large. Traditionally, this element ensured its survival as an essential component of the political structure of the bilad as-siba. The result is that, in addition to its instrumental role, it has sufficient prestige not only to ensure its survival but to displace any other claimants to the same position.

Furthermore, although the caliphate was originally an elective position in which the occupant had to fulfil certain specific functions, including ordering the Muslim world for the correct practice of Islam, the growth of religious orthodoxy during the first seven hundred years of Islam established the contrary principle, i.e. that the caliph – indeed, any ruler – should not and could not legally be displaced from his position.[32] This was particularly important in those regions where direct sultanic rule applied – the bilad al-makhzan – and where the sultan's power was traditionally absolute. Thus the Moroccan sultan's role as arbiter was bolstered by religious status and legal precedent.

In the postcolonial world, however, the vital assumption that the sultanate was weak could not apply. After all, the major legacy bequeathed to an independent Moroccan state by France and Spain in 1956 was the assurance that the forces of law and order operated equally effectively over the whole territorial extent of the modern state. Yet, at the same time, the political culture of the weak sultanate rendered vital to political stability by its mediating role survived. It was for this reason that a system of limited democracy, with a superficially constitutional monarch, became an essential part of the postcolonial political dispensation. In effect, however, behind this political culture, Morocco developed into a clientalist state in which the sultan-monarch became the supreme patron.

The key, then, to political survival in modern Morocco is to create structures which diffuse localized power and yet permit the local élites to be associated with the monarchist core of the political system. The formal parliamentary system is part of this process. However, it is buttressed by other components. Morocco's municipal system, for example, is decentralized through the system of the *collectivités locales,* in which municipalities and communes have autonomy over local expenditure and receive a subvention from the state which they may supplement in order to provide local services. The government has proposed that, once the Western Sahara question is finally resolved – presumably in Morocco's favour – a similar system of administrative and legislative decentralization should apply at provincial level, with Morocco's 50 provinces gathered into 8 regions, each in charge of its own internal affairs.

The system of the *collectivités locales* thus provides local, largely rural, élites with a vested interest in the system under a superfi-

George Joffé   55

cially democratic guise – for the officials involved are chosen in part by popular suffrage. Of course, the culture of patronage-clientage and cultural consenus ensures that élite members are actually selected. Nevertheless, formally at least, the process is democratic. It is bolstered by a further participatory system, that of the *associations culturelles.* These bodies, funded by the Royal Palace, control vast areas of cultural and communal life. They, again, tend to be dominated by élites. On this occasion, the élites involved are largely urban in nature and are thus tied into the formal structure of the administration, which, however decentralized it is formally, is also closely scrutinized by both the Royal Palace and the government.

A system of this kind, formally democratic at several levels but permeated with a consensual patron–client political culture, is extremely effective in neutralizing political threat and at preserving a basically conservative social order. In so far as it is dominated by the Royal Palace, given its monopoly of the instruments of legitimate state violence and its status as the religiously sanctioned ultimate legal authority as the embodiment of the caliphate, it also has the monopoly of arbitrary power under the cloak of legality. Thus, those who are not integrated into the system can be effectively repressed by it and, indeed, implicit violence of this kind is traditionally an intrinsic element of the political culture as well.

The very complexity of the system also means that many of the threats that face its neighbours in North Africa do not threaten the political system of Morocco in the same way. Islamic fundamentalism, although it certainly exists in Morocco,[33] cannot compete effectively against the religious prestige and status of the monarchy. Thus, no Islamist movement has been really effective in threatening the *status quo.* Similarly, violent protest has occurred in Morocco – in January 1984 and in December 1990. However, it has no political focus, because the political parties and their associated organizations, such as the trade unions, in Morocco are also integrated into the complex political game and have a vested interest in its survival. Attempts to form a new political focus outside the formal party structure are simply repressed, as the Front Progressiste discovered in the 1970s.

After all, the democratic system now in force was introduced in 1976 as a specific response to formal political party support over the Western Sahara issue. The parties know the limits of their power and the Palace encourages their participation. Indeed, the king frequently goes above the party political scene to achieve consensus among party leaders if some major step is contemplated, in a process that is redolent of the principle of *shura* – consultation and consensus. Conversely, however, this relationship can give the political parties some leverage over the Palace.

Similarly, misjudgement by the Palace, as occurred during the Gulf crisis in 1990–91, when King Hassan initially enthusiastically supported the American initiative, can also provide the political parties with leverage. The result has been that King Hassan's attempts to rebuild the formal political consensus have obliged him to concede that past elections have not always been 'free and fair'. He agreed, for example, to appoint two electoral commissions made up of all the party leaders, the first to oversee revisions to the electoral law and the second to observe the fair conduct of the legislative elections themselves, which had been repeatedly postponed, to allow the Western Sahara issue to be resolved before they took place. In the event, although the direct elections in which two-thirds of the parliamentary seats were decided were relatively free from official interference when they took place in June 1993, the indirect elections for the remaining seats – which deprived the opposition parties of the fruits of their electoral victory in June – were clearly not. The resulting dispute over the future of the interior minister, Driss Basri, blocked the anticipated democratic evolution of Moroccan political life until 1995. In the autumn of 1995 King Hassan proposed constitutional amendments to create a second, appointed legislative chamber, while the first – from which the government would be drawn – would become entirely elected. Once approved by referendum, these constitutional changes would set the scene for new elections and thus unblock Morocco's slow progress towards a truly democratic political system.

In fact, this crisis very neatly underlined the way in which the monarchy's control of power had personalized the political process in Morocco, despite its formal democratic nature. Indeed, in the king's very dominance in the Moroccan political process lies a major danger for the dynasty, and King Hassan must be aware that a genuine constitutional monarchy will have to be created if it is to survive. This implies a voluntary restriction of the monarch's arbitrary powers in order to legitimize the system of government he has created. It also implies the primacy of the legal process and the legislature over the executive, and the abandoning by the monarchy of its legislative function as sanctioned by Islamic constitutional tradition. Yet, by doing this, the monarchy will also lose its major source of current legitimization, even though, in theory, it will be replaced. Not surprisingly, this is a risk King Hassan is loath to take too speedily. Most observers anticipate that this will be a decision left to his successor.

CONCLUSION

Indeed, the real problem that faces governments in North Africa is not so much the process of democratization, in terms of 'procedural democracy' at least. It is the need to achieve 'substantive democracy' and political legitimization. This requires the development of political systems that are and are perceived to be limited in their powers by effective and independent legal controls. The difficulty, however, is that the preferred cultural expression of this limitation is religious in nature – *Sharia* (Islamic law). And that, in turn, seems to imply the rejection of any democratic experiment, although many moderate Islamists deny that this is in fact the case.

This contradiction reveals two other problems that face any process of political legitimization through democratization in North Africa. The first is that, in essence, democratic systems that are effective are secular in nature – they have to allow for cultural differences and they must require that religious commitment is an individual and not a communal matter. In that context, Islamists are right to reject the democratic option, since it, in turn, would reject them. The second problem is that democratic systems can only operate if there is a generalized consensus throughout society over the democratic object – the system itself. And that, in turn, assumes a society in which basic ideological confrontation over the nature of the political process does not exist, a condition which does not yet apply in North Africa.

Finally, democratic systems can only operate against the background of a democratic culture, a culture which, in addition to being secular and ideologically non-confrontational, is homogeneous enough to share a set of common political values. This can only be achieved once the process of nation-building is complete.

In North Africa, quite apart from the ethnic and linguistic divides that particularly pervade Algeria but which are also present in Morocco, the simple facts of economic development failure, growing disparities of wealth and accentuating inequalities as a result of inappropriate economic reform ensure that true nation-building is far from complete. In addition, democratic systems are self-limiting, in that to work effectively they must contain mechanisms which limit the power of government, even if it is already controlled by law. They need, in short, effective civil societies and a cultural infrastructure to sustain them. This is still lacking in North Africa, although the growth in the number of organizations to protect human rights suggests that civil society is beginning to develop.

So, what of the future? The fact is that political liberalization is still a very delicate flower in the Maghreb. It is profoundly threatened by Islamic extremism and by the dangerous doctrine of 'conditionality' which, because it is seen to be an alien imposition, is considered to automatically discredit the reforms it wishes to achieve, whatever their intrinsic worth. Governments, too, have a vested interest in discrediting a political system which will limit their arbitrary power. The contradiction between a divinely ordered social system, implicitly and explicitly perfect, and therefore neither capable nor desirous of change, and a secular, pragmatic, non-ideological political alternative cannot be easily resolved. Indeed, the one precludes the other. Although the vast mass of people in the Maghreb believe they want democratic choice, their innate political culture could well destroy the very choice they seek, unless economic equity and cultural evolution allow them to evaluate objectively the choices before them.

NOTES

1.   Hayek, F., *New Studies in Philosophy, Politics, economics and the History of Ideas* (Routledge & Kegan Paul, London, 1978), p. 152.
2.   A. de Tocqueville, quoted in Roper, J., *Democracy and Its Critics: Anglo-American Thought in the Nineteenth Century* (Unwin-Hyman, London, 1989), p. 22.
3.   *Al-I'lan*, November 1982, quoted by Hermassi, E. 'State Building and Regime Performance in the Greater Maghreb', in Salamé, G. (ed.), *The Foundations of the Arab State* (Croom Helm, London), ·p. 152.

George Joffé 59

4. The view is best expressed by the person who coined the term, Francis
Fukiyama, in his essay, 'The End of History?', in *The National Interest*
(Summer 1989), p. 3, when he wrote: '[T]he century that began full of
self-confidence in the ultimate triumph of Western liberal democracy
seems at its close to be returning full circle to where it started: not to an
"end of ideology" or a convergence between capitalism and socialism, as
earlier predicted, but to an unabashed victory of economic and political
liberalism.'

5. The requirement that economic aid is available only provided certain
conditions are met, including the modification of state practice in
government organization towards recognized democratic structures and
in human rights in accordance with internationally recognized and
accepted norms. 'The clash of civilizations' refers to the article of the
same name by Samuel Huntington, in which Islam is identified as the
future adversary. See Huntington, S. (1993) 'A Clash of Civilisations?',
Foreign Affairs, Summer 1993.

6. Roper, op. cit., p. 13.

7. Roper, ibid., p. 9.

8. Hayek, op. cit., p. 142–3: Roper, op. cit., 204–8.

9. Roper, op. cit., pp. 51, 139.

10. See Hayek, op. cit., pp. 110–11.

11. Roper, op. cit., p. 209.

12. Roper, op. cit., p. 212.

13. As required by the 1933 Montevideo Convention definition of the state
– in which the state has a defined territory, a permanent population and
a government which can enter into formal relations with similar state
entities elsewhere.

14. Gellner, E., *Nations and Nationalism* (Blackwell, Oxford, 1989), p. 1;
Hobsbawm, E. J., *Nations and Nationalism Since 1780: Programmes, Myth,
Reality* (Cambridge University Press, 1991), pp. 23–5.

15. See Ayubi, N., *Political Islam: Religion and Politics in the Arab World*
(Routledge, London, 1991), and Choueiri, Y. M., *Islamic Fundamentalism*
(Pinter, London, 1990).

16. See Joffé, G., 'The Moroccan Nationalist Movement: Istiqlal, the Sultan
and the Country', *Journal of African History*, 26, 1985.

17. Bessis, S., 'Habib Bourguiba', in Lacoste, C. and Lacoste, Y. *L'Etat du
Maghreb* (Editions Le Fennec, Casablanca, 1991), p. 75.

18. Kedourie, E., *Politics in the Middle East* (Oxford University Press, 1992),
60–2.

19. The terms is Zartman's (see Zartman, I. W., *Government and Politics in
North Africa*, Methuen, London, 1963, p. 13). It means a system which
may not be a 'procedural democracy, in the Western sense of parliamen-
tarianism' but is one 'in which popular aspirations are known and
satisfied despite the absence of formal parliamentary machinery'.

20. Zartman, op. cit., pp. 7–9.

21. A system in which 'a modernist hierarchical group controls the political life
of the country, relying on concentrated executive power and a high degree
of two-way contact with lower political echelons, resulting in an often
deceptive impression of a democratic system' (Zartman, 1963, p. 12).

22.   Joffé, E. G. H., 'A View from the South', in Thomas, C. and Saravana-muttu, P., *Conflict and Consensus in North/South Security* (Cambridge University Press, 1989), p. 165; and Joffé, E. G. H., 'Concepts of Sovereignty and Borders in North Africa', in IBRU, *International Boundaries and Boundary Conflict Resolution* (International Boundaries Research Unit, Durham, 1990), pp. 228–30.

23.   See Munson, H. Jr, 'Islamic Revivalism in Morocco and Tunisia', *The Muslim World* (1986), p. 76.

24.   See Bessarabski, N., 'Islamisme et arabisme, deux idéologies politiques de référence', in Lacoste, E. and Lacoste, Y., op. cit.

25.   Joffé, G., 'Iran, the Southern Mediterranean and Europe', in Ehteshami, A. and Varasteh, M., *Iran and the International Community* (Routledge, London, 1991), pp. 96–9.

26.   Details of these movements are given in Boulby, M., 'The Islamic Challenge in Tunisia since Independence', *Third World Quarterly*, 10, 2 April 1988, and Dwyer, K., *Arab Voices: The Human Rights Debate in the Middle East* (Routledge, London, 1991), pp. 40–6. Indeed, in the 1990s the Bin Ali regime ousted the An-Nahda party (the renamed MTI) out of political existence and forced its leadership into exile. The result is that there is now no effective organized expression of political Islam inside Tunisia.

27.   Roberts, H., 'Radical Islam and the Dilemma of Algerian Nationalism', *Third World Quarterly*, 10, 2 April 1988, p. 578.

28.   See Joffé (1991), op. cit.

29.   Lek Hor Tan, 'Democracy Scores an Own Goal', (*Index on Censorship*, 5, 1992), p. 20.

30.   Joffé, G., 'The Politics of Islamic Reassertion in Algeria', in Nonneman, G., *The Middle East and Europe: an Integrated Systems Approach* (Federal Trust, London, 1992), pp. 208–12.

31.   *Caliph*: title once used by rulers who were successors of the prophet Muhammed – the chief civil and religious rulers. *Caliphate*: ruler's position and residence. *Monarchy*: the royal family. *Sultanate*: a term used for the Moroccan monarchy. *Sharifian*: someone who is descended from the prophet Muhammed.

32.   Kedourie, op. cit., pp. 3–9.

33.   See Munson, op. cit.

4 The Yemen Republic: From Unification and Liberalization to Civil War and Beyond

Gerd Nonneman

TOWARDS UNITY

When the leaders of North and South Yemen met on 16–18 April 1988 and agreed to revive unity discussions, following this up with a summit in Sanàa on 4 May, observers could be forgiven a certain scepticism. Over the years, a range of previous declarations had gone essentially unheeded, and the gap between the North's relative traditionalism and free-market orientation on the one hand, and the only officially Marxist system in the Arab world on the other, was perceived by sceptics as too great. Yet on 30 November 1989, on the occasion of the celebration of Independence Day in Aden, South Yemen's Ali Salim al-Baidh joined with the North's Ali Abdullah Salih in signing an agreement for the unification of the two states. The draft joint constitution for the union was approved and published, and both legislatures were given six months to ratify it; subsequently the constitution was to be submitted to a referendum, within a year of the signing of the accord. According to the draft constitution, the new state – to be called the Yemen Republic – was to have its capital in Sana'a and have a five-man presidential council. It would be a democratic state, with a parliament elected every four years. Political groupings and trade unions would be allowed to organize. The 'Joint Committee for a Unified Political Organization' (JCUPO – first mooted in 1972) had already had its first meeting in October and now saw its mandate confirmed.

Still, the fate of previous efforts had led many observers to be dubious about the chances of yet another one. Reports about the difficulties encountered in subsequent negotiations notwithstanding, however, in May 1990 events suddenly accelerated beyond expectation: both parliaments ratified the agreement as well as the provisional new constitution on 21 May, and the following day the union between the two states was officially declared, forming the Yemen Republic. The referendum was dropped, and instead of the planned 6-month pre-unification transition period, a 30-month transition was now begun, after which elections would follow. Meanwhile, the JCUPO, contrary to its original remit, had in fact seen its recommendation of a multi-party system accepted. The new state has since survived a further five years, much of them under heavy economic and political pressure largely resulting from the Gulf crisis – and suffering yet another civil war in 1994.

ROOTS AND OBSTACLES

Clearly, the merger project of the late 1980s and early 1990s was at a different level from previous attempts. The lack of success on previous occasions is not hard to explain. In the first place, contrary to rhetoric, the two Yemens had rarely if ever been united in the past. Second, the merger initiatives themselves were unrealistic – overambitious political declarations taking little account of the real implications and constraints. Third, there were few urgent practical pressures for uniting the two states. Fourth, the ideological divergence over political and economic organisation was too great for an easy fit. And fifth, there were external pressures, mainly embodied in the Saudi government for North Yemen, and the Soviet Union for Aden. The Saudi leadership had long funnelled payments to Northern tribes supporting opposition to unification initiatives (and generally diluting the Sanàa government's hold over the northern reaches of their territory).[2] They are also assumed to have cautioned the North Yemeni leadership against unification, using their influence over the tribes, and their economic assistance, as a lever. The Soviet Union's regional interests, on the other hand, led it to oppose any merger of its client state with the North. Add to this the internal situation in South Yemen, with at best unstable truces between radical and pragmatic wings; and the political situation in the North, far less 'mature' than in the later 1980s, with a National Democratic Front seeking support from Aden.

The mood behind the 1990 merger can be traced back to the period before the 1986 civil war in South Yemen, when Ali Nasir Muhammad and his supporters brought the Yemen Socialist Party (YSP) round to a more pragmatic approach to international relations and North–South relations specifically. The South Yemeni leader was known to have developed a good personal rapport with President Salih of North Yemen. Yet he had to contend with powerful radical criticism within his own party, so progress could at best be halting. At the same time the Saudi government was trying to hold Sanàa back. Nevertheless, the 1981 agreement to set up a Supreme Yemeni Council (SYC) was eventually followed by that body's first two sessions in 1983 and 1984. Brief tension over the potentially oil-rich border zone in January 1985 was quickly contained, Salih already having suggested the previous month the possibility of joint oil exploration.[3] During 1985 further economic cooperation and coordination was agreed upon. The civil war in January 1986 erupted from an attempt by Ali Nasir Muhammad to preempt the radical wing of the YSP from toppling him and reversing his pragmatic/accommodationist policies. His removal, and flight to North Yemen, appeared to put an end, yet again, to the process of rapprochement. But the new leadership in Aden, with Ali Salim al-Baidh as its most prominent personality, stated it wished to continue the search for eventual unification.

THE NECESSARY CONDITION: THE THAW IN THE SOUTH

Although the leadership in Sanàa was in principle willing to move ahead, everything depended on the situation in Aden and the new leaders' attitude.[4] Initially, the picture in South Yemen looked far too unstable; in addition, the ideological statements of the Aden regime sounded radical, and any conciliatory attitude towards the losers in the civil war was absent. The developments of late 1989 were only possible because of the evolution that had by then become apparent in the South.

The new leadership in Aden consisted of differing components, including moderates from the previous government such as the Foreign Minister, Abdul Aziz al-Dhali. The main point, however, is that the chief ideological radicals were dead. Initially, at least

domestic policy rhetoric returned to more strictly Marxist formu-
las; Mr al-Dhali lost his seat in the Politburo, the ousted leader
was condemned, and suggestions of leniency for those tried for
treason were at first dismissed. But economic-cum-external pressures and opportunities led to a fairly swift turnaround, which
appears to confirm the continued existence of a pragmatic line all
along: the latter could now push through its points, supported by
facts and (foreign) friends. More specifically, a number of factors
can be listed.

First, a payments crisis was looming, worsened by the need for
an extra $120 to $150 million to cover the losses inflicted by the
hostilities. By the end of 1987, the country's international
liquidity had dropped below $100 million – the lowest in a
decade – and the 1988 debt servicing requirements were estimated at over $160 million.[5] An isolationist attitude was not the
way to cope with this. A change in policy was likely to, and
indeed did, bring more western and Arab aid (including from
Saudi Arabia, Aden's erstwhile foe). Second, many in the regime
realized the necessity of mobilizing investment capital from both
local and expatriate Yemenis to try to restore some health to the
country's economy. A logical follow-on from this was the tapping
of foreign capital. Apart from funds, technology inputs were also
desirable. All of this required a more pragmatic attitude domestically as well as internationally. Third, these developments were
both made possible and pushed along by the new Soviet policy
under Gorbachev. The latter's international accommodationist
line ('new thinking') which accompanied domestic *perestroika* and
glasnost, had its impact in South Yemen as well. During the latter
years of Ali Nasir Muhammad's leadership, Soviet interests in the
region had in fact fared rather well, as Aden's relations with
others improved. Moscow had no wish to see this reversed, and
was in a position to impress this upon the new leaders in Aden
in several ways. The USSR was the country's main source of
development aid, without which only a fraction of planned
projects could be realized – much less in the costly aftermath of
the civil war. The Soviet Union also in effect took care of the
country's oil exploration effort, and was by far the largest source
of arms. There was no substitute for the USSR, towards the more
radical-Marxist end of the spectrum. In addition to these elements of pressure, there were those of persuasion. Soviet advisers
had already for some time been telling the YSP leadership that

any effort to impose a strict orthodox Marxist mould on the country was in any case premature. Now they added to that Moscow's own reinterpretation of the old ideological concepts. The visit to Moscow by Mr al-Baidh and Central Committee member Salim Salih Muhammad in February 1986 was a good occasion for such a Moscow–Aden flow of suggestions to be increased.[6] It is understood that it was kept up in the course of frequent contacts between the two sides subsequently, while, in return, a number of economic assistance and cooperation accords were signed. At the time of the treason trials in 1986–87, the USSR was among those urging leniency. Moscow's position was further reinforced with the discovery of oil deposits in the Shabwa area in late 1986 or early 1987. The USSR had promised a $190 million loan to cover its oil exploration efforts until 1990, and later in 1987 signed an agreement to finance a pipeline from Shabwa and exploitation of the deposits.

The growing importance of oil was in itself another, fourth, factor helping to explain the changes in Aden. The country desperately needed to develop any oil wealth it might possess, but lacked both the finance and the technology to do so. As indicated, this increased the leadership's inclination to follow the USSR's pragmatic lead, but it also highlighted the importance of building bridges with the West, where more capital and more sophisti-cated technology were available. Finally, the likelihood that oil would also be found in the border zone with North Yemen, between that country's producing fields and South Yemen's own, eventually provided the most urgent argument in favour of détente and cooperation with Sana'a.

Evidence that all of this indeed helped bring a change of policy on the part of the Adeni leadership can be found in all fields. Domestically, rhetoric gradually changed, and there were clear echoes, from 1987 onwards, of Gorbachevian expressions on democratization. By February 1989, only twenty-five supporters of the ousted president remained in jail.[7] Calls for private and foreign investment were issued, and a South Yemeni version of *perestroika* was embarked upon, with Mr al-Baidh stressing that a pragmatic approach was necessary. A reform programme was published in July 1989, allowing for a more positive attitude towards Islamic and Arab traditions, a freer press, more demo-cratic procedures within the party, and a liberalization of some sectors of the economy.[8] In foreign policy, the accommodationist line was evident even earlier. Shortly after the civil war, the Foreign Minister went to North Yemen and four Gulf states, followed by an Omani visit to Aden in July. High-level visits to Kuwait followed a year later. Subsequently, Aden made a successful concerted effort to restore relations with all of the regional actors, including Saudi Arabia.[9] The country definitively left the 'steadfastness front' behind when it re-established diplomatic relations with Egypt in February 1988. And already in October 1988, President al-Attas was speaking about doing the same with the USA. The foreign minister, for good measure, stressed that the regime rejected the idea of 'exporting the revolution'.[10]

Considering all of the explanatory factors listed earlier, and given the rather dramatic evidence which had been accumulating especially since the autumn of 1987, the leadership in North Yemen was justified in concluding that the change in Aden was for real, and that the worst threat of instability was over. Indeed, this time round it was the presumed hardliners who, having taken on the mantle of Abdul Fattah Ismail, now turned pragmatist themselves, with relatively few real radicals of any standing left in positions to challenge the leadership. In addition, there appeared to be little desire on the part of most people to risk another 1986-type convulsion.

THE VIEW FROM SANA'A

While developments in the South, therefore, increased Sana'a's willingness to take Aden's declared wish for continued moves toward unification at face value, they also made the objective circumstances more conducive to such moves. The ideological chasm between the two regimes was much reduced (and looked like being further reduced) in terms both of international alignment and of political organization and economic policy. North Yemen also had to gain from, at the very least, cooperation on oil exploration in the border zone. Indeed, there were rumours in the international oil world that the South and the zone would prove to contain more oil than North Yemen could ever hope to have. This was especially crucial because President Salih

badly needed a political and economic success in the fall of 1989. Abroad, he was faced with a loss of momentum of his other major initiative – the ACC [which] had proved of little concrete benefit to most Yemenis. At home, the gap between Salih's consistently optimistic predictions about the oil bonanza and reality was becoming increasingly apparent.[11]

Another major economic spur to the unification idea, for Sana'a, was the access to the South's market which it promised. Finally, by late 1989 the problem of the presence in North Yemen of a substantial number of refugees, along with Ali Nasir Muhammad himself, had lost much of its obstructing quality. The refugees could no longer transmit radio programmes from North Yemen; the leadership in Aden stated that, as long as Ali Nasir Muhammad refrained from hostile moves, his presence in the North was not a problem; and the ousted president himself dropped his claim to power in 1989 and was even sounding carefully positive about some of the new Adeni rulers' policies.[12]

PRELUDE TO UNIFICATION

It is against this background that the 1989–90 *rapprochement* between North and South must be seen. Specific moves bringing the two Yemens closer together, included first and foremost the project for joint oil exploration in the disputed border zone, initiated at the summit meeting between Ali Abdullah Salih and Ali Salim al-Baidh on 4 May 1988, on which occasion the two countries' prime ministers also met and agreed to replace border posts with joint posts and to facilitate border crossings.[13] A joint company (Yemen Company for Investment in Oil and Mineral Resources – YCIOMR) was established in November 1988 to manage the exploration of the 2200-square-kilometre area, and the exploration contract was awarded at the end of 1989 to a fournation concern, including a Soviet group already involved in the south, and Hunt of the USA, already exploiting North Yemen's Marib/Jawf fields. In addition, road links were being upgraded. A project to link the two power grids was given the go-ahead in 1988, and the national telephone networks were connected in 1989. In accordance with agreements reached in the course of 1989, November of that year saw the YSP's Politburo agree that henceforth identity cards would be all that was required for citizens to travel between the two states; this was linked in with a simultaneous decision in Aden to lift all restrictions on citizens' travel to foreign countries.[14] Easier border crossing procedures had already been put into effect in July of the previous year, following the agreement reached at the May 1988 Summit.[15]

In the political arena, high-level as well as other meetings became a regular occurrence. From the May summit in 1988, it was clear that friction over ex-president Ali Nasir Muhammad was no longer an obstacle. The Supreme Yemeni Council was reactivated to draft a unified constitution. Throughout, both sides stressed the necessity for realism, and in November 1989 Mr al-Baidh spoke about 'taking gradual and practical steps' and the importance of finding a transitional federal formula.[16] It appears to have been the North's intention to propose a confederation (though not under that name) with joint Ministries of Defence and Foreign Affairs. But when President Salih went to Aden on 30 November, the result of the final deliberations turned out differently, as sketched at the beginning of this chapter.[17] The reasons behind the changes will be explored in the following section. They follow from, and at the same time illustrate, the kinds of contradictions which would eventually help lead to the 1994 civil war.

Meanwhile, however, the changes from the previous decades, and the momentum towards unity, were palpable. In the months before the official declaration of unity, a number of further significant decisions and statements were made. Inside South Yemen, the YSP on 11 December decided to adopt a multi-party system for the country, 'reinstating all the national forces which struggled against British colonialism'.[18] The following day North Yemen's foreign minister told Jordanian radio that 'there is no doubt that the new Yemeni state will announce its commitment to all treaties and charters to which the two parts were committed' (including the Arab Cooperation Council).[19]

Clearly, the new merger project was in a different class from any of the previous ones. Its chance of realization – in some form or another – was real from the outset, even if by no means unproblematic. First of all, there was an awareness of the importance of realism – previously usually lacking. (In the final few months before unification some of this awareness appears to have been overwhelmed by the immediate political imperatives for the leaderships on both sides; for more, see below.) Mutual flexibility appeared to go hand in hand with this. Mr al-Baidh said on 1 December 1989: 'We have agreed that we can agree and disagree for the sake of reaching consensus.'[20] Second, an important range of infrastructural and economic links had been, or were being, established. Third, economic interests pointed to integration: in oil exploration there was no alternative; the North could look forward to the Southern market; and the South could expect a better aid and investment climate. Fourthly, two political factors increased the likelihood of success. As argued above, the pragmatic line in Aden was less threatened than at any time since independence. The ideological chasm was no longer so unbridgeable. And externally, Saudi Arabia no longer appeared to be as adamantly opposed to the idea of a united Yemen. The new mood in Aden was noticed in Riyadh as well, and the Saudi leadership, by getting involved in development assistance and economic agreements with South Yemen, appeared to be favouring a cooptation strategy.

Yet equally, a number of question marks hung over the project's future. First, it remained to be seen how the conservative elements in the North would receive the idea: it was they, supported by the Saudis, who had often held the North Yemeni leadership back. Second, some uncertainty remained over Riyadh's attitude, as well as over that of the USSR: officials in Sana'a are reported to have said in early November 1989 that Soviet influence was proving an obstacle.[21]

The key question emerged only shortly before unification itself, when the eventual form of the union and its institutions, along with methods and time scale, became clear. There was some concern among observers of the Yemeni scene over whether the final merger plan was not too hasty, contrary to the original federal or confederal transition plans. One year could hardly be sufficient truly to merge two such different army structures, bureaucracies and economics. Indeed, although ministries were officially merged and the upper levels of the military establishment integrated, the situation obtaining in 1994 was one of continued North–South differences and duplication both in the bureaucracies and below the very top of the armed services. Finally, even if the North Yemeni president stated on 1 December 1989 that 'in serving this strategic cause we are willing to sacrifice to the limit, even to the extent of giving up our positions of leadership if that is what the people want',[22] it remained less than obvious whether genuine power-sharing in the five-man presidential council would in fact become a reality.

THE POST-UNIFICATION POLITICAL SCENE

As mentioned before, ministries and the armed forces high command were officially merged upon unification; foreign missions were unified. The central banks gradually merged their functions in the course of 1990–91. The joint committee for a 'unified political organization' had, in fact, recommended a multi-party system instead, which was inscribed in the draft constitution and indeed implemented following unification. Contrary to the original plan for a six-month transition period, before unified elections, the unity agreement specified a thirty-month transitional period *after* unification, with elections foreseen at the end of that period (i.e. in November 1992).

The change in the shape, modalities and speed of the unification scheme may be explained by a number of factors, but essentially by the recognition by both leaderships that a deal should be done while there was still a Southern leadership to do it. President Salih and his entourage always seem to have been confident of having the dominant voice in a unified state, not only because of the preponderance of the North in terms of population, but also because it was recognized that the position of the YSP in the South was not particularly strong. It is this very point which in the end made an acceleration of the process imperative. The initial measures to open up the economy by Aden's leadership were not having the hoped-for effects, and therefore also failed to shore up the political position of the YSP top. The newly liberated media reflected the regime's failing popularity. At the same time, the collapse of communist regimes throughout Eastern Europe undoubtedly increased the regime's sense of vulnerability. All this combined with a fear of potential challengers in the YSP itself, and with the undoubted enthusiasm of the population for the project of unity, to drive al-Baidh and the pro-unity YSP leadership towards the accelerated formula. Meanwhile, as indicated above, President Salih also increasingly needed a swift boost to his own popularity. The combination of the acceleration of unification with a postponement of elections (because the transitional period would now *follow* unification) suited both parties, but especially Ali Salim al-Baidh and the YSP: fearful that early elections would lay bare their weak position, they appear to have hoped that the symbolic appeal of unification, and the hoped-for economic effects, would over time boost their popularity enough to risk elections at a later date.

Even so, the YSP leadership also anchored its position in power by negotiating a fifty-fifty division of the key leadership positions in the government (after effectively ceding the position of head of state to Ali Abdullah Salih). They also appear to have felt they had reached an understanding that, regardless of precise electoral outcomes, this strategic partnership with the General People's Congress (GPC, the former North Yemeni unified political organization, transformed into a party proper) would remain secure.

The new constitution was approved by a large majority in a referendum in May 1991, although strong opposition was voiced by groups wanting to make Islam the only, rather than one, source of law. The largest and best organized of these groups was (and continues to be) the Islah party, led by the paramount shaikh of the Hashid federation, Abdullah bin Hussain al-Ahmar. The elections for the Council Representatives which were to end the transitional period had to be postponed – partly for technical reasons (definition of constituencies etc.) and partly because of an increase in political violence – but they did eventually take place in April 1993.

Over forty political parties were active by this time, but only three were of major significance: the Islah party, the GPC, and the YSP (the South's former single ruling party, which, as illustrated earlier, largely left its socialist ideology behind). The press was freed from censorship – although the broadcast media remained firmly in the hands of the government. Political debate became widespread, illustrated and enhanced by the daily tele-vized sessions of the Council of Representatives. In terms of ideology, the GPC is a centrist 'umbrella' party, intending to appeal both to modernist and left-of-centre technocrats, and to tribal/conservative interests. The YSP in effect became a 'social democratic'-type party, left of centre, and targeting 'the many Yemenis whose living standards have suffered since unification and who fear the growing strength of Islamic fundamentalism'.[23] The Islah contains two strands. The majority is probably ac-counted for by the traditional Yemeni, conservative/Islamic interests represented by Shaikh Abdullah al-Ahmar; yet these interests were allied with a more radical Islamist tendency led by

Shaikh Abdul-Majid al-Zindani, the party's spokesman (a clash between the two men over the party's orientation appears subsequently to have led Shaikh al-Zindani to leave for Saudi Arabia for a while).[24]

The Islamist opposition was indicative of the tensions between northern and southern social mores – traditional and markedly religious ones in the North versus more liberal and secular ways in the south, especially Aden. Apart from the question of Islam proper, there was general concern among northerners that the South's life style might affect their own; issues in point were the availability of alcohol in the South, and the status of women. These concerns had their mirror image among Southerners, particularly in urban areas. The regime was obliged to walk a thin line of compromise. Qat chewing became legal all week in the south, following the Northern rule. But President Salih confirmed in mid-1990 that men and women would be equal in terms of obligations and rights (mentioning in particular their participation in parliamentary life). Nevertheless, the judicial powers bill, confirming the acceptability of women judges, passed only with great difficulty in the Assembly in September that year; the south had some one hundred women judges, the north none. Equally controversial was the issue of female membership of the armed forces – prohibited in the north but allowed in the south.[25]

While these social and cultural contrasts and tensions were (and remain) certainly genuine in their own right, the extent to which they became politically significant and potentially acute must be explained in large measure by the contrast between, on the one hand, the promise and high expectations riding on the oil discoveries and unification itself, and, on the other, the economic difficulties being experienced. The latter resulted from the previous economic problems which the separate states had been suffering, from the shocks associated with the initial stages of the liberalization programme in the south, and, crucially, from the economic blows the Kuwait crisis dealt the new country.

THE KUWAIT CRISIS, ECONOMIC LIBERALIZATION AND THE FRUSTRATED SEARCH FOR PROSPERITY

Little more than two months after the new Yemen Republic's birth, Iraq invaded Kuwait and focused the attention of the whole region and the international community on the area. Yemen's stance in the crisis would cost it dearly. Yemen's position as the only Arab state with a seat on the UN Security Council meant both that the leadership felt a particular responsibility to put forward a balanced Arab view, and that all Arab governments were watching Yemen's initiatives very closely. In addition, North Yemen had been a fellow member in the Arab Cooperation Council with Iraq, Jordan and Egypt, and it had a history of friendly relations with Baghdad, which included arms supplies, military training, and economic assistance. The Yemeni decision to oppose the international operation to expel the Iraqi forces from Kuwait (even while condemning the Iraqi invasion), meant that Sanàa was immediately ostrazised by the Saudi and Kuwaiti regimes, as well as by the United States (and to a lesser extent other governments which were part of the alliance). Long highly dependent on labour export and the inflow of remittances, as well as on foreign aid, the country saw both slashed drastically. Most of the 1.8 to 2 million migrant Yemeni workers found employment in the Gulf states, and remittances for the north and south combined averaged some $1 billion per year during the 1980s (although this already masked a sharp drop in the second half of the decade after the end of the Gulf oil boom). The exodus from Kuwait was followed by the effective expulsion of at least 800 000 Yemenis from Saudi Arabia, where their conditions for employment and residence were tightened at very short notice. Some subsequently trickled back, and from 1992 there was evidence of the gradual integration of some of the returnees into the economy; also, there was a one-off surge in remittances as returnees repatriated those assets they were able to. Even so, unemployment in Yemen doubled, reaching an estimated 35 to 40 per cent by 1994, and government services and finances strained under the extra burden. At the same time, aid from Gulf sources was virtually halted (as were the more modest amounts from the USA and the UK, among others). Foreign grants and loans had in any case already undergone significant cuts before. Yemen's new status of oil exporter had lessened the generosity of some Western donors, and aid from the Eastern bloc had virtually dried up in the late 1980s. In the wake of the Kuwait crisis Saudi Arabia suspended all official transfers to the government (although some on-going projects were completed), and the United States cut its aid in 1991 by 90 per cent to $2.9 million.

(On the part of the United States at least, recognition of the counter-productive nature of this kind of pressure led to a softened stance, with at least $30 million being allocated in 1992.)[26]

As a result, the country's already dire financial situation became acute. The current account deficit rose to an estimated $800 million in 1991, and to well over $1.5 billion in 1992 and 1993.[27]

Yet beyond the immediate financial implications, the economic and foreign policy climate also had other effects. In the crucial oil sector, difficulties arose when Saudi intimidation over oil exploration efforts in Yemen's northern border region followed the rekindling of a territorial dispute. More generally, the climate of economic and political uncertainty, worsening considerably as a result of the crisis's effects, in turn inhibited the all-important investor confidence which the government was trying to stimulate.

The concerted effort of the new republic's government to boost economic growth through a strategy of economic liberalization, therefore, ran into overwhelming obstacles almost from the beginning.

On the day of the merger, 22 May 1990, a statement on economic policy by the leadership highlighted freedom of economic action, the attracting of local as well as foreign private investment, and the intention to make Aden into a free economic zone which was to become the focus of this endeavour. Subsequently, it was announced specifically that the private sector would be encouraged to invest in agriculture (the top priority sector among the productive sectors), fisheries and industry. A policy statement on 16 June stated that while the government would work 'to limit the prices of basic commodities and services', it would leave other prices to market forces.[28]

However, although the government indeed tried to ensure sufficient supplies of staple foods such as rice, sugar and flour at fixed prices, many other prices increased substantially after unification, both because of the liberal policy and because goods brought south from the north were sold with transport costs added on. This very soon caused major labour and social unrest in the south, with calls for strikes and work stoppages, and the demand – later acceded to – that the rights and wage grades acquired by southerners before unification would be kept. Also, the government in July 1990 standardized the price of some oil products, comparatively lowering them in the south.[29]

On the first anniversary of unification, 22 May 1991, Aden was declared a free zone, in the hope of recapturing the port's erstwhile glory.[30] The ministry of industry had by then already identified about fifty industrial projects for inclusion in the zone. Some local and foreign interest was expressed, and in July an official Yemeni delegation visited the UK for talks with British firms about investment in the zone.[31] However, the economic dislocation following the Kuwait crisis, and the potential social and political upheavals which might follow from this dislocation, as well as from dissension over the form of the unification (between northerners and southerners, modernists and conservatives), all combined to deter most potential foreign investors.

Nevertheless, the dismantling of the remnants of the Marxist system in the South continued. The minister of agriculture and water resources announced in July 1991 that 60 per cent of disputed land cases in Wadi Hadhramaut had been solved, including the return of nationalized property of over fifty landowners in Tarim and al-Qatn. This followed a March decision to establish a committee chaired by the prime minister to oversee the solving of such disputes: an official statement said that the 'mistakes' of the 1970 nationalization law would be corrected, on the basis of consent between the original owners and current beneficiaries of nationalization. The minister of housing and urban planning had already confirmed that all those affected by the nationalization of private houses under the socialist regime would receive compensation. Also in March, those intending to build private homes in the south were told they would be invited to meet representatives of the ministry in Sana'a to arrange the details and allocate plots of land.[32] And the return of commercial property appears to have begun as early as November 1991.[33]

In another move, a small enterprise support unit was opened by the Industrial Bank of Yemen in November 1990, with the aim of providing technical assistance to entrepreneurs, as well as foreign currency for the necessary imports of machinery and equipment. Some $5.1 million was foreseen in funding for it, from the government and international sources.[34]

The keystone of the new liberal edifice was the publication of the new *unified investment law*, valid as of July 1991. This covered domestic as well as foreign investors in the sectors of industry (except hydrocarbons and minerals extraction), agriculture and fisheries, tourism, health, training and education, transport, construction and housing, and any other field which the Council of Ministers would accept at the recommendation of the new General Investment Authority. The latter's board, chaired by the prime minister, further included the ministers of planning and development, oil and minerals, industry, supply and trade, finance, and foreign affairs, in addition to the governor of the Central Bank, and the Authority's general manager. Apart from sectors where foreign investment could be restricted or banned at the prime minister's discretion, foreign and local capital were given the same status. Investors were allowed to buy or rent land to establish commercial premises. The law ruled out nationalization or sequestration of private assets; impounding of goods without due legal process; and requisitioning of property without compensation.

Imports of fixed assets for an investment project were exempted from customs duties and taxes. Profits were given a tax exemption for five years, which the Council of Ministers could extend by a maximum further ten years. In a measure aimed at spreading investment across the country, the republic's territory was divided into two zones, 'A' and 'B', for investment purposes; if the project was in zone B, it might get an immediate seven- instead of five-year profit tax exemption. A similar rule also applied to projects owned by a company at least 25 per cent of whose capital was generated by public subscription: a stipulation by which the government wanted to mobilize local private capital further.

There was to be no compulsory pricing for products of these projects, provided they did not have a monopoly. In 'extraordinary' circumstances, the Council of Ministers was given the power to fix the prices of staple foods (flour, bread, milk), baby foods and medicines. Once licensed, a project could open a foreign currency account with a bank registered with the central bank, and net profits made as a result of foreign capital invested could be transferred abroad, provided the project remained within the limits of the credit balance of the foreign exchange account (in accordance with specific executive regulations). The investment law was explicit in requiring investment projects to employ as many locals as possible. However, expatriates could be employed under a licence, in which case they would receive a renewable working permit for three years. Expatriates working in administrative and technical jobs were given the right to transfer

60 per cent of their net earnings abroad, also within the limits of the credit balance mentioned above.[35]

In the *General Economic Memorandum* which the government presented to the 1992 UNDP-sponsored round-table conference with donors, three crucial policy objectives were identified: (1) to increase the rate of growth of the economy; (2) to reduce the deficits on the balance of payments, the current account and the government budget, as well as inflation, through reform of the exchange rate, monetary and fiscal policies; (3) to abolish state monopolies and to give the private sector the primary role in expanding economic activity and diversification. In the latter respect, the government saw its own role as one of providing the framework for the private sector to fulfil this function in. Government investment, therefore, was intended to be concentrated in infrastructure and training, while further liberalizing the economy (including imports) and reducing state commercial activity.[36]

Yet the effect of the new investment law and economic policy on boosting the economy was limited: the necessary precondition for any substantial success was absent: namely, a stabilization of the internal political situation, and full reintegration of the country in the regional and international community as regards trade, aid and other benefits that had been lost in the wake of the Iraqi invasion of Kuwait. The country's financial situation was catastrophic, and this affected both the general economic environment and the government's ability to build up the services and basic infrastructure within which (especially foreign) investors would be able to thrive. It also heightened the potential for socio-political disturbances and disenchantment, while limiting the governments resources to pre-empt or manage such problems through largesse, patronage or other means.

THE 1993 ELECTIONS[37]

Yemen's first free elections in April 1993 were greeted as a sign that the country's fledgeling democracy would not, after all, be stillborn. However, they also occurred against the background of increased tensions between the northern and southern leaderships, and of multiplying instances of violence and demonstrations. The latter, in turn, were related to the political rivalry between the competing parties, as well as to the country's economic difficulties, and in particular a certain sense in the south that its interests were not being sufficiently observed. The conduct of the elections was less than perfect, but nevertheless allowed an essentially democratic process to unfold. Two contradictory qualifications must be applied here, however. The first was the declaration by Ali Abdullah Salih and Ali Salim al-Baidh, that they would continue their cooperation after the election: this could be construed as holding out a perpetuation of the power-sharing deal which had been in place since unification. On the other hand, it was in fact inevitable that the smaller constituency of the YSP would now be reflected in its representation in parliament – implying either a conflict with the party's power-sharing expectation, or its relegation to junior-partner status, possibly even below that of Islah. Indeed, with only about a fifth of the population living in the south, and the election law provision that the 301 constituencies should have a roughly equal number of voters, such an outcome seemed inevitable. The very democracy which had arguably facilitated the original establishment of unity, therefore, was likely to put obstacles in the way of its further development. As Whitaker has expressed it, national unity and democracy in Yemen proved to be 'a marriage of inconvenience.'[38]

In all, 2.7 million people registered to vote – including over three-quarters of eligible males. A great majority of the 4800 candidates who registered were independents. Debate and campaigning were vigorous and widespread – even if punctuated with some intimidation and violence. In the end, the GPC predictably emerged as the largest party with 123 of the 301 seats, followed by Islah (62) and the YSP (57). The latter's success was mainly in former South Yemen – confirming the persistent geographical split in the political scene. There had been clear cooperation between the GPC and the Islah in the North, evidenced by candidate withdrawals in each other's favour in several constituencies, while there were only a few such arrangements between the GPC and the YSP in the South.

Following the elections, the three main parties formed a coalition government under the YSP's Haidar Abu Bakr al-Attas, and containing 15 ministers from the GPC, 8 from the YSP, 6 from the Islah and 1 from the Ba'ath Party (close to the GPC). This proved only the beginning of a further series of difficulties, however. The continued divide within the country had been glaringly demonstrated; the mutual suspicion between the parties (mainly GPC and Islah on the one hand, and the YSP on the other) had by no means been eradicated – and neither had their difficulty in cooperating effectively; there was sharp disagreement between Islah and the YSP over the former's demand for a change in the constitution to make Islam the sole source of legislation; and the YSP's al-Baidh – officially the country's vice-president – expressed his unhappiness at northern domination and the failure to resolve the assassinations of YSP figures over the previous months, by withdrawing to Aden in August 1993 and refusing to return to Sana'a.[39]

THE ROAD TO WAR[40]

Although the YSP leader was confirmed *in absentia* as the vice-president of the five-man presidency council in October 1993 – in a deal which saw the GPC drop one of its seats and give it to Islah – he still refused to return to Sana'a to be sworn in. A major part of his grievances centred around the question of security for his followers and YSP members. Later that month, his own nephew was murdered in Aden, and scores of YSP members (over a hundred and fifty, according to al-Baidh himself) had been killed by late 1993. As a condition for his return to Sana'a, he demanded the implementation of an eighteen-point programme, which included security guarantees, the arrest of those responsible for the assassinations, and greater administrative but especially economic autonomy for the south. The perception among the YSP leadership – and indeed in much of the south – was that the central control over the country's oil resources gave President Salih too much power relative to other (in particular southern) political actors. This rankled especially because September 1993 had seen the coming on-stream of oil production from the southern Masila fields, and the prospect that the south might in fact turn out to be more endowed with hydrocarbon resources than the north. In the latter part of the year the YSP leader hinted several times at the possibility that unity might have to be seen as a thing of the past.

Both the GPC and Islah next issued a list of demands of their own. Under pressure from prominent members of the Yemeni intelligentsia and of respected tribal leaders such as Shaikh

Mujahid Abu Shuwarib (of the Hashid tribal federation) and Shaikh Sinan Abu Luhum (of the Bakil), a national dialogue committee was established to come up with a compromise set of points for reform on which all sides might be able to agree. The Document of Pledge and Accord which emerged from several months of deliberation, was eventually signed by the main political leaders on 20 February 1994 in a ceremony in Jordan hosted by King Hussein. The king had been among the many Arab and other personalities trying to avert a crisis for the previous few months. The document reflected the main concerns of the YSP, indeed stipulating both a degree of devolution from the centre, and the investigation of the assassinations and the punishment of those responsible. This was the first time 'the two Alis' had met since the start of al-Baidh's self-imposed internal exile. Yet the lack of trust, indeed the antagonism, between president and vice-president was not hereby diminished. Al-Baidh returned to Aden, insisting that he wanted to see action on the agreed points, in particular on the punishment of those behind the assassinations. As there was a fairly widespread suspicion in Aden that Ali Muhammad Salih, one of the president's brothers and a senior general, was one of those involved, along with other members of his entourage, there were strong doubts about the northern leader's commitment to the pledge signed in Amman, which implied disbanding and reorganizing some of the security units accused of such involvement.

Military clashes broke out shortly after the signing and southern units moved to the oil-rich Shabwa province a few days later. The establishment of an international military mediation committee and the efforts of Arab and other mediators, including Sultan Qaboos and US Assistant Secretary of State Pelletrau, proved unable to turn the tide of increasing clashes. On 12 April, Prime Minister al-Attas left the country ostensibly for medical reasons. While in itself adding to the country's state of crisis, this move might also be interpreted as evidence that the southern leadership had decided it had reached the point of no return.

THE 1994 FIGHTING[41]

On 27 April, the anniversary of the elections, a major battle broke out at the Amran military base, involving over two hundred tanks and resulting in some two hundred or more wounded and killed. Both sides claimed the other side had started the fighting. In a brief lull, US Assistant Secretary of State Pelletrau made a final attempt at resolving the crisis, but on 5 May, a day after his arrival in Sana'a, the war broke out in earnest with the bombardment of Sana'a and Aden by planes from the opposing side. The Northern members of the presidential council dismissed al-Baidh and his fellow YSP council member as secessionists. Prime Minister al-Attas, still abroad, was also dismissed. The YSP in turn suspended its membership in the Yemeni parliament, and the leadership launched an assiduous campaign to attract regional support and international mediation.

In the fighting which followed, it appears clear that the southern leadership had calculated that its military could overcome the North's forces on their own territory. In fact, President Salih fairly swiftly succeeded in taking the battle to the south – all the while proclaiming his willingness to cooperate with mediation efforts but never halting his drive to take Aden and the Hadhramaut. The southern leadership issued calls for a return to the conditions of the Document of Pledge and Accord, but this was deflected by Sana'a as a ploy.

On 21 May the crisis moved into a new phase, with al-Baidh's announcement from his base in the Hadhramaut that a new Democratic Republic of Yemen was seceding from the united republic. Mediation attempts continued, including a UN Security Council Resolution (924) calling for an immediate ceasefire. Saudi Arabia actively supported the secessionists' plea for UN intervention, while the line from Sanàa remained that this was an internal Yemeni matter. The position of the Gulf Cooperation Council states, except Qatar, was made clearer when they issued a communiqué on 5 June calling on an immediate ceasefire, and warning the party which would not comply – a reference to the government in Sana'a – while depicting the secession as a reaction against the military offensive by Salih's forces.

This position can be explained (1) by the Al-Sa'ud's long-standing antipathy to the Salih regime, combined with a preference for a divided Yemen where they would in effect become the patron of the new Southern state; and (2) by these states' continued resentment over the stance of Sana'a in the Gulf crisis.

By this time, however, the group around al-Baidh was fighting a losing battle. They had withdrawn mainly to the Hadhrami town of Mukalla (al-Baidh himself and many of his entourage being of Hadhrami origin), and proved increasingly unable to counter the northern offensives. These were punctuated with a number of unilateral ceasefires declared by President Salih in response to UN Security Council demands – but without seriously slowing the northern advance. On 28 June the Northern forces succeeded in blocking off Aden's oil and water supply, combining this with intensified bombardment of the city.

On 6 July Aden saw Northern troops enter the city, distributing food and water to the inhabitants. A day later, all of Aden was in northern hands. On 6 July also, the inhabitants of Mukalla, having first persuaded the secessionist leadership to flee to Oman, surrendered in order to save the city and airport from destruction. The Southern leaders based in Aden also fled to Djibouti and hence to Saudi Arabia and other destinations. (Abdulrahman al-Jifri, the non-YSP vice-president of the breakaway republic, was in fact a Saudi citizen – having gone into exile from South Yemen at the time of the Communist takeover.)

The tensions and grievances between north and south, but especially between the respective leaderships, provide the context within which al-Baidh's chosen path – problematic and ultimately unsuccessful as it was – must be explained. But this context does not by itself provide a complete explanation. Moving from the general to the specific, a number of factors suggest themselves. As indicated earlier, many in the South felt that Southern political, social and economic interests were being marginalized by the Northern leadership. There was widespread resentment also over the economic hardship being felt in the south (even though this was as much a consequence of the freer play of market forces as of unification itself). By 1993 it had become clear also that, with southern oil production coming on-stream, the population of a separate southern Yemeni state would benefit from greater revenues than if they stayed part of the united republic. While this did not translate into general support for separation among the population, the prospect of greater economic autonomy, at least, did have a strong appeal for the leadership. After all, it had been economic collapse and the regime's weakness which had dictated the accelerated pace of unification in 1990; both of these could conceivably be reversed with oil revenues. Moreover, there is no doubt that the Southern leadership received support for their demand for autonomy, and subsequently separation, from the ruling families in Saudi Arabia and Kuwait.

As Whitaker has argued, none of this meant that al-Baidh and the YSP had a preconceived plan to secede:

A more accurate way to describe the YSP's position shortly before the war would be to say that it reverted to what it had been before 1990 and, indeed, throughout most of the history of the PDRY: support for unity in principle, but not under the regime in Sana'a. The consequence of this was that YSP policy ran along two different tracks at the same time: one unionist, the other separatist.. On the one hand they were trying to bring down Salih but retaining secession as a fall-back if that failed. On the other, they were seeking secession as a platform from which to bring down Salih later.[42]

It is true that since August 1993 the Southern leadership under al-Baidh was actively working to maintain or create separate institutions, whether at the level of the bureaucracy or at that of the military. At the same time, however, they remained involved in national politics and more specifically in attempts to build alliances with groups in the North who were seen as critical of the Salih regime.[43] This ambivalence was maintained until well into the war. The three-week delay in declaring secession, for instance, must be explained by the two reasons suggested by Whitaker:

The first was that [al-Baidh] opted for secession reluctantly. He knew it would be unpopular with the Yemeni public; it would cost him what support he had among disaffected northerners; and it risked splitting his own party (as indeed happened). The second was that he declared secession mainly for external reasons, when it became clear that his forces were losing the war and he badly needed international support[:] international recognition [would allow] sympathetic states [to] provide arms openly.[44]

The reasons for the failure of the YSP and the secessionists' bid can be summarized under four headings. First, they miscalculated the relative strengths of the northern and the southern militaries, and their ability to count on disaffected groups in the North. Several leading figures have since confided that they expected the fighting, when it came, to take place mainly in the north.[45] In fact of course, Salih quickly took the war to the south. Second, the forces loyal to former South Yemeni President Ali Nasir Muhammad, which were based in the north, played a major role in aiding the northern offensive; leading officers had inside knowledge of the defence layout of the southern forces and installations, and made this count in the northern victory. Third, once they opted for secession, support even among the population of the South dwindled, and the southern leadership itself became sharply divided. There was no real, major constituency for the short-lived secessionist government. And fourth, while the regional environment appeared to be propitious for an attempt at secession, the role of the US countered this: Washington's pressure on the Gulf states to desist, and its own explicit support for Yemeni unity, probably sealed the fate of the breakaway republic.

AFTER THE WAR: THE POLITICAL SCENE

After the fighting, President Salih promised reconstruction and reconciliation, following this up with an amnesty for all those who had been involved in the conflict on the Southern side, except for Ali Salim al-Baidh and fifteen others (by late 1995, even those fifteen appeared to be considered for an amnesty). Many indeed returned to Yemen, even though some of the key leaders established an opposition front (the so-called 'Mowj') based abroad, and headed by Abdulrahman al-Jifri. This front has comparatively little clout among Yemenis generally, however, in part because of the involvement of members in the secession attempt, and in part because of their foreign base and sponsorship. Nevertheless, the military victory did not take away President Salih's need for a delicate balancing game.

The Islah party, the GPC's partner in the North, demanded that the YSP be excluded from power, after its involvement in the separatist adventure. Indeed, the government formed in October 1994 contained no YSP ministers. The South was represented by non-YSP figures, including prominent members of the Ali Nasir Muhammad faction, under the GPC flag. The YSP, shorn of its separatist element, became in effect an opposition party. The Islah also imposed its views in other respects. The most important was the amendment of the constitution (as of 1 October 1994) to make Islam into the sole source of legislation in

Yemen.[46] Another instance was the destruction of the Aden brewery (until then the only brewery in the Arabian Peninsula). At the same time, however, the amended constitution held out greater devolution away from the centre. This held out the possibility of reconciliation with those who had supported the YSP's grievances. Indeed, by late 1995 the government was holding out olive branches to members of the southern opposition, as well as other opposition forces. It appeared that even the opposition front based abroad was being offered such overtures. This was very much in character for Ali Abdullah Salih. Having overcome the YSP challenge, he was not prepared to accept serious challenges from the Islamists either. As Schmitz observed,

In September [1994] fundamentalists mounted an effort to destroy religious sites in Aden that they felt were not proper; some 2000 armed men equipped with heavy construction equipment descended upon the city in a well-organized operation. The president responded by rushing military reinforcements to Aden, and the attackers were repelled.[47]

It seems clear, therefore, that the President is rebuilding an alliance with Southern and other non-Islamist elements, in order to contain the independent power of the Islamist wing of the Islah. It is in any case far from certain whether this party itself can stay together, given the more pragmatic, traditional-tribal instincts of the substantial part of its membership, which looks toward Shaikh Abdullah al-Ahmar as its leader.

While attempting to play the domestic balancing game, the Sanàa regime was also busy trying to build bridges with Saudi Arabia and the Gulf states. This culminated in the president's visit to Saudi Arabia in the Summer of 1995, and the official condemnation later that year of the Iraqi invasion of Kuwait by the regime. This followed the agreement on 26 February of a Memorandum of Understanding which reconfirmed the 1934 Taif signing on the border between the two states, and committed both sides to peaceful coexistence.[48] This had an immediate impact on the perception of the country's chances of recovery and stability, even if a Saudi statement that Yemenis would again be free to seek employment in the kingdom did not come until September 1995.

While future Yemeni prosperity will depend to a large extent on the degree of political stability which can be achieved or maintained, conversely, political stability will depend to a large extent on containing the economic crisis and its effect on people's lives. If the economic situation can be contained, the factor of socio-ideological differences will be less acute. Moreover, extra resources will allow the government to continue coopting the tribal forces. The two-way linkage between the latter factor and economic developments is illustrated perhaps most strikingly by the situation in the Marib and Jawf governorates where the North's original oilfields are located. There have been a number of armed clashes between government forces and local tribesmen, and these are certain to recur and perhaps gain in intensity unless the tribal leaders perceive that a suitable *quid* is received for the *quo* of sharing their control of the territory with the central state for the purposes of oil exploration; the government, on the other hand, absolutely needs to be able to rely on the oil revenues which can be generated in order to continue the state consolidation project and assure its own survival. Development allocations, therefore, are likely to give special attention to these areas, as well as to the tribal hinterland in general; this will fulfil both the function of extending the state's physical reach into these regions (and its ability to deliver services), and that of coopting the tribal leaderships. Yet in the aftermath of the 1994 civil war, the importance of the government's ability to direct resources into a coopting and pacifying exercise also ranges beyond the specifically tribal issue, especially as regards the south. Moreover, as the government has indeed recognized, some signs of economic recovery would be crucial if it is to come through these elections unscathed without having to subvert them.

THE POSTWAR ECONOMY

The four key economic variables which will impinge on Yemen's future are (1) the development of the hydrocarbons sector and revenues from it; (2) the fate of returnees (i.e. mainly the former migrant workers in Saudi Arabia); (3) the level of international aid; and (4) the success of the restructuring programme and efforts to attract domestic and expatriate investment. All four depend to varying degrees on the political situation, as demonstrated earlier. All are urgent imperatives, given Yemen's acute financial difficulties and high level of unemployment.

Yemen's situation of financial crisis is characterized by (1) continued balance of payments deficits; (2) continued government deficit spending; and (3) mounting foreign debt. The country's projected current account deficit for 1995 is $1.1 billion, rising to $1.5 billion in 1996. The government's budget deficit has been running at between 20 and 30 per cent of GDP in recent years. In 1993 and 1994 no budgets were issued, but the deficits in these two years can be estimated at some YR30 billion (about $550 million) and YR50 billion (nearly $600 million) respectively. The 1995 budget looked as if it was spiralling further out of control, until a retrenchment plan in worked out in May that year promised to bring it down from YR60 billion to YR37 billion (about $400 million). It is unclear whether the government will be able to deliver on this promise. The significance of these sums, as reflected in the rough US dollar equivalents given above, in part depends on the exchange rate used. The average rate of YR per $1 for these years was 29 (1992), 54 (1993), 85 (1994), and a projected average of 100 for 1995: this in itself indicates some of the difficulties the economy is suffering.[49]

Total official foreign debt – the inevitable result of years of heavy deficit spending – by the end of 1995 may be estimated at close to $10 billion. This includes $3 to 4 billion in debts to the former Eastern bloc (largely for arms deals); there is no agreement over whether and how to repay various parts of this Eastern bloc debt, and in particular over the exchange rate to be used. The above estimate is higher than some other published estimates: this is because the latter either exclude the Eastern bloc debt and/or use unrealistic exchange rates.

The resultant need for the resumption of larger aid flows is in large measure dependent on good foreign relations – especially with Saudi Arabia and Kuwait. Some modest success is already being achieved in this respect. Gross ODA inflows in 1995 may be projected at some $250 to 300 million, and improved relations with Western donors as well as with Saudi Arabia (the latter since the summer of 1995) hold out at least some further improvement. Yemen is unlikely, however, ever again to receive aid at the levels prevailing in the 1980s.

There is an urgent need to regain a higher level of expatriate employment, both to relieve the financial deficit and the extremely high level of unemployment. In mid-1995, it may be estimated that between 40 and 50 per cent of the labour force were either unemployed or underemployed. (The UNDP estimate for 1994 is 37 per cent unemployed.) This may acquire serious political implications, as well as being a huge social and economic problem, especially since the population is likely to double well within the next two decades – unless the rate of population growth is curbed. Again, therefore, the need for improved foreign relations with the Gulf states – where the majority of expatriate workers would go – stands out. It would appear that a breakthrough was achieved in this respect in late September 1995, with the announcement by Saudi Interior Minister Prince Nayif bin Abdul-Aziz that Saudi companies and individuals were free to bring Yemeni workers into the kingdom.[50] Again, however, the economic climate in the Gulf states means that the level of remittances obtaining in the 1980s will remain out of reach.

Whatever else happens, government spending must be kept under tight control. The May 1995 budget plan presented a step in the right direction, but the restraint should be consistent and long-term. This is not, however, to argue for cuts in areas such as primary education and basic health care provision: these are at the root of Yemen's future human potential, while also being important elements in any strategy to control population growth. In any event, the difficulty here is likely to lie in political constraints. Reductions in subsidies are bound to be politically unattractive, and patronage spending is likely to retain its role. In addition, military spending is unlikely to be scaled back significantly – however important that would be.

The need for IMF and World Bank aid, along with the economic stabilization and restructuring which such aid will be conditional on, cannot be avoided. Success in this respect of course depends in part on the control of government spending. A successful aid and restructuring programme could have three types of beneficial effects: (1) extra aid would flow in; (2) deficit spending would be reduced; and (3) the scope for domestic and foreign investment would increase. In the course of December 1995 and January 1996 a package of reforms and measures was agreed between the government and the institutions by January 1996, and both sides declared themselves moderately optimistic about the chances of the package proving successful. In the first three years this package would include $300 million in new aid. The hope is that the IMF/World Bank lead will encourage larger ODA flows from other sources, as well as increasing investor confidence. Importantly, a $50 million social fund is included in the plans, to safeguard those most vulnerable to the initial effects of the stabilization and restructuring measures. This is in line with the recent shift in World Bank thinking towards the recognition of the importance of poverty alleviation and social safety nets. This new awareness may give the implementation and outcome of such plans a greater chance of achieving some degree of success.

The agreement[51] also holds out a significant further liberalization of the economy and investment conditions. Among other things, the government promised that 15 to 20 public enterprises would be brought to the point of sale within a year. The prospect of shedding some 60 000 public employees was held out. It was hoped that the official exchange rate could be devalued to $1: YR115, while subsidies on energy, water, health and education would be reduced.

Oil, the great hope of Yemen's leaders at the time of unification, has certainly made a difference, but has not quite lived up to its promise. Today's estimates of Yemen's recoverable oil reserves stand at only 2.2 billion barrels – down from hopes of 5 billion barrels or more in the late 1980s. This is the equivalent of 15 to 16 years' production. Projected average annual production levels are 350 000 barrels per day (b/d) in 1995, rising to 360 000 b/d the following year and 390 000 b/d in 1997. These levels are based on the continued production of some 350 000 b/d from the Marib/Jawf and Masila field, and production starting up from the Jannah and East Shabwa blocs, which should be producing 25 000 b/d and 12 000 b/d by late 1996. In the course of 1997, production may be expanded to 400 000 b/d. It remains unclear how much the government is receiving from this in revenue. The details of initial hefty down-payment deals for the granting of concessions to companies were in many cases not revealed. Moreover, in the wake of disappointing results, some of these are now being challenged by the oil firms concerned. As regards income from oil produced, this again is difficult to ascertain. There are different cost recovery and royalty arrangements with different companies, and each of these operates on a sliding scale depending on the volume of production. Again, in the wake of disappointing results, some of these arrangements are being renegotiated.[52] It seems clear, however, that the government's share of oil revenue will remain under $1 billion in 1996.

Account must also be taken of the country's domestic requirements, which run at about 65 000 b/d.

With modest production, modest reserves, and generous takings by the oil companies involved for cost recovery and otherwise (takings which are being revised upwards in 1995 because of these firms' downward revisions in expected exploration results), it is clear that oil cannot by itself be the answer to the government's – and the country's – dilemmas.

Gas reserves are estimated at anywhere between 15–20 trillion cubic feet (cf) – potentially worth two or three times the value of the country's oil reserves. These reserves are located mainly in the Marib/Jawf concession, where Hunt is the lead operator. The government has an agreement with the French oil company Total for the development of a $5 billion LNG project which is meant to exploit these gas reserves mainly for export. The LNG plant and associated equipment are provisionally costed at $3 billion, while the necessary pipelines would come to $2 billion. The project will be 30 per cent government-owned, while 70 per cent of the capital will be in the hands of Total and other companies joining in the scheme. The project is scheduled to come on-stream in 2001, and have a 25-year life, during which 1 trillion cf would be produced for domestic consumption, and 10 trillion cf for export, probably via a terminal on the Red Sea. Potentially, this could be worth some $600 million a year in export revenue.

The difficulty is that the obvious partners for investment – the companies already involved in the Marib/Jawf concession, and Hunt in particular – are proving less than eager to join in at the terms which are being offered. While protracted negotiations are not unusual in these types of LNG schemes, it does seem to indicate a lesser degree of confidence in the scheme's long-term commercial attraction than the government and Total were assuming. This is particularly significant, since these firms are the very ones who developed the fields in the first place. The insecurity of expectations is in part due to the peculiar nature of LNG projects: they require enormous investments not just at the producing end but also by the consumers, necessitating a long-term, secure supply relationship. This in turn requires confidence both in the long-term level of production and in the ability to set a realistic long-term price. Given some apparent hesitations about the nature of the field, but especially about the political environment within which the scheme would have to be executed, it is by no means a foregone conclusion that the necessary billions in investment will in fact be found within the time envisaged. Serious delays, of course, imply the possibility that other suppliers would get in first.

The country's two areas of immediate need in the field of hydrocarbons, therefore, are (1) increased exploration and development, especially for oil, and (2) measures to increase confidence in the LNG project's feasibility. Both depend largely on political factors. Indeed, the prospects for oil exploration and development depend on (a) offering better conditions to oil companies (this is already being done); and (b) investor confidence. The latter in turn depends on improved domestic stability, and the consolidation of good relations with Saudi Arabia. Confidence in the future of the LNG project (necessary to persuade investors to sink the necessary capital into the project's development, and consumers to commit themselves to long-term supply agreements) again depends to a large extent on the assurance of a sufficient degree of political stability in Yemen.

Outside the hydrocarbons sector, and apart from the potential of the fisheries sector which remains thus far underdeveloped, it is clear that the economy generally, and the unemployment situation in particular, in the longer term require economic diversification and the growth of industry. Among other things it would be of the utmost importance to boost productive enterprise based on the returnees and their assets, as well as attracting expatriate and foreign investment.

The main opportunity for expansion and diversification of the country's industrial sector would seem to lie in the realization of the potential which the Aden Free Zone represents. The master plan was completed before the 1994 fighting, and the government had repeatedly held out development of the scheme as a key component of its economic plans. Following the end of the civil war, however, announcements that the government would not itself consider funding the scheme's development a priority indicated an apparent loss of interest. This led to speculation that the victorious powers were not interested in this essentially southern project, and indeed might wish to 'punish' the south. At the same time, this apparent lack of political commitment was combined with a falling away of investor confidence as a result of the political upheaval.

However, by the autumn of 1995, two international consortia were actively interested in taking on the main scheme – although their respective bids differed in scope. A group headed by the UK-based MBI International Group was proposing the construction of a container transshipment area on Caltex Island, while a consortium led by the Yemen Investment & Development Company (Yeminco) was putting forward a more comprehensive development, including expansion of the Maalla terminal, the building of an industrial estate and a world trade centre, and also the upgrading of Aden airport. It is worth noting in this regard, that Yeminco is in fact the local subsidiary of the Saudi Economic Development Company (SADCO), owned by the Saudi Bin Mahfouz family (itself of Hadhrami origin). The final contract was signed with Yeminco in March 1996.[53] This development both indicated confidence in Aden's potential, and is likely to engender further interest. Such potential – at least from the point of view of foreign investors – is in large measure due to Aden's position as one of the most impressive and best-located natural harbours in the world. Given the right political environment and a swift enough development, the prospect of the port reclaiming much of its former glory is not wholly fanciful. In addition to the economic benefits to be derived, there is of course the very important political effect it would have: first, it would contribute to the integration of the south into the nation and demonstrate that the interests of this part of Yemen can indeed be well served within a united Yemen; second, the contribution to the country's overall economic fortunes would be a major factor in favour of political stability and consolidation.

The same argument applies for other types of investment – whether by expatriate Yemeni or other foreign investment in the industrial diversification of the country. Whether for the Adeni scheme or more generally, the two key conditions remain (1) a stabilization and restructuring package with the World Bank and IMF which is seen to be effective, and (2) political stability.

In sum, Yemen's main economic opportunities would appear to lie in the following areas: (1) gas – but this remains somewhat uncertain and can in any case only be viewed in the longer term; (2) oil: this remains crucially important for the balance of payments, but will remain relatively modest; (3) the development of the fisheries potential; (4) the development of the Aden Free

Trade Zone, Aden Port and the Aden refinery; (5) the pursuit of labour export. Meanwhile, serious economic restructuring should open the way for significant foreign assistance, as well as, indirectly, investment.

CONCLUSION

The Yemen Republic's dire economic situation and the government's lack of resources have a four-fold political impact. They create greater hardship and dashed expectations for much of the population, thus undercutting the regime's support base and security; this in turn endangers the hoped-for liberalization and stabilization of the political scene generally (as exemplified by the upcoming 1997 elections). It also reduces the state's capacity to extend its grasp over territory and society. Third, it diminishes the government's ability to coopt or even temporarily pacify the tribal leaderships which it needs so much to keep on board (in the absence of effective state control over the tribal areas) in order to maintain political stability and to safeguard uninterrupted oil exploration and production. And fourth, it reduces the ability to tie in and stimulate the southern economy in a way that would diminish the local population's grievances over their lot in the united republic.

Yemen, then, needs all the help it can get, both in overseas aid and in investment. At the same time, the Yemeni government itself would need to focus its energies, politically, on domestic political reconciliation and consolidation, as well as the further improvement of regional relations. Economically, determined restructuring – while safeguarding the most vulnerable sections of the population – and the creation of an investment-friendly climate must be at the top of the agenda. These two clusters of imperatives are, of course, strongly interlinked. President Salih has long been renowned for his skill at playing the balancing game between tribes, army and modernizing technocrats. Much will depend on whether he is able to display the same skill when it comes to the 'new' constituencies of the Islamists and the southern population. As of 1996, the indications were that he would. Yet without tangible success on the economic front, this may yet prove insufficient.

NOTES

1. BBC, *Summary of World Broadcasts* (SWB) ME, 4 December 1989; *Neue Zürcher Zeitung*, 9 December 1989; and R. Burrowes, 'Prelude to Unification: the Yemen Arab Republic, 1962–1990', *International Journal of Middle East Studies*, vol. 23 (1991), pp. 483–506.
2. Burrowes, 'Prelude to unification', op. cit., esp. p. 470.
3. R. Burrowes, *The Yemen Arab Republic: The Politics of Development, 1962–1986* (Westview Boulder, Colo., 1987). This volume covers most events and political-economic developments, including inter-Yemeni affairs, until 1986.
4. Although one account interprets the North Yemeni leadership's position as, rather, 'playing to the gallery', trying to get Aden off-balance, in the expectation that the South Yemeni leaders would not respond positively to unification moves: C. Dunbar, 'The Unification of Yemen: Process, Politics and Prospects', *Middle East Journal*, vol. 46, no. 3 (1992), p. 460.
5. Figures from IMF, *International Financial Statistics*, and World Bank, *Debt Tables*, 1988–89.
6. *Economist Intelligence Unit (EIU), Country Report: Bahrain, Qatar, Oman, the Yemens, 1986*, no. 2. (Economist Intelligence Unit, London, 1986). On Soviet policy towards South Yemen, see also F. Halliday, 'Moscow's Crisis Management: the Case of South Yemen' in *Middle East Report*, March–April 1988, pp. 18–22.
7. *EIU Country Report: Bahrain, etc. Qatan, Oman*, 1989, no. 2.
8. *EIU Country Report: Bahrain, etc. the Yemens*, 1988 nos. 3, 4; *1989*, no. 3.
9. See for instance *Country Report: Bahrain, etc., 1988*, no. 3, and *Middle East Economic Digest* (MEED), 1 December 1989.
10. *The Middle East*, April 1989.
11. Dunbar, op. cit., p. 469.
12. *EIU Country Report: Bahrain Qatar, Oman, the Yemens*, 1988, no. 2; 1989, nos. 2, 3.
13. Yemini Office of Unity Affairs, *Al-Yaman al-wahid: silsila watha'iqiya 'an al-wahda al-yamaniya*, 4th edn, Sanàa, May 1990, pp. 236–8.
14. *SWB* ME, 18 November 1989.
15. Dunbar, op. cit., p 45.
16. *SWB* ME, 16 November 1989.
17. See also Dunbar, op. cit., p. 461.
18. *SWB* ME, 13 December 1989.
19. *Neue Zürcher Zeitung*, 9 December 1989.
20. SWB ME, 5 December 1989.
21. *MEED*, 17 November 1989.
22. *SWB* ME, 5 December 1989.
23. *EIU Oman, Yemen: Country Profile*, 1992–93, p. 36.
24. *EIU Country Report: Oman, Yemen, 1992*, no. 3, pp. 26–30.
25. *EIU Country Report: Bahrain Qatar, Oman, Yemen, 1990*, no. 3 pp. 37–8; and no. 4, p. 41.
26. *EIU Country Report: Oman, Yemen, 1992*, no. 2, p. 26; and *Oman, Yemen: Country Profile 1992–93*, p. 74.

27. See *MEED*, 3 May 1991, for a contemporary report. For a more extensive treatment of the Yemeni economy with the relevant estimates, see Gerd Nonneman, 'Key Issues in the Yemeni Economy', in George Joffé (ed.), *The Unity of Yemen: Crisis and Solutions* (London: St Malo Press, 1996).
28. *EIU, Country Report: Bahrain, Qatar, Oman, Yemen, 1990*, no. 3, p. 39.
29. *EIU, Country Report: Bahrain, Qatar, Oman, Yemen, 1990*, no. 4, p. 41.
30. For a digest of the draft legislation on incentives for foreign investors in the Free Zone, see *MEED Country Report: Oman, Yemen, 1992*, no. 2, p. 31.
31. See *MEED*, 30 August, 1991, quoting statements by Vice-President Ali Salim al-Baidh; also *Middle East Economic Digest*, 26 April 1991; 12 July 1991.
32. *MEED*, 29 March 1991; 5 April 1991; 9 August 1991.
33. *EIU, Country Report: Oman, Yemen, 1992*, no. 1, p. 22.
34. *EIU Country Report: Oman, Yemen, 1991*, no. 1, p. 25.
35. See *Middle East Economic Digest*, 26 July 1991.
36. *EIU Country Report: Oman Yemen*, 1992, no. 3, pp. 34–5.
37. The best treatment of these elections can be found in Sheila Carapico, 'Elections and Mass Politics in Yemen', *Middle East Report*, November 1993, pp. 2–6, and Renaud Detalle, 'The Yemeni Elections Up Close', in ibid., pp. 8–12. The reader is referred to these sources for a detailed account and analysis.
38. Brian Whitaker, 'National Unity and Democracy in Yemen: a Marriage of Inconvenience', a paper presented at the Conference on The Unity of Yemen: Crisis and Solutions London, SOAS, pp. 25–26 November (to be published in G. Joffé, op. cit.).
39. See for instance Eric Watkins, 'Not a Happy Family', in *The Middle East*, December 1993, pp. 14–16; and Eric Watkins and Patrick Makin, 'Yemen's Crisis Threatens the Country's Unity', *Middle East International*, 19 November 1993, pp. 18–19.
40. Good coverage of this period can be found in the contemporary issues of *Middle East International* and *The Middle East*. A useful chronology of the period from January to October 1994 is given in the Royal United Services Institution's *International Security Review 1995*, pp. 227–34.
41. See the chronology in RUSI's *International Security Review 1995*, pp. 227–34.
42. Whitaker, op. cit., p. 4.
43. See also C. Schmitz, 'Civil War in Yemen: the Price of Unity?', in *Current History*, January 1995, pp. 33–6.
44. Whitaker, op. cit., p. 4.
45. Ibid.
46. See *The Constitution of the Republic of Yemen*, translation published by the Information Services and Translation Center, Sanàa, 1994.
47. C. Schmitz, op. cit., p. 36.
48. For more details on the agreement, see *MEES* (Middle East Economic Survey) 6 March 1995.
49. Sources: author's estimates, IMF; official statistics, EIU.
50. *Middle East Economic Digest*, 27 October 1995.

51. See the report by Abdulaziz al-Saqqaf in the *Yemen Times* of 4 December 1995.
52. See for instance *Middle East Economic Digest*, 22 May 1995 and 7 August. 1995.
53. For a summary of the MBI-led bid, see *Middle East Economic Digest*, 29 September 1995; for the Yemico-led bid, see *Middle East Economic Digest*, 3 November 1995. For a report on the final contract, see *Yemen Times*, 25 March and 1 April 1996.

5 Security Structures in the Middle East: An Overview
Anoushiravan Ehteshami

INTRODUCTION

In the Middle East, unlike perhaps in Europe, the issues at stake in the post-cold-war environment are not simply to reshape the past to fit a new reality, but rather to shape the future in view of the new realities – which themselves stem from the end of the cold war, the disintegration of the USSR and the changing alliance patterns within the region itself and among the regional actors.

To speak of 'security structures' in the Middle East, therefore, is largely to speak of a need to establish new realities and modes of interaction among and between the states and peoples of the region.

IS TALK OF THE NEED FOR CREATING SECURITY STRUCTURES IN THE MIDDLE EAST PREMATURE?

Some years ago, the realistic answer to the above question might have been in the affirmative. A glance at the history of conflict in the Middle East since 1945 reveals why. In the 1945–91 period, the region experienced five Arab–Israeli wars, the two Gulf Wars and a handful of other (largely) inter-Arab conflicts. In addition to the unnecessary loss of life in these wars, the material damage done in each conflict has been enormous. To illustrate the point with reference to the two Gulf Wars, it is estimated that the Iran–Iraq War cost the two belligerents some $1 trillion,[1] and the 1991 Gulf War cost all parties concerned some $310 billion ($250 billion in damage to Iraq and $60 billion the cost of Operations Desert Shield and Storm).[2]

In my view, the recognition of the need to establish viable security structures in the Middle East in the post-cold-war international system stems not from some utopian dream, which

97

in itself is not an unworthy endeavour, but rather the fact that since 1991 new and golden opportunities have presented themselves for making the Middle East a less unstable regional subsystem.

In other words, judging by what went before, the absence of superpower rivalries in the Middle East should make the exercise a realizable one. In addition, the disappearance of the established 'norms', and the evaporation of unquestioned external patrons, makes the enterprise a necessity if the post-cold-war dislocation is not to lead to another war in the Middle East in the not-too-distant future.

Moreover, the post-1945 European experience teaches us that when great divisions tend to keep countries apart and suspicious of each other's motives, procedures can be initiated whereby the chances of miscalculation and the overwhelming feeling of insecurity can be dramatically reduced. The Middle East in 1992 had reached the important turning point that Europe was facing after the Second World War; tired of war and exhausted of the need to prepare for war, its actors were instinctively looking for new ways of association and interaction, but remained fearful of each other's motives.

To facilitate certain security minimums in such an environment pushed Europe in two directions simultaneously: alliance-building within power bloc structures and formalization of ties into a potentially prosperous economic community. The Helsinki process of the 1970s and 1980s, which brought the two ideological camps of Europe under the same roof, provided the evidence for the feasibility of broad measures designed to reduce the prospect of war as well as to address the problem of representation and human rights. All three areas mentioned here regularly feature in any catalogue of 'problems of the Middle East'.

Ultimately, much in the Middle East depends on the role of those outside powers and the part international organizations and agencies are willing to play. As regards the outside powers, the role and attitude of the United States is paramount in any security scheme. The power of the United States is illustrated by the fact that barely a year after leading a major conflict in the Gulf region it was leading a process which brought the parties to the most intractable conflict in the Middle East (the Arab–Israeli conflict) around the same table.

Whether one can rely on Washington to act consistently is another question, however. Paradoxically, while the United Nations provided efficient machinery to counter Iraq's aggression against Kuwait, and was the main vehicle of US policy during the crisis, the Arab–Israeli peace process was initiated outside the UN machinery, even though the Madrid process is, explicitly and implicitly, based on Security Council Resolutions 242 and 338.

THE ESSENCE OF SECURITY STRUCTURES IN THE MIDDLE EAST

In the last analysis, security structures in the Middle East aim to provide for the prevalence of those conditions in the region which would allow both the weak and the powerful and the poor and the rich states alike to exist side by side and without fear of aggression and subversion by other regional actors, in addition to attempting to reduce the prospects of armed conflict.

Having provided a working definition of the problem, I propose to proceed to analyse the nature of some of the obstacles standing in the way of introducing new Middle East security structures.

(i) The Middle East is divided into subregions, which are in turn interdependent with each other. This situation I refer to as a condition of 'strategic interdependence'. The net result of this strategic reality is that while certain security problems can be addressed in isolation and within a given geopolitical environment, inevitably they have an overarching dynamism which hinders finding solutions to the security dilemmas of states at the subregional level. By extension, security mechanisms can not easily be found in isolation.

(ii) Many domestic problems (whether economic, political or a combination of both) tend to weaken regional actors in a balance-of-forces equation, and hence inhibit Middle East states from acting 'independently', unilaterally, at the regional level. Structural vulnerabilities thus compel most regional actors to pursue alliances. This is typically the case in the Arab system.

(iii) The Middle East is a highly militarized part of the world, and continues to receive attention from supplier states. These include the successor states to the Soviet Union, the Western countries and the new arms exporters of the Third World.

(iv) Rejectionism (in terms referring to regime legitimacy) at both the state and substate levels is a political reality which tends to complicate interstate relations by threatening to undermine the authority of the state.

(v) Alliances remain shifting and impermanent in the region, in sharp contrast to the European situation during the cold war. This greatly adds to instability in the region and tends to fuel the ethos of opportunism.

(vi) External alliance structures are essentially bilateral rather than multilateral in the Middle East subsystem. In the Persian Gulf subregion in particular, the Gulf Cooperation Council states have put a renewed emphasis on entering into defence and security pacts with the US, Britain and France as 'over-the-horizon' guarantors of their security.

(vii) In a general sense, at the broader regional level political dialogue between adversaries is still the exception rather the rule. Dialogue may develop between adversaries and competitors but at specific times and for a limited period. In addition, dialogue of this nature is usually issue-specific. Certainly in the recent past such exchanges have not tended to lend themselves to generalising dynamics.

(viii) Since 1991, the region has been experiencing an expansion due to the Soviet Union's implosion and the regionalization of the Afghani conflict. The emergence of new (mostly Muslim) republics in the Asian landmass of the former USSR has offered itself as a virgin area for the established Middle East actors to exploit and influence. The approach of the respective Middle Eastern actors in the Central Asian–trans-Caspian region is seemingly an extension of their existence in the Middle East, and as such the new republics could be turned into new battlegrounds for the Middle East actors. Conversely, the intricacies of the socio-economic and political life of the new republics can suck in the Middle East states and in turn cause further instabilities in the traditional Middle East region.

PRECONDITIONS TO THE CREATION OF SECURITY STRUCTURES IN THE MIDDLE EAST

The discussion in this section is based on three levels of engagement: (1) political dialogue, (2) confidence and security-building measures and (3) implementation of arms control measures.[3]

Political dialogue under international auspices is an essential ingredient and the precursor to any acceptable security framework for the Middle East. The establishment of such dialogue is in itself an achievement. If political dialogue can be sustained, however, then every hope exists that the parties concerned can develop an instinct for negotiations and collective 'problem identification'. The 1991 Madrid process, which followed Iraq's military defeat, provides a useful example of what is possible. Even if this process fails to fulfil the aspirations of all the parties involved in it, it nevertheless sets a precedent for political dialogue between apparently mortal enemies, which is now possible and practicable in the post-cold-war environment of the Middle East. If the process fails then we can devote energies towards finding the right ingredients to make it work, rather than abandoning the entire effort.

It is vital that the mechanisms for confidence and security building measures at both the political and military levels are provided for if durable security structures can be built in the Middle East. Such measures would typically include further disengagement agreements, fewer military exercises, voluntary reductions in force projectability, the placing of multilaterally agreed ceilings on defence proportion of GDP, reaching an international agreement on the provision of satellite intelligence on military activities at the regional level, adopting measures that can help in the democratization of the decision-making process, involving voters' representatives at the politico-military leadership level, reducing conscription periods, and taking steps to minimize the size of the reserve military forces. The adoption of all these measures is not likely or possible in one go, but a graded process designed to intensify the CSB mechanisms is not at all impossible.

The pursuance and implementation of arms control (and eventually arms reduction) measures at the subregional and regional levels must be regarded as a priority for the international community. International examples abound of successful arms control exercises, some with more relevance to the Middle East subsystem than others. These include: the Missile Technology Control Regime, the Non-Proliferation Treaty, conventions on manufacture and storage of chemical and biological/bacterial agents, and the Security Council Resolution 687 (the ceasefire resolution) in the 1991 war against Iraq. The latter provided a comprehensive framework for the disarming of Iraq. Iraq was obliged to lose all of its CBN capabilities and research facilities, plus its SSM force with a range in excess of 150 kilometres, to go without new military supplies, and, ultimately, to suffer the consequences of a potent international military force charged with checking the regime's political excesses against (some of) its own citizens (i.e., the Kurdish region and the Shii districts). If some of the measures adopted against Iraq were used as an arms control model for the region as a whole then the future in this endeavour could be said to be bright. As it is, however, the West, Russia and the Soviet Union successor states, China, North Korea and others have continued to supply other states in the region without considering the strategic implications of their military transfers. It is estimated that planned arms transfers to the Middle East in 1991–92 topped $35 billion, most of the supplies originating in the US.[4]

Arms control measures and arms reduction talks, therefore, are likely to prove the most difficult part of any security building blocs envisaged for the Middle East. Still, discussion needs to take place on controlling the flow of conventional arms to the Middle East; on stabilizing (and aiming to reduce) the military and security budgets of Middle East states;[5] and on reducing the non-conventional capabilities of the regional actors, including Israel, which remains the only state in the Middle East to possess nuclear weapons.

In addition, at the international level a deeper knowledge of offensive and defensive capabilities must be incorporated in the discussion of regional arms control. The distinction becomes particularly important in the context of adopting confidence-building measures.

SPECIAL CIRCUMSTANCES OF MIDDLE EAST SUBREGIONS

We can divide the Middle East region into five functional subregions; the Persian Gulf and Arabian peninsula, the Levant,

North Africa, the Red Sea, and the broader Mediterranean region. Taking these in turn, the Gulf and Arabian Peninsula (AP) subregion is dominated by the three states of Iran, Iraq and Saudi Arabia. The last-named, since 1981, has been heavily involved in tying the security of the smaller Gulf Arab states to that of its own, thus complicating somewhat the balance of force structures in the Gulf and AP subregion. The Gulf Wars have underlined the reliance on the military solution to disputes in this subregion, and the competitive nature of the subsystem continues to fuel the local arms race. The isolation of Iraq since 1990 has increased the influence of both Iran and Saudi Arabia, sometimes bringing these two actors together around an anti-Saddam axis and sometimes setting them against each other on matters pertaining to the general security of the subregion and the role of outside powers in providing for the security of the GCC states.

The role of Turkey in maintaining the status quo in the Gulf subregion has become apparent since 1990, a role which has been growing since the early 1980s. Turkey's close alliance with the West and its increasing influence in the Central Asian/trans-Caspian regions may have a direct impact on its relations with Iran and other Gulf states. Also, Ankara's interest in defeating Kurdish nationalism in Turkey and on its borders threatens to bring it in direct confrontation with Iran and Iraq, and, less likely, with Syria. The prospects of Turkish expansionism could filter through to affect the balance of power in the Gulf and AP region, acting as a force to forge new alliances.

The Levant subregion's security challenges are dominated by the Arab–Israeli conflict and the Syrian–Israeli standoff. Here, the pursuit of 'nationhood' has been the most destabilizing force – first by the Jews and then the Israelis, followed by the people they displaced, the Palestinians. In addition to some six wars which have originated in this subregion, the level of tensions has continued to underlie inter-state and sub-state relations in the Levant. In trying to avoid a direct confrontation (since the 1973 war), Israel and Syria chose Lebanon as the battleground. Syria's search for military parity with Israel since the early 1980s has been instrumental in sustaining the arms race in the Levant, particularly as Israel has been striving to maintain its own military superiority in all categories.

Jordan's role in this bilateral race has been marginal, but in the broader balance-of-forces equation in the Levant, Jordan has a vital role to play. As an Arab state and host to the Arab world's largest concentration of Palestinians, Amman has a direct stake in the Arab–Israeli conflict: nor can it afford to be a bystander when the fate of the Palestinians in Lebanon are being determined by Israel and Syria. Jordan's military power, however, does not match its geopolitical situation. To redress this imbalance, King Hussein sought the patronage of its powerful Gulf state neighbour, Iraq, in the 1980s and 1990. This act complicated Jordan's relations with the two dominant actors of the Levant at the same time as leaving it open to GCC criticism when the alliance between the GCC and Iraq was reduced after 1988 and gave way to open hostilities in 1990. Iraq's military defeat in 1991 and the Madrid process have once again tied the fate of Jordan to that of the Levant region. Without other regional allies, Jordan has felt vulnerable to Israeli and Syrian machinations. As such, it has sought to (a) end its isolation in the region and in the West, and (b) strengthen the bond between the East and West Bankers of the River Jordan, and the PLO and Jordan.

The role of Turkey in the Levant must also be emphasized. First, its control of the Tigris and Euphrates waterheads can cause friction between the main beneficiaries of these rivers, Iraq and Syria. Iraq and Syria have already chosen to bury some of their differences in the interest of presenting a united front against Turkey on the water issue. Second, Turkey's interests in the Levant region has made the country an indirect partner to the peace process. Its overwhelming power can help to tip the regional balance of power decisively in Syria's or Israel's favour.

In the past, the Libyan regime's uncertain behaviour tended to mar the attempts at North African subregional cooperation. Since 1989, however, serious steps towards collective cooperation have been taken. These efforts have been formulated around the Maghreb Arab Union, which has endeavoured to deal with the bilateral disputes of its member-states as well as attempting to formulate Maghribi policy towards the rest of the region, the Mediterranean and the EC. The direct challenge of militant Islamic movements to the *status quo* in North Africa since the end of the cold war has provided an added impetus to cooperation at the regime level, but the status of the Polisario movement and the Western Sahara continue to complicate relations between Algeria and Morocco and militate against closer cooperation over threats to subregional security. Regime stability is vital to cooperation and collective action in North Africa and, because of Algeria's problems with FIS, Tunisia's efforts to contain the spread of militant Islam and the continuing confrontation between Libya and the US have tended to push to their limits the parameters of collective action.

All indicators show that the Red Sea subregion is likely to become a hot spot of the 1990s. The end of superpower rivalries in the Horn of Africa, coupled with Yemen's unification and the spread of civil unrest, has made the Red Sea subregion more unstable now than at any time since the Yemeni civil war. The nature of the security challenge in the Red Sea subregion is such that it encompasses inter-state relations directly, for example Somali–Ethiopian, Saudi–Yemeni or Sudanese–Egyptian relations, as well as the internal stability of many Red Sea states: the Sudanese, Somalian and Ethiopian civil wars serve as sufficient examples to illustrate the point.

For the moment, Saudi Arabia and Egypt remain the most influential and stable Red Sea states. So long as they remain allies they can aim to provide a relatively durable twin-pillar security structure in the Arab Red Sea region to contain the threats of Islamic militancy from Sudan and the spread of civil unrest. Egypt's military might is well complemented by Saudi Arabia's financial power, and in the Red Sea subregion this combination forms the strongest unit. Whether Red Sea security structures can be built around a Cairo–Riyadh axis, however, is debatable. This is due partly to the fact that the national interests of the two parties diverge rather than converge on Arab and international issues, and partly because the end of the cold war did not in fact end direct outside interest in the Red Sea subregion. The US (and its allies) and the UN became involved in the internal affairs of many of Red Sea states before the end of the cold war, and their involvement has not ended with it. Thus, the scope for a Saudi–Egyptian-led Red Sea security system is rather limited. Nonetheless, the subregion's poverty and its marginality in terms of regional issues tends to move most parties to ignore the destabilising dynamics of the Red Sea subregion and the ways in which these can be fed into the broader problems facing the Middle East subsystem. The lack of political influence of most of its state actors notwithstanding, most of these states are an integral part of the Middle East and as such can bring influence to bear, albeit indirectly.

Finally, one needs to consider the issues arising out of considering the Mediterranean region as a security extension of the Middle East. Out of some 20 independent Mediterranean actors, 9 have direct Middle Eastern 'connections', of which 7 are Arab states and a total of 8 are Muslim states. If we add countries which tend to gravitate towards the Muslim Middle East then some northern Mediterranean states, such as Albania, can be regarded as those with strong ties to the region. Military and economic power in the Mediterranean strongly follows the global division of the world along North–South lines, but the geographical line of poverty and socio-economic weakness has slowly shifted northwards since the collapse of communist regimes in the Balkans. However, although Albania may be regarded as the poorest European country, in the Mediterranean it has to vie for bottom position with some North African states (whose economies are in any case much more dynamic than Albania's). Uneven distribution of wealth and power in the Mediterranean merely add to an already complicated security picture. Apart from the Arab–Israeli conflict, which dominates the politics of the eastern Mediterranean, the Turkish–Greek rivalry, Cypriot nationalism, Black Sea security and ideological disputes (as in Algeria) threaten to undermine the security of the entire Mediterranean region. Unlike other subregions of the Middle East, however, Western European states, largely due to the EC's own direct interests here, can afford to be proactive in the Mediterranean without being regarded as 'colonial actors'.

Implementation of security regimes in the Mediterranean, therefore, *à la* CSCM, can have very positive results for the subregional states concerned. Also, such a regime, because it will have to incorporate all Mediterranean states to be viable, can influence directly and positively the conflicts brewing in the eastern and southern parts of the Mediterranean. Strategic interdependence ensures that the virtues of any CSCM spread to the rest of the Middle East, even affecting bilateral relations among the non-Mediterranean, non-signatory states. CSCM, for instance, would be well placed to seek lasting solutions to the Arab–Israeli conflict, discuss economic problems of the subregion, and hold talks on arms control, as well as attempt to introduce political pluralism to the less 'liberal' parts of the

Mediterranean. In so far as these are shared problems, their addressing by the CSCM will have a knock-on effect on the rest of the Middle East, hopefully encouraging the non-member-states to shadow and implement policy recommendations arising from CSCM meetings.

CONCLUSIONS

If attempts at finding lasting solutions to the security dilemmas of Middle East states are sought, then we must be prepared to take on board the less tangible and less quantifiable aspects of insecurity in the region. These would necessarily include a discussion of socio-economic issues (poverty, the uneven distribution of wealth and resources, rapid population growth, etc.), the efficient management of shared resources (e.g. water, oil and natural gas, land usage, pollution control and such like) and the need to create region-wide institutions to deal with the non-state, non-military aspects of insecurity.

Since the end of the cold war the UN has been promoted as the best vehicle for advancing humanity's interests: in resolving conflicts, fighting hunger and poverty, reforming political systems, and acting to deter aggression within and across nations, the world body has been seen to have a place. And yet, as the UN's own leadership acknowledges, the organization has shown little progress in its own structures to reflect new global realities. The reform of its decision-making process, its command and bureaucratic structures and its global brief have been sought by the developing countries for some years now, but it is only since the early 1990s that prospects for the reform of the UN's internal system have presented themselves.

Assuming that the UN continues to act as the world body, we must seek answers to a number of urgent questions. Can the UN be flexible enough to respond effectively to the challenges of the next fifty years? Is it likely to remain hamstrung by the narrow vision and interests of its members? Will the power struggle of its members and increasing regionalism destroy the UN system at the moment of its glory? Is the organization capable of making the transition to a New World Order and learning to question its own charter in ways that would help in advancing the interests of humanity as well as state actors?

On balance, the UN's own prognosis has been that it can rise to the challenges facing the world. The secretary-general's views of the UN indicate that the organization's leadership both is aware of the global problems and is prepared to overcome the internal (structural) and other obstacles in its way. In the words of Mr Boutros-Ghali: 'the UN Secretariat needs to seize this extraordinary opportunity to expand, adapt and reinvigorate the work of the United Nations so that the lofty goals as originally envisioned by the charter can begin to be realized'.[6] Areas for reform which the secretary-general has focused on indicate precisely a recognition of the new role of the UN in the much expanded international system: new modes of peacekeeping, efficient peacekeeping systems, financial reform, development needs and development assistance, changed views of sovereignty, global cooperation on 'human problems', and reforming the UN system and its 'culture'.[7] The need for the UN to be able to move between peacekeeping and peacemaking is readily recognized by the UN Secretariat.

On international and regional arms control, too, the UN Secretariat has been much more active since the end of the cold war. It has attempted to set up an independent international register of arms sales and put on the UN agenda a discussion of factors which lead to regional arms races, with the ultimate aim of curbing the arms race through implementation of regional arms control regimes. In the end, we are back to the point where we started from: the outside actors in the Middle East. In today's post-cold-war international environment, reliance on such outside actors as the UN is not only not a negative attribute but, in unstable regions like the Middle East, an essential factor and actor in the march towards implementation of viable security structures.

NOTES

1.   See Kamran Mofid, *The Economic Consequences of the Gulf War* (Routledge, London, 1990), pp. 120–42.
2.   Author's estimates.
3.   These issues are discussed in greater detail in A. Ehteshami, 'The Ingredients of Arms Control and Cooperation in the Gulf and Arabian

Peninsula', in G. Nonneman (ed.), *The Middle East and Europe: Stability and Integration* (Federal Trust, London, 1993).

4. Tony Walker *et al.*, 'Weapons Deals Hit Prospects for Middle East Stability', *Financial Times*, 11 May 1992. Saferworld Foundation estimated that Middle East states had ordered some $35 to 45 billions' worth of arms in the two years following August 1990. See *Financial Times*, 24 August 1992.

5. For example, Saudi Arabia's military and security budget for 1992, according to the Saudi Finance Ministry, was set at $16.44 billion (SR61.63 billion), and Iran was estimated to be allocating as much as 21 per cent of the 1992/3 (March to March) budget to the military sector. See *Mideast Mirror*, 5 January 1993, 6 January 1993. Similar patterns are repeated in such countries as Israel, Syria, Egypt and Turkey.

6. Boutros Boutros-Ghali, 'Empowering the United Nations', *Foreign Affairs*, vol. 72, no. 5, Winter 1992–93, p. 89.

7. For details see ibid., pp. 88–102.

6 The Arab–Israeli Conflict in the New World Order

Emma C. Murphy

INTRODUCTION: TWO FACES OF THE NEW WORLD ORDER

In March 1991, President Bush proclaimed the existence of a New World Order, one in which 'The principles of justice and fair play protect the weak against the strong.'[1] The war which had just been concluded in the Gulf had demonstrated that the bi-polar competition of the cold war era was no longer a feature of international relations and that the states of the Middle East would henceforth be required to adjust their own foreign, domestic and security policies to take account of a new 'code of conduct' that would be determined principally by the remaining superpower. The moral will and military might of the United States, reflected in a more forceful and effective United Nations, combined to dictate that this code of conduct should ensure the protection of weak and vulnerable states from the roguish elements of the international community. Such elements would be excluded from that community, or even penalized by it, for non-conformity with the newly determined 'international consensus'.

In the Middle East, Bush asserted, the national interests of the United States depended upon a secure and stable Gulf. American policy towards the region would be based upon four component paths: regional disarmament, regional security, regional economic development and the revitalization of the Arab–Israeli peace process. These priorities merged well with the general ethos of the New World Order: the moulds of international confrontation and competition should be broken and new paths towards dialogue, political reforms and regional security pursued, to be accompanied, preferably, by the regional (and later global) integration of market-oriented economies.

If the United States was setting the political agenda, global capital was providing dynamic enforcement of a wider agenda shared by the world's developed states. The breakup of the Soviet Union, and the rejection of central planning by the governments of the newly independent states, gave added momentum to a new phase in the development of the world capitalist economy. Harry Magdoff has termed this the phase of 'globalization', pointing out that, while capital has always contained within it the need to expand, it has since the 1980s been able to 'globalize' this expansion in a way which threatens the character of the nation-state itself.[2] The advent of new technology, the opening of new geographic territories, and a slowing down of growth in the established capitalist states, have proved to be the engines behind a new pattern of growth. This one is characterized by a great leap in direct foreign investment globally, the globalization of finance markets and increasing competition between Third World producers to export to the developed world in order to improve their own economic standing.[3] To take advantage of the burgeoning opportunities, investment capital required that those states which formerly attempted development through central planning in some form or other should now undergo substantive economic restructuring, something which could usually be done only with the help of the large international financial institutions. The latter, dominated by the interests of the developed countries of the North, imposed their own criteria of political liberalism and international conformity upon states whose economies they helped through structural adjustment loans and programmes.

As many Arab states abandon the central planning of former years,[4] and as Israel itself is also forced to undergo major economic structural change,[5] they are all sucked into this process of the globalization of capital, and are forced increasingly to subjugate their national political interests to the pressures of integration with the prevailing and developing economic system. The states of the Middle East are not unique in being caught between the pincers of a newly hegemonic United States, willing and able to assert its own international agenda,[6] and an acceleration in the expansion of capitalist forces which they have been unable to resist. Thus there were two faces to the New World Order; the romantic idealized one pronounced by President Bush, and a second, more real one which has resulted from the synthesis of new global political and economic conditions. This chapter argues that the Middle East peace process, in its Madrid, Oslo and present forms, has been shaped by the second face of the New World Order, rather than by the visions and hopes of the first.

AMERICAN POLITICAL HEGEMONY IN THE REGION

For the on-going conflict between Arabs and Israelis, the New World Order had specific and immediate implications. The Kuwait crisis had demonstrated to the United States that this running regional sore had the potential to disrupt American interests throughout the region. While the Western powers, with the collusion of their Arab allies, had fought hard to undermine Saddam Hussein's attempts to link the two conflicts in any peaceful resolution of the crisis, they could not ignore the massive popular support for the Iraqi leader which was evident throughout much of the Arab world, and which was largely based on his championing of the Palestinian cause on behalf of the Arab nation. The hypocrisy of the Western position (taking a moral stand against Iraqi occupation of Kuwait but unwilling to take action against similar Israeli action against the Palestinians) rekindled Arab grievances against historic and arbitrary Western imperialism in the region. It was only possible for the United States to draw in Arab participation in the multinational military force by committing itself to convening an international peace conference after the war which would bring Israel to a table at which the 'land for peace' proposal was the central agenda. Hence Bush's New World Order speech emphasized United Nations Security Council Resolutions 242 and 338 as the basis for the new peace process, one which would take account of new strategic realities created or illustrated by the Kuwait crisis, as well as those which had resulted from the end of the cold war.

With the disappearance of the latter as the defining factor in a state's usefulness to American national interests, America was forced to deal with individual states on the basis of bilateral or regional rather than global interests. While under President Reagan Israel had been promoted as the bastion of Western-style democracy in an area otherwise under threat from Soviet-backed communist intrusion, the Kuwait crisis proved that even a former Soviet ally – Syria – could have common interests with the United States. By contrast, the war provoked a reassessment of Israel's role as an American strategic ally. During the course of

the war itself, the status of the Israeli–American special relationship had come under fire as their close ties to Israel proved to be
something of a liability for American military planners. Meanwhile, the possibility that Israel might respond to Iraqi SSM
attacks, and become actively engaged in the war, threatened to
rip the coalition apart and divide America from the Arab allies,
who lent regional credibility to the whole operation. As Avi
Shlaim so eloquently puts it:

> Here was a conflict which threatened America's most vital
> interests in the region and the best service that Israel could
> render to her senior partner was to refrain from doing any-
> thing. Far from being a strategic asset, Israel was widely
> perceived as an embarrassment and a liability.[7]

The retreat from the region by Soviet policy makers under
Gorbachev enabled America to reassess its evaluation of Israel's
importance to its own interests. It was inevitable, and made plain
by the Arab states, that Israel's relative centrality to US policy
making should be downgraded to facilitate less complicated
dealings with themselves. A trade-off had to be found, for
example, in US dealings with Syria. From 1989 Gorbachev had
made it clear to President Hafez al-Assad that the USSR would
no longer support the goal of strategic parity with Israel –
promising only strategic defence capability.[8] Without a superpower patron willing and able to fund the practicalities of
rejectionism, Assad was forced to seek a path to reconciliation
with the United States, a process already visibly underway in his
courting of US approval for his operations in Lebanon prior to
the Kuwait crisis. The drying up of Soviet injections of cash and
military hardware had a further implication. It exacerbated the
economic crisis facing many Arab states. Formerly committed to
various forms of state planning, many Arab states were increasingly being forced to liberalize their economies in the face of
accumulated debts, inflated bureaucracies and oppressive bal-
ance-of-payments deficits. This already painful process was made
harder by the withdrawal of Soviet aid and demands for payment
of goods in hard currency. For countries like Syria, the need for
reintegration with the world capitalist system (and specifically to
attract foreign investment and trade) has made it difficult to avoid
toning down anti-American and anti-imperialist rhetoric, or to at
least to exclude it from practical policymaking.

Thus we can see that in 1991 the United States was in a position to develop new ties with the Arab world and to strengthen existing ones, unhindered by prior considerations of superpower competition. Equally, the Arab states no longer had a choice of patrons and were forced to come to terms with a new global balance of power in which confrontation with the United States was a lonely venture. A key factor in their policy realignment was the altered relations between the United States and the PLO. At a press conference in Geneva on 14 December 1988, Yasser Arafat had explicitly acknowledged Israel's right to a peaceful and secure existence and unequivocally renounced terrorism, thereby removing the obstacles to direct dialogue with the United States. However, an unreceptive America, together with the PLO's disastrous display of siding with Saddam in 1990, combined to substantially weaken the PLO in regional and international affairs. The Arab states, having elicited the promise of a peace conference from the United States, were free after the Gulf War to pursue their foreign policymaking more independently of the Palestinian issue and their commitments to – or problems with – the PLO leadership.

Israel, aware of its diminished status as strategic ally and unamused by American pressure to attend the peace conference, was alarmed by the developments in American–Arab relations. If ever there was a time when a peace process was least likely to develop in its favour it was now. Its concerns were heightened as it became increasingly evident that the 'regional disarmament' pillar of the New World Order was illusory. In fact, the post-Gulf-War era proved to be one of massive regional rearmament, with the United States itself being a principal supplier. The end of the cold war had indeed resulted in a global retraction of the 'cold war army' elsewhere, with military commitments on foreign soil being steadily reduced and more onus being placed by the US administration on providing weaponry (at a price) for allies to defend their own regions. In the case of the Gulf Arab states, however, the threat to Western interests – combined with the threat perceived by the Arab regimes themselves – has ensured that the allies of 1990 have maintained a direct presence in the region.[9] This has been bolstered by vast new purchases of Western-produced arms by the Gulf Cooperation Council (GCC) states. Saudi Arabia, Kuwait, Bahrain and the UAE alone bought arms amounting to $25 billion between the end of the Kuwait

Crisis and October 1992;[10] this included a single sale of 72 F15-E jet-fighters to Saudi Arabia. The new Middle East arms race was fuelled by the combination of a proliferation of potential suppliers, American willingness to begin supplying current technology hardware to Arab allies, the failure to implement regional security agreements and the panicked response of the Gulf states to Iran's rearmament programme. While it was natural that Iran should seek to re-equip itself after the devastating war with Iraq in the 1980s, its more assertive regional policy,[11] combined with its purchase of two submarines from the former Soviet Union in 1992, led the GCC states to interpret the increased Iranian defence budget as potentially threatening and to increase their own in response.[12] This policy has been hampered since 1993 by the fall in oil prices, reducing Gulf Arab budgets in general, but the implications are still profound. While the United States remains committed to sustaining Israel's qualitative technological edge, it has upped the level of that which it offers to the Gulf Arabs. The proliferation of former Soviet Union and developing country producers willing to upgrade existing or sell new weaponry has meant that the open market reigns and arms sales to potentially unstable regions like the Middle East are decreasingly subject to political considerations.[13] The recent entry of China into the high-tech arms sales business is an excellent example.

Israel also initially viewed warmer US–Arab relations as economically challenging. Conscious that the United States was itself undergoing severe recession, Israelis feared that the administration, especially under President Clinton, would prioritize domestic rather than foreign policy budgetary needs. Pressure has indeed been levied on the American government to cut back on foreign aid, but so far this has not been a factor in congressional considerations of aid to Israel. Another contributing factor to Israeli nervousness in this area has been the new competition for financial help from the countries of the former Soviet Union and Eastern Europe. These states offer enormous potential for US capital to exploit investment and consumer markets and offer stiff and attractive competition for limited US funds in a time of a weak domestic economy.[14]

Israel tried to resell itself to the United States as a culturally familiar bastion of democracy and stability in a region progressively destabilized by Islamic fundamentalism. The argument found some sympathy, but did not generate the kind of support which evolved from cold war politics. While 'Islamic terrorism' and Islamic revolution hold certain fears for the West, the Islamic revolution of Iran has not been repeated on the same scale and intensity elsewhere. The reverberations of North African Islamic tensions have been felt by and large in Europe rather than in the US, and the tough policies adopted against 'militant' Islamic movements within the region by governments in Algeria, Tunisia, Jordan, Egypt, Saudi Arabia and elsewhere indicate a broad cross-regime resistance to Islamic politics among America's allies.

All the above arguments point to the redefinition of American interests in the New World Order and their implications for the parties of the Arab–Israeli conflict. The other side of the coin, however, was the package of regional changes which had taken place during and after the Kuwait crisis.

REGIONAL REORDERING AND THE ARAB–ISRAELI CONFLICT

The war in the Gulf had a profound impact upon the regional balance of power and its play on the Arab–Israeli conflict. Iraq's star, which had been steadily rising since the mid-1980s, was (at least temporarily) removed from the power play, leaving Saudi Arabia as the dominant state in the Gulf. Saudi Arabia, backed and bound by what is likely to prove a durable alliance with the US, does not present any military threat to Israel. It may well bankroll the Palestinian HAMAS[15] as some have claimed, but that is essentially a symbolic concession designed for a domestic audience.[16] The Saudi regime, since it is not a front-line state, is able to create a distance between its own interests and those of direct parties to the conflict. Moreover, the regime does not derive its legitimacy from adherence to the Arab-nationalist ideal. It is therefore able to take a foreign policy line in support of a political solution to the conflict – increasingly so now that Iraq is unable to project its radical rejectionism and Syria has abandoned the latter in all but rhetoric.

Syria, of all states, was best able to capitalize on the opportunities offered by the crisis. By siding with the American-led coalition, President Hafez al-Assad gained immediate US acquiescence for his operations in Lebanon. As the Israelis saw it:

Assad was hopelessly stuck in Lebanon for 15 years, never daring to advance on Beirut for fear of American and Israeli reprisals. As soon as he joined the US coalition he received the green light from the Americans to enter Beirut, and today Syria controls Lebanon.[17]

The Kuwait crisis ended Assad's isolation in the Middle East, reinforcing a recently developed Egyptian–Syrian alliance, facilitating participation in talks on a new regional security arrangement, and immediately leading to over $2 billion worth of aid from Saudi Arabia. With the loss of Soviet sponsorship, the removal of an eastern option (however unlikely) including alliance with Iraq, and in spite of siding on the same team as his erstwhile greatest enemy, Israel, Assad emerged from the crisis in a position of far greater strength than he went into it.

The same cannot be said of King Hussein's Jordan. Although there was a degree of international sympathy with Jordan's position during the war – sitting as it did on the border with Iraq and always conscious that it would be unable to withstand any Iraqi decision to make a drive for Israel through an annexed Jordanian corridor – Jordan ultimately suffered enormously from its Kuwait crisis balancing act. The economic stress of lost trade, the influx of refugees and being cut off from former Gulf Arab patrons, combined with the domestic pressures created by the groundswell of popular support for Saddam, created an atmosphere of crisis. In the aftermath of the war, King Hussein tried to regain Western favour by proclaiming his willingness to become re-engaged in the peace process. His motives were numerous: he was keen to forestall any Israeli attempts to take advantage of Jordan's weakness and instigate the transfer policies long feared by Palestinians; he was eager to 'cuddle up' to a diplomatically restored Syria so as not to be isolated from any peace process that did materialize; he wanted Gulf Arab 'forgiveness' (in dollar form) and perhaps, as Adam Garfinkle has naughtily suggested, he could not resist the opportunity to give a little kick to Arafat's PLO when it was down by dropping previous Jordanian qualifications that such a peace process could only proceed with direct PLO participation.[18]

If the Iraqi invasion of Kuwait marked the end of the dream of Arab unity, then the sacrificial lamb was the Palestinian cause. The war effectively demolished the option of using Arab unity for

Palestinian empowerment. When Arafat embraced Saddam, he inadvertently made it possible for Arab states to openly place their own national interests above those of the common Arab cause. The leadership of the PLO did not welcome the Iraqi invasion of Kuwait, drawing attention as it did from the Intifada and the campaign against settlement of Soviet immigrants in the Occupied Territories. When his initial strategy, of offering himself as a broker for an Arab solution to the crisis, failed, however, Arafat was increasingly pressured by the swell of popular Palestinian support for Saddam to take the latter's side. The Palestinian position should be understood as the result of their perceptions of the end of the Cold War as it appeared prior to the Kuwait crisis. The decline of the Soviet sponsorship of the radical Arab states had weakened the rejectionist camp; 200 000 Soviet Jews had flooded into Israel; transfer was being widely and openly discussed and settlement activity was accelerating in the Occupied Territories. Talks with the US were frozen, despite the brief respite after Arafat's historic acceptance of the Israeli state in 1988, with the United States demanding a halt to the Intifada before they could progress. The Intifada itself was fizzling out under the immense pressure of Israeli economic strangulation and the brutal 'Iron Fist' policy. With every day the PLO became more marginalized and the Palestinians more desparate. Thus, while some senior PLO figures (such as Salah Khalaf) condemned the Iraqi invasion of Kuwait, and in spite of widespread reservations about Iraqi motives and methods, there was a mass of popular support for Saddam's linkage of his own withdrawal to an Israeli withdrawal from the Occupied Territories and an enthusiastic welcome for his willingness to back words with weapons.

As the Palestinian journalist Hanna Siniora has explained the Palestinians' reaction to Saddam, when 'a drowning man sees land disappear slowly in front of him, and suddenly a man throws him a rope, he will not ask who that man is.'[19]

Saddam's defeat left the PLO demoralized and vulnerable, not to say near bankrupt after its Gulf funding sources were cut off in retaliation. Yet, while the PLO was temporarily isolated and suffered acid rebukes from the US, the Bush–Baker team were well aware that, as with Jordan, if the 'window of opportunity' for peace was to be taken advantage of, the PLO could not be wholly excluded. The period leading up to the commencement of a formal peace process thus became one of negotiating the extent and nature of Palestinian participation in the talks, during which Arafat bargained from a position of extreme weakness and was forced ultimately to accept a formula that denied him formal PLO participation. Aware that Syria, Egypt and Jordan were all now prepared to begin direct negotiations with Israel, Arafat could not risk the possibility that those states should between them decide the future of the Palestinians. As one Israeli academic put it:

> In the past it was clear that if the Palestinians did not participate in a peace conference, there would be no conference. When Egypt made peace with Israel, it was Egypt that remained isolated in the face of a united Arab world. In 1991 the tables turned. The Palestinians understood that if they didn't join the peace process, they would be the only ones left out. Syria, Jordan, Lebanon and Saudi Arabia would participate in the talks without them.[20]

The Palestinians in the Occupied Territories were clearly prepared, for this very reason, to participate in the US proposed peace conference. Arafat, remembering the unpleasant experience of being caught on the hop when the Intifada began, and with no real bargaining power left, was forced to accept that the PLO should have an indirect role only and that personalities from within the West Bank and Gaza Strip should represent the Palestinians, albeit with reference to Tunisia.

The last party needed to make any peace process meaningful, Israel, was brought kicking and screaming to the table by a United States government determined to take advantage of the combination of all the sea-changes wrought by the end of the cold war and the Kuwait crisis to resolve the instabilities of the region. The Israeli prime minister, Yitzhak Shamir, was commited to a right-wing agenda that rejected any land-for-peace equation. He attended the conference only under immense pressure from George Bush and James Baker, who linked American financial support of Jewish immigration to Israel with the latter's good behaviour in the peace process.[21] Although he was determined to drag the talks out, making no concessions but stalling such criticism of Israel as the intransigent party, Shamir did come to see the benefits of direct face-to-face talks with the Arab states as an equal. Thus, when Syria accepted to join direct talks in July 1991, Shamir convinced his cabinet that they should attend, if only to convince America of their good will and because, as Shamir said, 'The negotiations have to begin because that will signify recognition of Israel's existence by the Arab states.'[22] On 18 October, the Soviet Union re-established diplomatic relations with the Jewish state in anticipation of a peace conference, a gesture which served to encourage Shamir's government in the belief that if it showed willing in this New World Order then it could reap benefits without having to make tangible concessions to the Palestinians.[23]

Thus, on 30 October 1991, Bush's peace conference got under way in Madrid, apparently symbolizing that at least one of the four pillars of his new Middle East Order was edging towards achievement. Regional security arrangements, after a much vaunted start with the Damascus Declaration and the six-plus-two formula, had evaporated as Gulf Arab states turned increasingly to bilateral security arrangements with beyond-the-horizen partners. Regional economic development was proving equally elusive, given the new unwillingness of GCC states to share their wealth after what they saw as the betrayals of the pro-Saddam Arab masses of the poorer states. Regional disarmament had been whittled down to the dismantlement of the Iraqi NCW capability and US efforts to restrict Iranian acquisitions of the same. By the end of 1991, the Madrid peace conference seemed to remain as the sole beacon for positive change in the region's security agenda. The Arab world seemed to many to be caught in a malaise of post-Arab nationalist sentiment. Arab unity seemed now to be condemned to a hollow grave; while intellectuals berated their political leaders, Islamist political movements gained strength among the masses, advocating a return to Islamic values and traditions and rejection of imported, secular ideologies. Arab regimes, released by Palestinian participation in the Madrid Peace Conference (albeit a weak form of participation which reflected continued angst at the PLO position during the Kuwait Crisis) from adopting the more-Palestinian-than-the-Palestinians lines of previous years, were now free to pursue their own national state interests first and foremost. However, this was not yet to be translated into significant advances in diplomatic compromises because the Israeli position remained arrogantly defiant and unbending.

THE MADRID PEACE PROCESS

It would be easy but incorrect to dismiss the Madrid talks as having been essentially irrelevant to practical advances in peacemaking. The first five rounds of the bilateral Madrid talks quickly became bogged down in procedural matters and mutual suspicions, with Israel in particular refusing to make any compromises whatsoever on substantive issues.[24] Equally, the multilaterals, which centred round five different regional working groups on refugees, economic development, water resources, environmental issues and arms control, were characterized by boycotts and procedural complaints.

The election of Yitzhak Rabin in Israel in June 1992 on a land-for-peace slate created optimism that real progress might now be possible. Rabin certainly moved quickly to make goodwill gestures towards the Palestinians: he promised to halt all but strategic settlement building, released eight hundred Palestinian prisoners, accepted diaspora Palestinians at the multilaterals and sought to repeal the ban on contacts with the PLO. As a result, in August 1992 President Bush approved the requested loan guarantees. In the actual talks with Palestinians, however, Rabin was virtually as uncompromising as the former Israeli prime minister, Yitzhak Shamir, had been before him, and concentrated on using the bilaterals as a route to agreement with Syria and Jordan. His position was strengthened with the election in the United States of a new, pro-Israel president, Bill Clinton,[25] although the new Secretary of State, Warren Christopher, was keen to sustain improved US–Arab relations.

If Shamir's revisionism had been the greatest obstacle to peace prior to June 1992, Rabin's concentration on the Syrian and Jordanian tracks proved a hindrance thereafter. Rabin had made it clear in the sixth and seventh rounds of the talks that the exchange of part or all of the Golan Heights in return for a full peace with Syria was now on the agenda. While Syria could not afford to ignore the possibilities being offered, neither could it feasibly make advances on that road until some resolution of the Palestinian problem was accomplished. Jordan, keen to make formal peace with Israel and to restore good relations with the US and its conservative Gulf Arab allies, was equally unable to commit itself until both its domestic political situation had stabilized[26] and its northern neighbour could be sure to approve.

Meantime, cracks were appearing in relations between Chairman Arafat's PLO in Tunis and the Palestinian representatives at the talks. Arafat, feeling the tide of time working against the Palestinians and watching the tentative manoeuvring between Syria, Jordan and Israel, was more willing to make significant compromises than the team from the Occupied Territories, who reflected more clearly the aspirations of those they represented. As Arafat became more authoritarian in his demands on the team, the latter became less willing to defer to Tunis. Meanwhile, in the Occupied Territories themselves, the PLO faced increasing competition from a HAMAS-led rejectionist front (which included the PFLP, the Front for Popular Struggle, Islamic Jihad, the Revolutionary Communist Party, the DFLP, the PFLP-GC, the PFL, Sa'iqa and Fatah-Intifada). The longer the peace process was dragged out with no tangible results (and bearing in mind that Rabin's promises to halt non-strategic settlement activity amounted to only a very small reduction in actual construction and settlement), the greater the public sympathy for HAMAS.[27] The Israeli expulsion of 414 suspected HAMAS leaders to the slopes of Lebanon in December 1992 not only stalled the talks but reinforced Palestinian perceptions of Israeli insincerity and the pointlessness of dialogue.

The deportations created the first big test for the Clinton administration. The latter inherited the Bush administration's endorsement of UNSCR 799, which strongly condemned the act and called for immediate repatriation of the deportees. Clinton dispatched Warren Christopher to negotiate with Rabin, making it clear that the US was sensitive to Israeli concerns but that an Israeli climbdown was necessary if multilateral diplomacy was to continue. The agreement reached in February, that Israel would repatriate a hundred of the deportees immediately and the remainder by the end of the year, was seen by the PLO and the Arab states as evidence that Clinton's administration would not be an honest broker. While Christopher stated clearly that 'I am not in the business of pressuring the Israelis to do anything',[28] he was adamant that the Palestinians should not be allowed to use the issue to stall the talks any further. The US itself, in refusing to allow any UN action to be taken against Israel to force it to comply with a Security Council resolution, had undermined one of the basic principles of the so-called New World Order. It had shown that a strong state would indeed be allowed to defy the norms of acceptable international behaviour when it suited US interests and that the UN was not to be allowed to play the role of enforcer of the code of conduct independent of superpower dictats.

By mid-1993 it was becoming clear that the Madrid peace process was going nowhere. It was true that a vital bridge in peace making had been crossed; the Arabs and Israelis were at least now talking directly to one another. Major flaws existed, however, in the process as a whole. Under Clinton, and a State Department team dominated by dedicated Zionists like Martin Indyk and Dennis Ross, the United States had retreated from Bush's at least partial attempts at evenhandedness. Peace in the region was now being defined by the US in terms of Arab compliance with American and Israeli strategic objectives.[29] The bilaterals and multilaterals may have allowed Israel to sit with the Arab states, but the former's unwillingness to negotiate sincerely with the Palestinians prevented the Arab states from negotiating unreservedly with Israel. Meanwhile, the concentration of the international community and media on the progress of the talks was, conveniently for Israel, distracting attention from what it was actually doing in the Occupied Territories. For all his talk of peace, Prime Minister Rabin had proved unable or unwilling to stop the relentless Zionist ambition of expansion by creating facts, or to in any way reverse the process of colonization and consolidation of the occupation.

RESTRUCTURING THE ISRAELI OCCUPATION: OSLO'S HIDDEN AGENDA

The process of Zionist colonization of the Occupied Territories has a logic and momentum of its own. It has been carried out throughout the decades regardless of any political debate within Israel or between Israel and the international community. However, while the process of colonization itself continued under Rabin's premership, he and his ministers were increasingly aware that since the late 1980s the occupation had no longer been the profitable enterprise for Israel that it once was. The Intifada had raised the cost of security, even as the deliberate underdevelopment of the territories had impoverished the taxable base and diminished the captive consumer market. Closures during the

Intifada and the Gulf War began to adjust Israelis to the idea of substituting new Soviet immigrants or foreign workers for Palestinian labour, and the slow but inevitable drive for economic liberalization meant that guaranteed markets were no longer considered the simple answer for Israeli trade. Moreover, the linkage made between the Israeli occupation of Palestinian lands and the Iraqi occupation of Kuwait meant that international scrutiny of the practices of occupation was more intense.

The occupation had to be restructured so that the benefits of political control were maintained, but the responsibility for economic conditions passed on to someone else. Although the West Bank still had significant political, strategic and economic value for Israel, the Gaza Strip – exhausted of resources, and riddled with unemployment and chronic poverty – had become a liability. It was better for Israel to maintain control and prevent competitive development but to allow sufficient economic growth as to reduce unemployment through domestic channels. If economic conditions in the Ocupied Territories improved then it was logical to think that international concern would diminish and secure control more easily achieved.

In the event, this was not exactly a new line of thought. After the Kuwait crisis, the Israeli Civil Authority had adopted a new policy aimed at stimulating employment opportunities inside the Occupied Territories themselves. In March 1993 the International Labour Organization reported that

> Measures include tax facilities for investors, the establishment of investment centres and industrial parks, the lowering of certain fees such as those paid to cross the Jordan bridge, and steps taken to allow the strengthening of the local banking system.[30]

UNCTAD, in its assessment of the apparent shift in Israeli policy, noted that:

> the new approach was in line with the basic economic policy followed by Israel since 1967 which called for a maintenance of the established subcontracting relationship between the Palestinian market and the Israeli market under more flexible terms.[31]

In the meantime, and despite promises by Prime Minister Rabin that all non-strategic settlement should be halted, settlements continued to expand and spring up throughout the West Bank, indicative of the contradiction between a growing Israeli popular consensus in favour of peace (and Rabin's responsiveness to it) with an equal national unwillingness to actually take real steps towards relinquishing territory. Rabin was faced with the dilemma of finding a way to break the stalemate with Syria and Jordan (thereby achieving the promised 'peace' for his domestic constituents) and maintaining the benefits of continued occupation of the Palestinian lands.

As the Madrid talks got nowhere, Rabin grew increasingly aware that he would have to find some way to break the stalemate first with the Palestinians themselves, although in a way that left Israeli options for the future open. It was clear that the Madrid forum was not the place for this; the Palestinian representatives from the Occupied Territories could not and would not make the compromises necessary, the involvement of third parties meant the imposition of qualifications and multiple interests. Rabin had also personally come around to accepting that to make peace, Israel would have to deal directly with the PLO sooner or later. The alternative was to watch the Occupied Territories come more and more under the influence of rejectionist Islamic groups. Rabin was thus eventually convinced by his foreign and deputy foreign ministers, Shimon Peres and Yossi Beilin, to give official sanction to a secret dialogue between the PLO and prominent Israeli academics which had been carried out in London and Norway since December 1992.

The opportunities offered by the Oslo channel came at a critical time for Chairman Arafat, who was coming under stern criticism from the Palestinian team in Madrid (not to mention the increasingly popular rejectionist groups inside the Occupied Territories). Oslo offered him a chance to personally regain the initiative and, more importantly, for the PLO to negotiate directly with Rabin via his own, chosen aides. He was aware that he would be negotiating from a position of weakness, not having the weight of Arab (especially Syrian) support behind the Palestinian cause. He was also aware that, to get what he wanted, he would have to sacrifice many of the aspirations of the Palestinians of the Occupied Territories. But direct negotiations also meant Israel did not have America to constantly fight its corner, and it meant the personal recognition for which Arafat had struggled so long.

Although the Declaration of Principles contained what many Palestinians, particularly refugees in Lebanon from the 1948 war, considered to be wholly unacceptable concessions from their side, it was greeted by the world as a whole, by most Israelis and by a majority of the population of the Occupied Territories with optimism, tinged with wariness. It was a short document, with just seventeen articles, four annexes and a few paragraphs of agreed minutes. The essence of the document was as follows: within three months (i.e., by 13 December 1993) agreement should be reached on the details of Israeli military withdrawal from the Gaza Strip and Jericho, the withdrawal to be completed by 13 April 1994. Palestinians would take control of internal affairs in those areas, including taxation and policing. During a five-year interim period, taking effect from the signing of the DOP, the principle of 'early empowerment' would be applied to the rest of the West Bank, while elections for a Palestinian council would be held no later than 13 July 1994. Israeli military forces would be redeployed outside Palestinian population areas, but would remain to protect settlements. Final status talks would begin no later than December 1995, with the difficult issues of Jerusalem, refugees and settlements left for negotiation until then. During the five-year interim period, Israel would maintain control over foreign affairs, overall security and settlements. The thorniest issue of all – what was to be the final status of the territories – was not discussed in the document. The Palestinians saw transition as leading to statehood, a concept ruled out by Rabin, who envisaged a form of autonomy or self-rule in the territories.

Today, when one sees the reality of the achievements of Oslo, it is difficult not to be cynical. Given that Israel had already embarked upon a policy of restructuring the occupation in 1991 to give responsibility but not power to the Palestinians, to revive the Palestinian economy but not allow full competitive development, it is hard not to think that Israel has used the Oslo Accords as a strategic disguise to achieve just that. The Oslo Accords allowed the United States, the European Union and the Arab world to act as if the Palestinian–Israeli conflict was all but over. The perception is that, since the Palestinians and Israelis have resolved the principal stumbling block to progress in the wider peace process, the rest of the world can now leave that aspect to the two parties involved and themselves get on with attending to their own agendas. This has been in many ways the culmination of a process whereby, as Anoushiravan Ehteshami has said, 'the "Palestine problem" has been reduced to a set of negotiable proposals since November 1988, reinforced by the Kuwait crisis and the subsequent Madrid process.'[32]

The United States and the international community effectively divested themselves of any responsibility for ensuring that the spirit and letter of the Declaration of Principles was observed by the parties concerned, or that subsequent agreements on the interim arrangements or final settlements included any element of justice or adherence to UN Security Council resolutions. This was now a matter for direct PLO–Israeli negotiation – no matter that one party was in a vastly stronger bargaining position than the other. To make matters worse, the United States embarked on a fund-raising mission to provide a $2 billion sweetener for the bitter pill that the Palestinians of the Occupied Territories had to swallow. While the aim of providing aid and relief to the Palestinians was admirable, the precedent has been set that, not only is Israel not to be held financially responsible for its deliberate underdevelopment of the Palestinian economy over nearly thirty years, but also the political requirements of the Declaration of Principles are to be 'bought' by reducing Palestinian popular opposition through economic improvements.

In the event, the implementation of the Oslo Accords has been anything but smooth. It was not until May 1994 that agreement was reached on Israeli withdrawal from Gaza and Jericho, and by September 1995 agreement on elections had still not been reached. Israel did indeed withdraw from the Gaza Strip and a minute parcel of land around Jericho, but in reality the military occupation exists virtually as it did prior to the Declaration of Principles. Contrary to its commitments in the Declaration, Israel has pre-empted final status talks by continuing its building of settlements in the West Bank, as well as expropriating an additional 33 000 dunums[33] of Palestinian land, over 11 000 of which are being used for the construction of a massive new road network which will link settlements to Jerusalem and one another and bypass Palestinian population areas. This kind of massive infrastructure investment by Israel makes it patently clear that no real return of territory is envisaged for the future at all.[34] Israel has used the past two years to almost finish its programme of settlement building around Jerusalem, 'Judaizing' the city, isolating Palestinian villages and suburbs, erasing former borders and making sure that Jerusalem will stay forever wholly in Israeli hands.

The Palestinian Authority has, meanwhile, been allowed to furnish itself with an extensive security apparatus, amounting to 18 000 men, which it has used principally to assert its authority over the Palestinian people. This security apparatus, which amounts to something far more sinister than a police force, has become quickly known for its abuse of human rights, its detention of political suspects, its extra-judicial killings, its 'state security courts'[35] and its hunting down of suspects wanted by Israel in regard to Islamic terrorist activities inside Israel itself. Arafat has used it to repress actual and potential opposition to his administration and many Palestinians are now deeply fearful that it will be further used to effectively 'fix' any elections which might finally take place. Israel has made the Palestinian Authority responsible for acts of rejection against the peace process. Thus, to remain in control of what little it has, the Palestinian Authority must act, in effect, as an Israeli henchman.

THE PRICE OF PEACE

Some might say that it is in the field of economics that most progress has been made. The Declaration of Principles laid extensive weight on new economic arrangements between Israel and the Occupied Territories, to be linked to a regional economic development programme which would end Israel's economic isolation in the region. A Protocol on Economic Relations was agreed in Paris in April 1994 and appended to the Cairo Agreement in May 1994. The new arrangements were virtually dictated by Israel and amount to a customs union between Israel and the Palestinian economy, with Israeli import tariffs, trade taxes and import licensing and standards imposed upon the latter. The terms of the customs union prevent the Palestinian territories from acting as a conduit for third party cheap imports into Israel; it ensures a continued subcontracting role for Palestinians, using cheap Palestinian Labour and Israeli and international capital[36] to produce what will be effectively Israeli industrial and agricultural exports. The Palestinians take on the burden of economic welfare and social provision for their population, but are given only a limited hand with taxation revenue raising and economic planning. Israel retains the right to subsidize and protect its own industries, to determine VAT rates throughout the union, issue currency, and control energy and water supplies. The relationship of Palestinian dependence upon the stronger Israeli economy is modified but not replaced; Israel's ability to ultimately control Palestinian production is only marginally reduced and prospects for independent Palestinian development are nil.[37]

The injection of foreign donor funds (the $2 billion promised from the international community) was supposed to kick-start the Palestinian economy. After twenty-seven years of systematic underdevelopment by Israel, it was always unrealistic to expect a rapid revitalization in a matter of months. In the event, Arafat's refusal to delegate authority to the body set up to channel the money into the Occupied Territories in a planned and accountable way[38] and his use of funds to distribute political patronage meant that only a proportion of the expected funds arrived, and that most of them were spent on either supporting the new security apparatus or funding the budget deficit.[39] This deficit has persistently exceeded planned amounts due to the difficulties of tax collection, non-payment by Israel of owed tax and licence revenues, excessive public sector employment[40] and, most ominously of all, the prevention of Palestinian labourers from working in Israel.

In the Paris Protocol, Israel committed itself to posing no obstacles to the labour migration of the 100 000 or so Palestinian workers who have, in the past, had access to the Israeli labour market. Without this source of national income (about 30 per cent), the Palestinian economy cannot be revived but will stagger beneath the burden of massive unemployment. Even with the anticipated Palestinian diaspora and international investment in the Occupied Territories, the existing economy cannot absorb either the current unemployed or the 15 000 new labourers who come onto the jobs market each year. Despite its commitment, Israel has sought to deliberately decrease its own dependence upon Palestinian labour. Between March and December 1994, for example, 54 000 foreign workers from Eastern Europe (especially Romania), Turkey and the Far East were given work permits to take jobs previously filled by Palestinians. A series of 'closures', which restrict Palestinians from entering Israel to work, has been imposed, with a ceiling of 15 000 Palestinians being allowed back at any one time. The former Israeli prime minister Rabin had himself said:

> We have to free ourselves from our dependency on workers from the territories. This dependency forces us to take decisions which put Israeli lives in danger. The long-term aim is to reduce dramatically the number of Palestinians working in Israel.[41]

Security considerations have been used to advance what is now termed a policy of 'total separation', a policy which has come to mean that in the reconstructed occupation, Palestinian labour continues to work for Israeli capital but is confined geographically to the Occupied Territories.[42] The Palestinian Authority will administer and take responsibility for the welfare of the Palestinian population (relieving Israel of the obligation – which it never fulfilled anyway) but Israel will continue to control and exploit the resources of the Occupied Territories, including land and water. This is true bantustanization and is the logical climax of Israeli apartheid policies over the years.

THE WIDER CONFLICT

It was widely hoped that the signing of an accord between Israel and the PLO would open the door to advances in other tracks of the peace process. Sure enough, on 26 October 1994, Israel and Jordan formally ended the state of war which had existed between them since 1948. The PLO's unilateral action had made it possible for Arab states to pursue their own paths without the opprobrium faced by Sadat in 1979. While King Hussein had to move cautiously for fear of being seen to weaken his Syrian neighbour's position, the risks were outweighed by the benefits. Jordan can now be sure of a secure western border and a friendly Israeli neighbour. It is easier for Jordan to counter any attempt by Syria to pull Jordan into its orbit and sweeteners in the form of American aid, greater access to water, and a special position with regards to Muslim shrines in Jerusalem, made the deal extremely palatable. It is notable, however, that the agreement was reached at the expense of the Palestinians: the Jordanians accepted Israeli settlements on 'returned' Jordanian land – a bad precedent from the Palestinian position. Jericho was bypassed as an economic transit point for trade between Israel and Jordan, with new crossings being opened north and south of the West Bank. Furthermore, acknowledgement by Israel of Jordanian rights in Jerusalem was a direct slap in the face to the aspirations of the Palestinians for the return of their capital city.

With formal agreements signed with Egypt, Jordan and the PLO, Israel is left with only Syria and Lebanon to deal with. Although high-level negotiations have continued, Israel and Syria still have substantially opposing positions. Signs that Israel was prepared to make substantial withdrawals from the Golan Heights were not translated into any tangible deals during the period of Israel Labour Party premiership. Indeed the negotiations between Israel and Syria had essentially run to a standstill. The new Israeli prime minister, right-wing Benjamin Netanyahu, is already setting preconditions on further talks which are fundamentally unacceptable to Assad. Operation Grapes of Wrath, the fierce Israeli bombardment of Lebanon in early 1996, served only to strengthen Lebanese resistance to a separate deal with Israel and to demonstrate the reality of Israeli interpretations of peace; effectively imposition through occupation. Assad is aware, however, that while he may hold the high ground of Arab nationalism, his Arab brothers are all around him folding beneath the wave of 'regional economic integration'.

REGIONAL ECONOMIC DEVELOPMENT AND THE NEW WORLD ORDER

Much to the delight of the European Union, which has been promoting its own model of integration to the Middle East for several years, and the United States (remember the four pillars of its new Middle East policy), the Arab world has seen the advances in direct peace making between Israel and the frontline parties as the green light for a vigorous attempt at regional economic development. The idea goes thus: now that Israel is in the process of establishing normal relations with its neighbours (and ignoring the fact that this is still an extremely distant reality), the Arab world need no longer be divided between moderates and rejectionists. A principal cause of disunity has been removed and therefore a new approach is possible which links all Arab states into a regional economic framework for their mutual benefit. Israel too may have a place in this, although not without some reservations about its comparative strength compared with the other parties. This thinking is in line with the general movement to liberalize trade, to court international markets and to lift barriers to foreign direct investment. The movers and shakers of international capital, the international financial institutions, the multinational corporations and the governments of the G7 countries, have all welcomed and encouraged moves by the Arab states to initiate regional development projects and conferences.

This means, of course, that the Arab boycott has begun to disintegrate.[43] By the beginning of January 1995, Israel had official relations with five Arab League member countries. In September 1994, the Gulf Cooperation Council states, led by Kuwait, announced that they would no longer enforce the secondary boycott, and Morocco and Tunisia openly admit that they no longer do so. Jordan and Egypt, with peace agreements, are also not applying it. Indeed, Egypt has only recently agreed a joint project with Agrexco, the Israeli agricultural produce marketing company. Djibouti, Oman and Qatar have all initiated some level of contact with Israel.[44] Even Saudi Arabia has opened its airways to El Al flights. The primary boycott is still formally in place, but is being bypassed in an array of ways. The Casablanca Summit of November 1994 effectively marked the beginning of the end for the boycott, gathering together as it did 2500 businessmen and government officials from the Arab world, the United States, Europe, Asia and Israel. The Israelis produced a glossy, confident document, outlining their perspective regarding the potential for regional cooperation, which stated that Israel's goal is 'the creation of a regional community of nations, with a common market and elected centralized bodies, modelled on the European Community', with three stages of binational or multinational projects, international consortia and regional community policy.[45]

Already the first and second stages of this process are well under way, although it will still be a long time before the third can develop. Through the multilateral talks on the Middle East, projects have been established in the sectors of tourism, telecommunications, environment, water and energy resources which draw governments and the private sector into economic cooperation. It is true that common markets require forms of democratic and accountable government which simply do not exist as yet among most Arab governments, not to mention political stability and some degree of economic parity between member states. Israeli hopes are thus certainly premature. Yet it is equally true to say that the Arab boycott is being steadily weakened and is likely to be wholly dismantled in the not-too-distant future. Normalization of economic relations in the Middle East is a long-cherished Israeli dream and appears to be closer to attainment.[46]

Israel is also benefiting from a restored international profile. In the eyes of the world it has made peace with the Palestinians and may thus be appropriately rewarded, regardless of the true nature of that peace. Israel improved its active diplomatic ties rapidly after Oslo, from 116 countries in 1992 to 142 by March 1994. More have followed. In October 1994 the prime minister visited China, Indonesia and Singapore to set up new trade (including arms) deals. Many Asian countries, although not tied to the Arab boycott, had simply ignored Israel in the past. Now they are eager to link up with what they think will be the lynchpin of the future Middle Eastern economy. Vietnam, South Korea and Japan have all courted Israel in the last two years, have opened their markets to Israeli exports and joint ventures and have quoted Israeli stocks on their financial markets. In July 1995, Israel and the EU reached a wide-ranging economic accord giving Israeli agricultural and high-tech producers improved access to European markets. Even countries as far away as Uruguay and Venezuela, or as radical as Cuba and North Korea, have made direct contact with Israel. In total, as Aharon Klieman says,

> Clearly, incontrovertibly, the long international siege of Israel has been lifted, as a consequence of which the external political milieu is altered almost beyond recognition, whereby vast zones of potential opportunity replace zones of enmity and exclusion perviously designated as off-limits to Israeli entrepreneurs, tourists or good-will ambassadors.[47]

The result is that Israel is increasingly being seen as the success story round the corner. In recent years it has managed to combine economic growth (which averaged 5.5 per cent a year in 1989–93) with, until recently, falling inflation and unemployment. It has an experienced and highly educated workforce, a diversified and high-tech industrial base, an improving per capita export ratio, a sovereign currency debt ratio which places it above Mexico, South Africa and Greece, and a GDP per head comparable with New Zealand and Ireland. In short, it is expected to reach 'developed nation' status by the end of the century.[48]

Israeli attempts to attract foreign investment have been boosted recently by the accelerated progress of trade liberalization, labour market reforms, market deregulation and privatization. Israeli companies are for the first time turning to European finance capital and finding a receptive ear. European and Japanese banks are competing in what was previously an American domain – that of underwriting privatizations – and the Tel Aviv Stock Exchange is considered to be one of the potentially most exciting in the world.

Israel is clearly already reaping the rewards of peace, regardless of the fact that the Oslo Accords have not led to a just and equal settlement of the Palestinian dispute, nor are likely to. The truth is that international capital is not interested in waiting for such an outcome before it sucks the Middle East region into its expanding visions. The Oslo Accords were in fact convenient because they removed the procedural obstacle to advancing a far more important and dynamic agenda. Their ultimate outcome will not be judged by the reasonableness of a final settlement, by any moral or legal criteria set by the United Nations. They will be counted a success simply by having broken one of the barriers to the tidal wave of capitalist expansion into and within the region as a whole.

CONCLUSION

It has been argued here that President Bush's New World Order has failed the Palestinians: far from protecting the weak and vulnerable, the powers of that order have facilitated and colluded in a process which has reduced the Palestinian cause to a localized dispute, made it exempt from criteria of justice, fairness or legality and even provided material reward to Israel for continuing and restructuring an occupation condemned many times over by the United Nations itself. Bush claimed that American national interests required regional stability and security in the Middle East, not least because America is a lynchpin in the world economic system that also required the removal of political obstacles to economic activities. Given the collapse of alternative options and its own weakening economic status, the Arab world as a whole has proved unable to resist what may in retrospect seem to have been inevitable. Israel, ready and waiting, impelled by its own logic and that of its American sponsor, has been able to politically adjust itself to the compromises necessary to sieze the moment. In the middle are the Palestinians, their rights and requirements overridden by the states around them galloping towards one another, unprotected by the United Nations or the idealism of any New World Order.

NOTES

1. Stephen Graubard, *Mr Bush's War* (Tauris, London, 1992), p. 165.
2. Samir Amin argues that it is not the nation-state itself that is under threat, since capitalism has a political and social dimension so far organized or represented by the state. Globalization, however, undermines the economic efficiency of the state, even as its political and social functions remain. See Samir Amin, 'Fifty Years is Enough', in *Monthly Review*, April 1995, pp. 8–50.
3. Harry Magdoff, 'Globalization – To What End?', in Ralph Miliband and Leo Panitch (eds), *New World Order? Socialist Register 1992* (Merlin, London, 1992), pp. 44–75.
4. See Tim Niblock and Emma C. Murphy (eds), *Economic and Political Liberalisation in the Middle East* (British Academic Press, London, 1993).
5. For an analysis of Israel's attempts to restructure its economy, see Emma C. Murphy, 'Structural Inhibitions to Economic Liberalisation in Israel' in *Middle East Journal*, vol. 48, no. 1, Winter 1994, pp. 65–88.
6. For an analysis of Bush's conception of a New World Order, see Yasumasa Kuroda, 'Bush's New World Order: A Structural Analysis of Instability and Conflict in the Gulf', in T. Ismael and J. Ismael (eds), *The Gulf War and the New World Order* (University Press of Florida, Florida, 1994), pp. 52–76.
7. Avi Shlaim, 'Israel and the Conflict', in A. Danchev and D. Keohane (eds), *International Perspectives on the Gulf Conflict 1990–91* (Macmillan, London, 1994), p. 77.
8. See G. Joffe, 'The Implications of the New World Order for the Middle East and North Africa', in *The Middle East and North Africa* (Europa, London, 1992).

136   *The Middle East in the New World Order*

9. In 1995, for example, the United States gave a clear indication of its intention to retain a long-term naval presence by formalizing the creation of the Fifth Fleet to police the Persian Gulf.
10. *Christian Science Monitor*, 16–22 October 1992.
11. Take for example Iran's provocative reassertions of ownership of Abu Musa in September 1992, when it refused a ship carrying passengers from the UAE entry to Abu Musa and demanded that all non-Sharjan residents produce Iranian permits. See *Strategic Survey* 1992–93, International Institute for Strategic Studies (Brasseys, London, 1993), pp. 120–1.
12. In 1993 Kuwait was alleged to have planned for defence expenditures of over $12 billion for the next decade, while King Fahd announced that Saudi Defence expenditures should rise by 9 per cent. See *Strategic Survey 1993–94*, International Institute for Strategic Studies (Brasseys, London, 1994), p. 143.
13. Such arms sales have seriously dented the Israeli–American relationship, especially in light of 1992 allegations of illicit Israeli transfers of US technology. The Saudi deal was opposed by 237 Congress members and 72 Senators but was supported by McDonnell-Douglas and 2000 subcontractors who emphasized the 'US jobs now' theme.
14. In September 1992, then-Governor Bill Clinton told the B'nai B'rith national convention that: 'Without a growing economy, without a strong, stable and secure American middle class, America's commitment to Israel will always be under pressure.' See *Jerusalem Report*, 22 October 1992.
15. *Christian Science Monitor*, 16–22 October 1992.
16. After the Gulf War, the Saudi regime was faced with increasing demands from religious scholars and groups to persue a stricter interpretation of Islam in its policy making. The government responded with a combination of concessions and clampdowns. In 1993, it introduced measures to ensure that all private/mosque donations to Islamic causes were disbursed through official channels, after Egypt complained of private Saudi financial support for extremist Islamist groups in Egypt.
17. Jacob Goldberg, 'Syria and the Palestinians: The Change is Real', *New Outlook*, January/February 1992, p. 24.
18. Adam Garfinkle, 'Jordan', in Robert B. Satloff (ed.), *The Politics of Change in the Middle East* (Westview, Boulder, Colo., 1993), p. 101.
19. Muhammad Muslih, 'The Shift in Palestinian Thinking', *Current History*, January 1992, p. 22.
20. Jacob Goldberg, 'Syria and the Palestinians: The Change is Real', *New Outlook*, January/February 1992, p. 24.
21. Shamir's concerns centred around Bush's delays on considering $10 billion in loan guarantees for the settlement of new immigrants and James Baker's statement that there was no greater obstacle to peace than Israel's settlements in the West bank and Gaza Strip. See Marvin Feuerwerger, 'Israeli–American Relations in the Second Rabin Era' in Robert O. Freedman (ed), *Israel Under Rabin* (Westview, Boulder, Colo., 1995), pp. 9–23.
22. Ian J. Bickerton and Carla L. Klausner, *A Concise History of the Arab-Israeli Conflict*, 2nd edn, (Prentice-Hall, Englewood Cliffs, NJ, 1995), p. 258.

23.   Interesting analysis of the positions of the Palestinians and Israel during this period can be found in the following references: Kathy Glavanis, 'Changing Perceptions and Constant Realities: Palestinian and Israeli Experiences of the Gulf War', in Haim Bresheeth and Nira Yuval-David (eds), *The Gulf War and the New World Order* (Zed Books, London, 1991), pp. 117–135; various chapters in Gad Barzilai, Aharon Klieman and Gil Shidlo (eds), *The Gulf Crisis and its Global Aftermath* (Routledge, London, 1993); Marvin Feurwerger, 'Israel, the Gulf War and its Aftermath' and Helena Cobban, 'The Palestinians and the Iraqi Invasion of Kuwait', both in Robert O. Freedman (ed.), *The Middle East after Iraq's Invasion of Kuwait* (University Press of Florida, NJ, 1993) and Cheryl A. Rubenberg, 'The Gulf War, the Palestinians and the New World Order', and Meir Porat, 'Israel and the New World Order', both in T. Ismael and J. Ismael, (eds) *The Gulf War and the New World Order* (University Press of Florida, Florida, 1994).

24.   Shamir was adamant that settlement activity in the West Bank would not be stopped and that 'autonomy' for the Palestinians would be discussed only in terms of autonomy for the people, not the land. Talks between Israel and Lebanon and Israel and Syria were obstructed by continuing Hizbollah rocket attacks on the Israeli-occupied zone in Southern Lebanon and by Syrian purchases of new tanks and Chinese SCUD 'C' missiles.

25.   Prior to his election, Bill Clinton repeatedly made clear his commitment to Israel and drew heavily on Jewish support. His campaign attorney, David Ifshin, was a general council of AIPAC and headed a twelve-member 'Jewish Council' for Clinton. The new President stated that he believed the principal obstacle to peace was not Jewish settlements but rather the Arab boycott of Israel and the rearming of Syria. During his campaign he pledged to support $3 billion in annual assistance to Israel, and promised to enhance US–Israeli military and technological cooperation and to create a joint American–Israeli high-tech commission. See Marvin Feuerwerger, op. cit., p. 10.

26.   King Hussein's attempts in the late 1980s to introduce gradual democratization into Jordan, including a National Charter guaranteeing political freedoms, brought greater power for the Islamic fundamentalists during and immediately after the Gulf War. By the early 1990s, the fragile alliance between Islamists and secular oppositionists was falling apart over socially divisive issues such as gender segregation. While Hussein was now able to gradually reassert the regime's authority over plauralist forces, he was deeply aware of the popular support for HAMAS-style opposition to full peace with Israel.

27.   Even before the December 1992 Israeli expulsions of 414 suspected HAMAS leaders, it was estimated that HAMAS accounted for between 30 and 50 per cent of the population of the West Bank and Gaza Strip (*Christian Science Monitor*, 18–24 December 1992).

28.   Alan Elsner, 'Christopher Hopes Arab–Israeli Talks Resume Soon', *Reuters*, 24 February 1993.

29.   For an interesting discussion of this, see 'The American Peace Process – August 1994' in Edward Said, *Peace and its Discontents* (Vintage, London, 1995), pp. 84–90.

30. International Labour Conference, 80th Session, *Report of the Director General*, Appendix II, International Labour Organization, Geneva.

31. *Prospects for Sustainable Development of the Palestinian Economy in the West Bank and Gaza Strip*, UNCTAD/DSD/SEU/2, 27 September 1993, Geneva.

32. A. Ehteshami, 'Palestinian Perspectives on the Gulf Conflict', in A. Danchev and D. Keohane (eds), *International Perspectives on the Gulf Conflict 1990–91* (Macmillan, London 1994) p. 100.

33. The dunum was a Turkish unit of land measure equating to 919.3 m^2 which the British adopted in metric form to equal 100 m^2.

34. *Challenge*, July–August 1995, no. 32, p. 3.

35. The State Security Courts usually operate at night, just hours or days after arrests are made. No defence counsel is allowed, no appeals can be made and charges can be invented without regard to any legal code.

36. The most tangible example of this is the plan for new industrial parks to be established on the borders between Israel and the Palestinian auonomous areas. For more information on the disadvantages of these, see Samih Aboudi, 'Palestinian Industrial Parks' in *Peace Economics*, The Economist Intelligence Unit, 2nd quarter 1995.

37. For a full analysis of the implications of the Paris Protocol by this author see *Israel and the Palestinians: The Economic Rewards of Peace*, CMEIS Occasional Paper No. 47, University of Durham, March 1995.

38. This body was called PECDAR, or the Palestinian Economic Council for Development and Reconstruction.

39. Of $760 million in aid pledged for 1994, only $140 million had actually been disbursed by November 1994. The two US disbursements of $5 million in May and $4 million in October were not sufficient even to pay the Gaza Municipality electricty bill (*Financial Times*, 22 November 1994). In August 1995, the US raised $100 million to cover the 1995 budget deficit (*Arab Press Service*, 26 August–2 September 1995, SP 145, p. 17).

40. In 1995 the PA had approximately 29 000 public employees on top of the security services. The salaries have increasingly been paid by bank loans.

41. *Israel Radio*, 10 April 1994.

42. However, in August 1995, the Israeli Histadrut trade union agreed with Palestinian trade unions to help pressure the Israeli government to replace 80 000 immigrant workers from Asia with Palestinians (*Arab Press Service*, 26 August–2 September SP 147, p. 19).

43. The journalist Avi Temkin said of the Arab boycott 'since its inception [the Arab boycott against Israel] has been a relatively effective weapon. Official estimates put the damage caused by the boycott, mainly in its secondary and tertiary aspects, at some $40 billion. Even if this figure is inflated, the boycott was clearly effective in blocking the formation of working relations between Israel and multinationals, from Europe and Asia in particular'. See 'The Arab Boycott: Prospects for Dismantlement and Its Implications for the Israeli Business Environment', in *Economic Dimensions of the Middle East Peace Process* (Economist Intelligence Unit, London 1994).

44. Qatar has confirmed its approval for the marketing of liquified natural gas by its joint venture partner, Enron, to Israel.

45. *Development Options for Regional Cooperation* (Compiled by the Ministry of Foreign Affairs and Ministry of Finance, Government of Israel, Tel Aviv, October 1994).

46. In August 1995, the US fined the French company L'Oréal for joining the Arab boycott against Israel. Commerce Department Assistant Secretary John Despres said that companies would continue to be fined for joining the boycott 'until the boycott is completely ended'. It is clear that the United States cherishes the dream of an economically integrated Israel as deeply as the Zionist state itself does.

47. Aharon Klieman, 'New Directions in Israel's Foreign Policy', in *Israel Affairs*, vol. 1, no. 1, autumn 1994, p. 99.

48. David Brodet, the Israeli treasury budget director, estimates that current income per capita of $14 000 will increase to $20 000 by the end of the century. See *Jerusalem Post International*, 10 September 1994.

7 Pan-Islamism and Pan-Arabism: Solution or Obstacle to Political Reconstruction in the Middle East?

Haifaa A. Jawad

INTRODUCTION

Pan-Islamism and pan-Arabism are two major political movements which have a profound effect on the politics of the Middle
East. Pan-Islamism emerged during the late nineteenth century;
it aims to unify the Muslim world via its commonly held Islamic
beliefs. It emphasizes the universality of Islam and hence the
union of Muslim peoples by arguing that 'the idea of political
unity is inherent in Islam, whose character is a priori international, no less than a complete moral, cultural, legal, social and
political system.'[1] This comprehensive character of the religion of
Islam therefore has deeply influenced and affected the politics of
pan-Islamism. The precedent to which the proponents of pan-Islamism look is the dynamic period of early Islam, the 'golden age'
in which the Muslim peoples were united.

Pan-Arabism[2] or Arab nationalism (*al-quwmiyya al-arabiyya*) is a
later movement and is typified by the ideal of unifying the Arab
peoples. Arab nationalists consider the Arab world, which stret-
ches from the Atlantic Ocean to the Gulf area, and from the
Arabian Sea to the Mediterranean, to be a single, homogeneous
whole, and the Arab people to be a single nation bound by the
common ties of language, culture and history.[3] The concept of
Arabism and the idea of unity are the major and common
elements of pan-Arabism: 'Arabism or Uruba, is a quasi-mystical
term denoting the essence of being an Arab, the sense of
belonging to the Arab nation, the possession of Arabic as mother

tongue, and the fact of having been born an Arab in an Arab land'; unity or *Wahda* 'is implicit in the feeling and awareness of Arabism: it involves political unity, and restores to wholeness what has been violated by history, adversity and accident.'[4]

While pan-Islamism is multilinear and more universal in concept in the sense that it seeks to unify all Muslims, Arab and non-Arab, pan-Arabism is more unilinear, secular and ethnically exclusive. The promotion of Muslim political unity and of Arab unity has been taking place since the late nineteenth and early twentieth centuries respectively. Each competes with the other, claims to be the legitimate force and believes it can provide the proper solution to current political, social and economic decline in the region. This chapter will look at the roots and developments of the two ideologies. Such a perspective on the origins of pan-Islamism and pan-Arabism may help further understanding of current events in the region. The divergent roles of the two movements will be considered, plus the type of political concepts that have been utilized, and the reasons for their implementation or the lack thereof. Finally, the chapter will assess the successes and failures of the two movements and offer some conclusions as to whether they constitute a solution or an obstacle to political reconstruction in the Middle East.

THE HISTORICAL DEVELOPMENT OF PAN-ISLAMISM

During the fifteenth and sixteenth centuries the world of Islam was incorporated into three major empires: the Ottoman, the Safavid and the Mughal. All the present Arabic-speaking countries, with the exception of some parts of Arabia, Sudan and Morocco, were included in the Ottoman empire. The empire also contained Anatolia and south-eastern Europe, which included the whole of present-day or recent Romania, Yugoslavia, Greece, Bulgaria, Albania and Cyprus, as well as part of Hungary and the Crimea. The capital of the empire was Istanbul. It was thus one of the largest political structures to exist after the disintegration of the Roman empire. It ruled over lands with various political cultures, many ethnic groups and different religious communities. Turkish was the language of the ruling family and the military and administrative elites. The empire was a bureaucratic state, controlling various regions within a single administrative and fiscal system. Moreover, it was the last major Muslim empire; it defended the frontiers of Islam, expanded them when possible, and preserved and upheld the Islamic law (*Sharia*). Under Ottoman rule, the special position of the Arabic language was reinforced. Hence, the sciences of religion and law were taught in Arabic in the great schools of Istanbul, Cairo and Damascus, and works of religion, law, history and biography were all written in Arabic. The empire also guarded the holy places of Mecca and Medina in Arabia and Jerusalem and Hebron in Palestine. This boosted Ottoman credibility and gave the system a legitimacy and a claim to the attention of the Muslim world beyond that of any earlier Muslim state. In the early stages, the empire succeeded in maintaining public order, running an adequate administrative system and achieving economic growth. However, from the eighteenth century onwards, the empire's power in relation to the outside world, especially Europe, started to decline. First, the balance between Ottoman central and local governments changed. Second, there was a change in relations between the empire and the European countries. The gap between the technical skills of some European countries and the Ottoman empire started to grow wider. During the centuries of Ottoman rule, there had been no advances in technology, and there was a decline in the level of scientific knowledge, with general intellectual stagnation. This was compounded by increases in authoritarianism and corruption. Hence, whereas the empire had expanded into Europe in its early centuries, by the later part of the eighteenth century it was under military threat from western Europe. Conscious of this decline in power and independence, the ruling élite inaugurated an era of half a century of reforms known collectively as the Tanzimat. These reforms in the military, the legal system and education were based upon European models. The aim was to bolster the empire to meet the European threat. While the reforms did little more than superficially alter the basic infrastructure, the Tanzimat nevertheless had major ramifications within the Arab provinces, which were at the time falling prey to direct Western intervention. The first major conquest of an Arab country was that of Algeria by France (1830–47). This was followed by the conquests of Egypt, Tunisia, Morocco and Libya. The Ottoman empire also in due course lost most of its European provinces and became more of a Turkish–Arab state.[5] The rise of Western influence throughout the empire and later the outright invasion and occupation of the Arab provinces by the European countries illustrated the failure of the Ottoman system to protect the nations of Islam against foreign intervention. The attack on the Muslim world and especially on Islam during this period generated responses from thoughtful Muslims, who tried to defend Islam and explain the reasons behind the backwardness and crisis in the world of Islam. Haim explains the situation as follows:

> The assault which Islam had to endure in the nineteenth century was twofold. It consisted, in the first place, of military attack on Muslim states or their political subjugation by different European powers, and, in the second place, of criticism of Islam as a system of beliefs and a way of life, a way of life that was belittled, ridiculed, and made to seem backward and barbaric in comparison with the achievements of western learning, philosophy, and technical advance. The latter was perhaps even more dangerous and insidious than political and military subjugation, for it could penetrate the spiritual defen- ses of the Muslim community and of its intellectual leaders, thereby effecting a dissolution of Islam such as foreign rule, by itself, could hardly accomplish. In so parlous a situation, Islam was bound to make many attempts at its own defense[6].

The Traditional Reformists

The early reformists sought reform within the context of pre- existing Islamic structures. They were concerned with the reasons for the Islamic world's comparative backwardness in relation to the West. To many of them, though, they differed in their conclusive analysis; it was the rigidity of the socio-religious aspects of the Islamic world which was at the core of its decline and comparative cultural backwardness.[7] They sought to revi- talize pre-existing structures in the hope of countering the exter- nal threat, their ideas shaped by what they perceived as the necessities of their time. In particular, they searched for a vehicle to revitalize their culture. Among this group of early pan-Islamic intellectuals was the Egyptian scholar and writer Rifa al-Tahtawi (1801–73). His ideas are within the tradition of Islamic political thought. At every point he cites the example of the Prophet and his companions, attempting, however, to give them new momentum. For him, the best way to improve the situation in the Muslim world was through the introduction of a modern education system. He advocated a return to the study of the rational sciences, which had blossomed in the Muslim world, but which had subsequently declined. Also, he insisted that Islamic law should be reinterpreted to suit modern needs without endangering Islamic principles. In order to do so, the Ulama (who are the interpreters of the *Sharia*) must know modern developments in this field. Moreover, al-Tahtawi encouraged political education for all citizens so that they would know the laws as well as their rights and duties. He emphasized that the ruler should try to please his citizens and take into consideration their opinions. It must be noted that, although his ideas were radical for the time, his emphasis was not on the adoption or introduction of new institutions, but rather on the revival of the Islamic principles of the past.[8]

The same problems were considered by the Tunisian thinker Khayr al-Din Pasha (1820–89). His major work is a political study entitled *Aqwam al-Masalik fi Marifat al-Mamalik* (The Straightest Road to Know the Conditions of the State), first published in Tunis in 1867. His concern was with the history, political structure and military strength of the European countries. He encouraged Muslim leaders to try to take from them what was best for the welfare of the Muslim community and the development of its civilization, arguing that the only way to save and strengthen the Muslim states was to take over the best of the European ideas and institutions. By doing so, the Muslim community would not be abandoning Islam; on the contrary, it would be adopting the modern equivalent of the ancient institutions of the Islamic *umma*. He believed that the power of the ruler must be restrained: first by law, second by consultation. The ruler should consult the Ulama and notables. They should be able to speak to him freely, guide him to what was right, and away from what was wrong. The Islamic Umma in its original form had been like that, the author argued, and as long as it upheld the Islamic law, it enjoyed prosperity, strength and stability. Thus, the first step toward healthy reforms was that the religious leaders as well as statesmen should be in agreement and that the religious leaders must be in touch with the spirit of the times.[9]

The most liberal and influential of all these thinkers was Jamal al-Din al-Asadabadi (1838–97), commonly known as al-Afghani.

His main concern was the state of Muslim affairs. He believed that the Muslim people were in a deplorable condition because their governments were corrupt and unable to protect them from foreign intervention. To remedy the situation, he called for Muslim people to challenge their governments, to force them to act effectively, and to unite under the banner of Islam so as to contain European expansion. For him, Islam was the only effective means of solidarity and union among Muslim people – a means through which Muslims could create and maintain a strong and stable state.[10] To challenge the Western military, political and, most important, cultural assault on the Muslim world, therefore, al-Afghani advocated unity – pan-Islamism.

A contemporary colleague and co-founder of the influential newspaper *al-Urwa L-Wuthqa* (The Indissoluble Link) was Muhammad Abduh (1849–1905), who believed that the only way to solve the crisis of the Muslim world was through political reform and constitutional government. He differed greatly from al-Afghani on the role of Islam as a vehicle for unity and emancipation. For him, it was through social evolution via education that in the long term the lot of Muslims in the empire would improve. His erudite approach, based on humanist principles, was in keeping with pre-orthodox Islam in its 'golden age'.[11] Indeed, it should be stressed that it was the classical al-Mutazila school which first advocated this approach.

Abduh's ideas for the socialization of Islam, through reuniting Islam and reason, and a return to Islam's golden age, had great impact on the best known of his disciples: Muhammad Rashid Rida (1865–1935). Like his teacher, he was discontented with the situation of the Ottoman empire and eager for reform.[12] In his opinion, the reason for the backwardness of the Muslim people was that Muslims had lost the truth of their religion, a process exacerbated by flawed political rule. Islamic civilization, he argued, was created out of nothing by the Qur'an and the moral principles embodied in it, and, could therefore, be revived if Muslims would return to the Qur'an. While following Abduh's concept of revitalization via a return to Islam's golden age, Rashid Rida's interpretation differed in that it was more ethnically oriented than his predecessor's.[13] This, in conjunction with the fact that Syria remained under strong Ottoman influence, led him to believe in the superiority of Arab rule within Islam. It is important to stress, though, that he did not argue this from a purely ethnic principle. Indeed, non-Arab Muslim scholars such as al-Mawdudi, and, in medieval Islam, al-Jahiz, advocated the same idea.

Al-Kawakibi (1849–1903) followed a similar if not more extreme line of pro-Arab pan-Islamism.[14] He also believed in the contemporary importance of revitalization via Arab ascendancy, and of the historical precedent of the golden age. His starting point was the inner crisis of Islam. Islam had declined, he maintained, because of illegal innovation, blind imitation and despotic rulers who supported false religion and encouraged evil – hence corrupting the whole of society. To save Islam from this, he advocated a reform of the law, religious education and a shift in balance of power inside the Umma from the Turks back to the Arabs. He believed that the Arabs were the only people who could save Islam from decay, because of the special position of the Arabian Peninsula in the Umma and of the Arabic language in Islamic thought.[15] In the wake of these thinkers, and in the face of perhaps even greater challenge, the question of solving the crisis of Islam continues unabated today.

THE MUSLIM BROTHERHOOD

At present the most powerful movement advocating pan-Islamism is the Muslim Brotherhood.[16] The movement is similar to, and in part derived from, that of the *Salafiyya*. It was founded in 1928 by an elementary-school teacher, Hasan al-Banna, who was born in 1906 in the Egyptian city of al-Mahmodiyya. He received his first education there at the al-Rashad school. In 1920, he joined the *dar-al-mualemin* (College of Education) in Damnhor city, then went to Cairo to study at the *dar-al-Ulum* (House of Science). In 1927 he completed his studies and started his first job as a teacher in Ismailiyya. He published the periodicals *The Muslim Brothers* and *al-Nazir*. He also published a collection of letters called *Rasail al-Banna*, before being assasinated in 1949.[17]

Initially, the movement became a major political force in Egypt then spread to Syria, Jordan,[18] the Sudan and other Arab and Muslim countries. The movement played an effective role in the political life of Egypt. It participated in the Arab revolt in Palestine between 1936 and 1939 and the Arab–Israeli war of 1948. After the independence of Egypt in 1952, the Muslim

Brotherhood offered guidelines for the policies of the new government. But soon relations with the government became hostile, culminating in 1954 when members of the group attempted to assassinate President Nasser. This resulted in some members being executed, while others, such as Said Ramadan, Salih al-Ashmawi and Mustafa al-Alim, fled to Jerusalem where they became associated with the Higher Islamic Council. In the 1960s the exiled Muslim Brothers moved their base to Saudi Arabia and from there, unsuccessfully, attempted a *coup d'état* against the regime in Egypt.[19] Since then the movement has served as the most effective channel of opposition and continues to offer an alternative model for a just society.

The Muslim Brotherhood started as a movement aiming at reforming the individual as well as society, based on an analysis of what had gone wrong with the Muslim world. The movement believes that Islam has declined because of the spread of blind imitation, along with the excesses of *Sufism* (mystical Islam). In addition, they argue, Western missionary activities and imperial domination have brought alien values and immorality. To remedy the situation, it is advocated that Muslims should return to the Islam of the Qur'an and try to apply its teachings to every aspect of their lives.[20] For the founder of the movement, Hasan al-Banna, the teachings and doctrines of Islam are all-comprehensive and govern the affairs of all human beings for all ages and at all time, in this world as well as the next, because Islam is religion and state, spirit and work, holy book and sword. Also, as the source and foundation of Islam are the Qur'an and the Sunna (the validated Islamic traditions, sayings, etc.), it follows that the Umma could never go astray if it abided by them.[21] Al-Banna's writings both constitute and advocate *dawa* (call). This call, 'divine' and 'universal', has as its main goal to teach reverence for God, to all humankind throughout the world. Such *dawa*, he argues, is particularly important in the modern era because human knowledge, despite its material advancement, has failed to solve the problems encountered by people throughout the universe, and because the Muslims and other non-Western peoples have suffered long enough from European political domination. His call aims at a spiritual awakening based on the principles of Islam. This, in turn, would have an impact on the individual, the household and the nation. The individual's spiritual awakening, he argues, can be achieved when one learns to distinguish the noble from the base and right from wrong, when one engages in daily acts of worship and assumes the basic principles of Islam as one's own and when one struggles to acquire the moral virtues prescribed by Islam. The household's spiritual awakening can be obtained when the Muslim man creates the right circumstances for an Islamic upbringing of his children and when he treats his wife with due respect as a fellow Muslim. As for the spiritual awakening of the nation, al-Banna identifies two aims. The first one is to liberate the fatherland from all foreign rule. Once liberation is obtained, a free Islamic state must be established in accordance with the principles of Islam, which are set forth in the Qur'an. Other secondary goals are: accomplishing a better economic distribution by eradicating foreign monopolies, providing better health care for the people, offering general education to all citizens, reducing crime in society and setting up a decent army. These goals can be achieved through deep faith, work and careful organization.[22] Like Rashid Rida and al-Kawakibi before him, al-Banna emphasizes the special position of the Arab people within Islam, and believes that Arab unity is a prerequisite for the re-establishment of the Muslim state or union. To al-Banna:

> the Arabs are the core and guardians of Islam. Arab unity is an essential prerequisite for the restoration of Islam's glory, the reestablishment of the Muslim state, and the consolidation of Muslim power. This is why it is the duty of every Muslim to work for the revival and support of Arab unity.[23]

The most prominent leader of the movement after Hasan al-Banna was the Egyptian schoolteacher Sayyid Qutb (1906–66), who played the role of an ideologue for the group. He was imprisoned in the 1960s for his political activity and released by the government in 1964 for health reasons (it is said that the former Iraqi leader Abdel Salam Aref exerted pressure on the Egyptian government to release him), but was executed in 1966 after the Brotherhood's attempt on Nasser's life. Like al-Banna, Qutb's writings call for the renewal of the Islamic life, because contemporary Muslim society is not truly Islamic. To achieve this goal, he stresses there birth of religious belief and the restructuring of legislation so that all facets of public life could be ordered in accordance with the Islamic framework. His teaching focuses on the belief that Islam offers adequate solutions to the problems of human kind 'because Islam alone unites spirit and matters, or heaven and earth, thereby responding to all needs of mankind'.[24] To illustrate how Islam responds to these needs, he explains the Islamic principles of social justice in his famous book *al-Adala al-Ijtimaiyya fil-Islam* (Social Justice in Islam).[25] Here he states that for Muslims there is no gap between faith and life. All human deeds can be regarded as acts of worship, and the Qur'an and Hadith offer the rules on which action should be based. Man is free only when he is free from all subjection to powers except that of God. Among the rules to be derived from the Qur'an is that of the mutual responsibility of people in society. Despite the fact that human beings are equal in the eyes of God, they have various tasks which correspond to their different positions in society. For example, men and women are equal spiritually but different in function and responsibility. Rulers, too, have special obligations: upholding the law, enforcing morality and creating a just society. This includes maintaining the right to property, but ensuring that property be used for the common good of society. Wealth should not be used in dishonest ways; rather, it should be taxed to serve the interests of society. The necessities of communal life should be owned in common and not left in the hands of individuals. The rulers should be obeyed only if they uphold the fabric of a just society. If they cease to do so, the duty of obedience lapses. A genuine Islamic society can be revived only via the establishment of a new mentality by means of good and proper education.[26] These writings have special appeal to the Muslim people of the Middle East, and the Muslim Brotherhood continues to attract large segments of Muslim populations throughout the world, but especially the Arab world. To understand this phenomenon we need to look at the reasons and causes for this popularity.

CAUSES OF SUPPORT FOR THE CONTEMPORARY ISLAMICIST MOVEMENT

Two main factors explain the continued support for the Islamicist movement in the Middle East. First, Western values are penetrating the Muslim world and the countries of the Middle East are undergoing cultural alienation. Evidence of this is seen in increasing secularization, widespread moral corruption in society and the threat of fragmentation or even a breakdown of traditional institutions. Hence, many are longing for the application of Islam as a way of life. Second, there is the growing social and economic discontent among most strata of society. There is an increasing gap in income between rich and poor as a result of (1) the failure to provide adequate economic growth; (2) declining legitimacy of political systems because of corruption within the state apparatus and public sector; (3) the failure to counter Western influence; (4) the loss of Palestine to Zionism; (5) the inability to achieve Arab unity; and (6) the rising consciousness of the urban middle class. The combination of these factors has led to frustration, aliena-tion, and identity crisis, thus creating a fertile ground for the Islamic opposition groups to gain support and popularity among various social strata. The opposition groups stress that the Mus-lim world is experiencing difficulties because their rulers have strayed from the right path of Islam, and that greed, corruption and atheism are threatening to fragment society and prevent it from effectively confronting its external enemies. To remedy the situation, they emphasize the need for a recreation of the unity and integrity of the Muslim society which was envisaged in the Qur'an and the tradition (Sunna).[27] Hence, Muslims are increas-ingly turning away from secular ideologies (whether nationalist, leftist or other) and moving towards a religious framework. Secular ideologies have been viewed as foreign, alien and unsuc-cessful imports. In sum, then, it is hardly surprising that Muslims have been turning to Islam as a result of the perceived failure of other options.

It must be noted here that resorting to Islam can take different forms. On the one hand, people may turn to Islam as a refuge which offers comfort and peace. On the other, Islam may become a symbol for socio-political protest. Internally, this protest may be directed against the corruption or the injustice of the political system; externally, it may be channelled against foreign influen-ces, which represent a cultural, economic, political or strategic threat to the Muslim community.[28] The West, especially the United States, tends to be the main target of this protest. The reasons for this can be summarized under six headings. (1) The memories of the Crusades between Christendom and the *Dar al-Islam* (the world of Islam – the believers) have not been erased.[29] (2) The sensitivities which were created by the contra-dictions between a glorious past (Islamic civilization was a direct source of learning for the West) and a miserable present (recent Western domination of Muslim societies) have engendered a sense of grievance and injustice. (3) The effect of European colonial experience, followed by American supremacy, has been particularly painful to Muslims. (4) The creation of the state of Israel in the heart of the Arab world and the special support which it received from the West have created bitter feelings, especially among Arab Muslims. (5) The perception that Western states have often allied themselves with repressive regimes in the Middle East and the Third World has thrown into question the integrity of these powers, bringing a mixture of doubt, fear and hatred in its wake. (6) The prevailing images in the Middle East of the West as a permissive and decadent consumer society make the West both an alluring and a despicable place.[30]

In assessing pan-Islamism in the Middle East, one is neverthe-less driven to the conclusion that the movement has not been able to achieve its goals at the political level, despite its wide public support and despite the fact that Islam is an important source of national solidarity. Although the movement has been an important means of opposition, it has never reached the level at which it could force significant social, economic and political changes. On the contrary, the movement has suffered successive setbacks (in Egypt, Syria and Algeria). This may be attributed to the fact that it has no cohesion; it is fragmented, lacking a clearly defined common goal, as became evident during the Gulf War, when one faction (in Jordan) supported Iraq, while the other (in Egypt) sided with the Coalition. One could also add that the movement lacks the charismatic leader who could provide it with a sense of confidence, let alone one who could help overcome the faction-alism which distracts the movement from focusing on the import-ant issues. Finally, and most importantly, the movement has not been able to produce a comprehensive programme which could constitute a viable alternative to the current social, economic and political vacuum in the region.

PAN-ARABISM: AN OVERVIEW

While there is no precise date for the beginning of Arab nation-alism, it is possible to discern, toward the end of the eighteenth century, a number of factors which worked together against

Ottoman rule and ultimately gave rise to Arab national feeling. (1) There was a sense in the non-Turkish communities that they were not equals, the concept of equality being applied only to the Turkish race. (2) European economic and political penetration of the empire and its provinces exposed the Arabs to European culture and ideas, and prompted them to re-examine their cultural heritage and employ it against Ottoman control. (3) The decline of Ottoman authority over the periphery gave the élite groups in the Arab world an opportunity to enjoy a degree of autonomy; by the nineteenth century, especially after Greek independence, the concept of an Arab nation gained strength and clarity. (4) The so-called Arab renaissance[31] was encouraged by the work of European and American Christian missionaries who were concerned with the Arabic language. This cultural awakening weakened Ottoman control while at the same time serving European objectives.[32]

THE EMERGENCE OF ARAB NATIONAL FEELING UP UNTIL THE FIRST WORLD WAR

During the despotic rule of the Ottoman Sultan Abdul-Hamid (1878–1909), the Europeanized forces, who had supported the Tanzimat, were harassed and prosecuted. In the 1860s, the Westernized intellectuals whom the Tanzimat had produced started to articulate their ideas through the so-called 'Young Ottoman' movement. They believed that the Empire could be reformed through adopting contemporary European methods without making fundamental changes in its structure. This movement came to an end when Abdul-Hamid assumed power. It was replaced in the 1880s by the 'Young Turks' movement, from which emerged the Committee of Union and Progress (CUP). Arab officers of the Ottoman army were represented in the Committee. They offered their cooperation against Hamidian rule on the grounds of a new interpretation of Ottomanism. They played an important role in the 1908 *coup*, when the constitution of 1876, which had been abrogated by Abdul-Hamid in 1878, was restored by force.[33] Shortly after the coup, a new society, the Ottoman Arab Fraternity, was set up. Also, the Sharif of Mecca, Hussein ibn Ali, was released and appointed as Governor of Hijaz, Keeper of the Holy Places and Prince of Mecca.[34]

When Abdul-Hamid launched his counter-coup in 1909 against the Young Turks, the Arab officers played an important role in putting down the *coup*. Hence, in the summer of the same year, leading Arabs formed the so-called Arab Literary Club in Constantinople, which became a centre for Arab nationalists.[35] However, this Arab–Turkish honeymoon did not last long. The Young Turks, once they established themselves firmly in power, soon began to reveal their own national ideology – that of Turanianism. In doing so, they alarmed other ethnic groups, especially the Arabs, since it implied the abandonment of Arab culture and the acceptance of the policy of Turkification. The Ottoman Arab Fraternity was therefore banned and Arab nationalists who demanded cultural expression within the empire were harassed and prosecuted. The situation became worse when the Young Turks increasingly adopted a policy of centralization and proceeded to tighten their hold on the central bureaucracy.[36]

It must be noted that, until then, Arab demands did not go beyond a decentralized administration and a natural cultural autonomy.[37] But when the Arab leaders lost all hopes of reaching an accommodation with the CUP government, they decided to go ahead and press for separation. This was the aim of the Arab revolt of 1916. The European powers, especially Britain, supported the Arab separatist movement and exploited it for their own ends. The British government approached the Sharif of Mecca, Hussein ibn Ali, and persuaded him to lead the Arab revolt within the context of the so-called McMahon–Hussein corespondence.[38] In return, Britain pledged support for an independent Arab kingdom under the leadership of the Hashemite dynasty. This pledge proved to be illusory. The Arab national movement did not achieve independence. Instead, the Arab world was divided into British and French spheres of influence, according to the Sykes–Picot agreement, which was signed secretly between Britain, France, and Russia in 1916 (Russia, after the revolution of 1917, disclosed the terms of the agreement). This was complemented by the notorious Balfour declaration of 1917, in which the British government promised to set up a Jewish homeland in Palestine.[39] The failure of the Arab revolt to achieve economic and political independence at that juncture meant that the task of the movement now become one of achieving self-reliance and of fighting European domination and its agents. These efforts gathered increasing force from the end of the Second World War, in part because the question of Palestine began to act as a fermenting agent for the Arab national movement.[40]

THE RISE OF ARAB NATIONALISM: THE CASE OF NASSER

The prime mover for the rise of Arab nationalism was no doubt the growth of Zionism in Palestine, reaching its peak with the creation of the state of Israel in 1948. The success of Israel in 1948 made the neighbouring Arab countries more aware of their Arabness and set the cry for Arab unity growing in earnest.[41] The defeat also destroyed the political legitimacy of the foreign-installed governments and offered a good opportunity for the new classes which were challenging the *status quo* imposed by the foreign powers to replace it with a new one. Hence a succession of military *coups* took place in the core Arab countries such as Syria (1949), Egypt (1952) and Iraq (1958). These new regimes managed to pass laws limiting the size of landholdings, nationalizing foreign enterprises and expanding the public sector. Given the foreign-imposed conditions which the Arab national movement had to remove, the rhetoric of the movement tended to assume revolutionary overtones similar to those of the national movements throughout the Third World in the search for political and economic independence after the Second World War.[42]

The rise of Arab nationalism reached its climax under the leadership of Nasser. When Nasser and his military officers assumed power in Egypt in 1952, their concern in furthering the aim of a pan-Arab movement was not clear. In his book *The Philosophy of the Revolution,* Nasser spoke of Egypt not as being simply Arab, but rather as being at the core of three circles, of which one was Arab and the others African and Islamic.[43] The main goals of the leadership were to improve the political, social and economic lot of the Egyptian people. Nevertheless, in the pursuit of its own policy, political circumstances placed Egypt in a position to play a leading role in shaping and directing the forces of Arab nationalism.[44] Egypt's refusal to bow to Western pressure, and its willingness to buy weapons from the Eastern bloc in 1955, after having been denied such weapons from

Western sources, constituted a step forward on the road towards political independence. As an act of sovereignty, it enhanced the leadership status of Egypt and Nasser in the Arab world. This position was further enhanced when, a year later in 1956, Nasser nationalized the Suez Canal. His decision to do this had various ramifications for the forces of Arab nationalism. It demonstrated the willingness and determination of a poor country like Egypt to defy the domination of foreign powers which had shaped the political and economic structure of the Arab region. Also, it illustrated that an Arab country like Egypt, contrary to general belief, could efficiently run the complicated operations of a major international waterway. The success of the nationalization set Egypt and Nasser as the standard by which the acts of other Arab leaders had to be judged. Egyptian leadership within the Arab world was again enhanced as a result of the invasion launched in November 1956, by Israel, Britain and France in an attempt to oust Nasser and return the Suez Canal to foreign ownership. The ultimate failure of the invasion had a positive impact on the Arab national movement. It strengthened the forces of Arab national-ism in general and the position of Nasser as a leader of these forces both in Egypt and the Arab world in particular. The success of Nasser in challenging foreign domination set a stand-ard of legitimacy for other Arab leaders and countries. The failure of other regimes to follow the same policies could throw into question their legitimacy, as indeed proved the case with Iraq. In 1955, the Iraqi monarchy decided to join the Baghdad Pact, along with Iran, Turkey, Pakistan and Britain. The aim of the organization was to contain the threat of Communism in the Middle East. Arab nationalists believed, however, that the threat to their security was coming from Israel and its Western allies, rather than from the Soviet Union. Hence, they regarded the Baghdad Pact as a means to contain and weaken the forces of Arab nationalism. The invasion of Egypt confirmed this percep-tion. Egypt's example of defying the West strengthened the opposition in Iraq and led to the overthrow of the monarchy in 1958. The new nationalist regime decided to withdraw from the Pact, and at the same time open negotiations with the oil companies to achieve a better deal. This heyday of Arab nation-alism also found itself reflected in the 1958 Syrian–Egyptian union under the leadership of Nasser (even though it lasted only until 1961).

THE DEFEAT OF 1967 AND THE DECLINE OF ARAB NATIONALISM

The defeat of 1967 constituted a watershed in the retreat of Arab nationalism and the rise of the conservative forces in the Arab world. The Arab regimes had lost Palestine in 1948; to this was now added some of their own territories: Sinai, East Jerusalem, the Golan Heights, the West Bank and Gaza. The defeat altered the balance of power in the region. It shifted the leadership of the Arab world from the core countries – Egypt, Syria and Iraq – to the conservative oil-producing countries. This became apparent during the Khartoum Arab summit in 1969, when the nationalist regimes reached compromises and understandings with the oil regimes of Saudi Arabia and the smaller Gulf states. This signalled the rise of the more prominent role of Saudi Arabia in the region. The shift in the balance of power was accelerated and dramatized in the aftermath of the October War of 1973, when the oil-producing countries decided to reduce their oil exports and place selective embargo measures on their oil sales for a few months in the name of the Palestinian cause. The decision was successful in the sense that it dramatically increased their income, wealth and, most importantly, their political power within the Arab world. They became, in fact, the main arbiters of many Arab issues.

The increase in oil income created a wide gap in the distribution of wealth between the Gulf states and other Arab countries, and in one way or another disrupted economic development in many Arab countries, as well as establishing patterns of consumption largely insupportable by local resources – thus increasing Arab dependency on the West. In addition, the shift reduced the weight of the pan-Arab agenda. This process reached its peak with the foundation of the Gulf Cooperation Council in 1980. The GCC, under the leadership of Saudi Arabia, has a different agenda from those who hoped for fair distribution of Arab national wealth among the Arab countries. Saudi Arabia, together with other oil-producing states, succeeded in counteracting the larger thrust of the Arab nationalist political agenda. Under Saudi impulse, an 'Islamic bloc' was created in the form of the Islamic Conference Organization; the Organization of Arab Petroleum Exporting Countries was established (OAPEC), arguably, at least in part, in order to remove oil from the pan-

Arab agenda; the Palestine question was moved to the sphere of American diplomacy; and aid-receiving Arab countries were pressed to reorient their economies toward the private sector and international capitalism. Against this background and given their wealth, the nature of their income, and their heavy economic, military and political dependence on the West, it would seem unrealistic to assume that the GCC governments would adopt the pan-Arabist aims of unity and non-alignment.[45]

An assessment of the pan-Arabist movement, then, as having by and large failed, would not seem unduly harsh. The movement has never lived up to or fulfilled the expectations of the people who believed in it. We would agree that this is because Arab nationalism and pan-Arabism, from their inception, have never moved beyond being middle-class political movements without solid roots in society; they have not been able to reflect the hopes and aspirations of the majority of the Arab masses. The failure of the movement was manifested in various aspects. Palestinian self-determination was not achieved, and Israeli expansion remained uncontained. Social and economic equality, and the reduction of dependency on the international capitalist system, remained elusive. Despite the claim to represent the masses, there was little attempt to broaden the basis of its political support. The movement, of course, never even came close to realizing the central theme of pan-Arabism – the unity of the Arab states. The tendency has, rather, always been to focus on regional interests rather than those of the Arab nation as a whole. The defeat of 1967 crippled the movement, the October War of 1973 took away much of its substance and the Gulf War of 1991 proved to be the last nail in the coffin of pan-Arabism as presently constituted.

CONCLUSION

Pan-Islamism and pan-Arabism have had, and will continue to play, an important role in the politics of the Middle East. However, given their current weakness it would seem highly questionable whether they will, in the near future, be able to perform any remotaly effective role. It is difficult to imagine that the Arab nationalist movement, with its history of failure, will be able to offer a viable solution to current political crises in the

Middle East. The pan-Islamic movement might perhaps stand a chance if it succeeds in uniting its aims and means, and manages to produce a constructive programme in tune with the social, economic and political needs of the people in the area; even so, their chances look fairly slim. This is because the 'fundamentalists' or the politicized Islamic groups tend to confuse and overlook the whole issue of Islamic revival in the Muslim world. The fact that they nearly always speak of or use the term 'ideology' shows that their orientation is implicitly Western, secularistic and worldly, however much they may formally denounce Westernisation, claim to be speaking in the name of Islam, and proclaim their belief in a Hereafter. In contrast, the vast majority of traditional Muslims refer to their religion as *al-Din* and live that religion to the best of their ability.[46] Also, they posit the *Sharia* as their exclusive concern; they overlook and decry the other essential complementary dimension of the Islamic tradition, the spiritual. Without the spirituality diffused throughout society by the Turuq, the legality of the *Sharia* would have been impoverished, rigid and imposed more by force than through consent. The fact that the fundamentalists are nearly always opposed to the forms and doctrines of *Sufism* goes hand in hand with their unrealistic extremism in attempting to impose the Sharia. Moreover, the very term 'revival' or 'resurgence' leads one to overlook an indisputable feature of the Islamic world: namely, the *continuation* of belief in Islam among the masses throughout the recent upheavals of history – for them there is no need for a 'revival' in personal terms of faith, because Islam had in fact never been 'sick' as far as they were concerned; revival is only necessary for something which is dying. The persistence of belief and orientation towards Islam is something which, being of a spirtual and moral order, is much less noticeable or newsworthy than the actions of politicized groups claiming to speak in the name of the Muslim masses. And it is their actions and programmes that are unfortunately identified as the key elements in the 'revival' of Islam. There has of course been a revival within the Islamic world, but one that conforms to the traditional concept of *tajdid*, that is, 'renewal' in the sense promised by the prophet Muhammad about a *mujaddid* coming at the beginning of every century. It is important to stress that this renewer is always first and foremost a spiritual authority: al-Ghazzali, al-Jilani, al- Sirhindi, etc. For an ailing society, inner renewal and purification is the first step towards a more general cure for society as a whole; there are moral, intellectual and spiritual efforts by numerous scholars, thinkers, sufi brotherhoods and professionals, which may more accurately be referred to as the 'renewal' of the contemporary Islamic order. These efforts may not be so sensational as the actions of violent groups, nor are they so susceptible to evaluation by conventional tools of political analysis, but this should not blind one to their significance. This aspect of Islamic revival, which is moral, cultural and spiritual, may not have immediately tangible political manifestations, but it certainly cotributes to a more balanced, authentically Islamic 'political culture' and thus to an ambience within which more moderate forces can be expected to develop.[47]

NOTES

*   Some of the material in this article has previously been published in my earlier articles 'Pan-Islamism', *The Islamic Quarterly*, no. 3, 1993, and 'Arab Nationalism: Dead or Alive?', *The Gulf Report: The Gulf in the 1990s* (Gulf Centre for Strategic Studies, London, 1992).

1.   J. M. Landau, *The Politics of Pan-Islam Ideology and Organization* (Oxford University Press, 1990), p. 4.

2.   For more Information See N. Ziadeh, 'Arabism', in E. Kedourie, *Nationalism in Asia and Africa* (Frank Cass, London, 1971), pp. 294–303.

3.   H. B. Sharabi, *Nationalism and Revolution in the Arab World* (Van Nostrand Reinhold, London, 1966), pp. 4–5.

4.   *Ibid.*, pp. 96–7.

5.   A. Hourani, *A History of the Arab Peoples* (Faber, London, 1991), pp. 207–64.

6.   S. G. Haim, *Arab Nationalism: An Anthology* (Cambridge University Press, 1962), p. 6.

7.   P. Piscatori, *Islam in a world of Nation-States* (Cambridge University Press, 1986), p. 77.

8.   A. Hourani, *Arabic Thought in the Liberal Age 1798–1939* (Cambridge University Press, 1983), p. 73–82.

9.   *Ibid.*, pp. 84–94.

10.   S. G. Haim, *Arab Nationalism: An Anthology*, op. cit, pp. 6–12.

11.   See P. Piscatori, *Islam in a World of Nation States*, op. cit., p. 83.

12.   For an elaborate discussion of his concept of the Islamic state, see H. Enayat, *Modern Islamic Political Thought* (Macmillan, London, 1991), pp. 69–83.

13.   A. Hourani, *Arabic Thought in the Liberal Age 1798–1939*, op. cit., pp. 222–44.

14. For more information see A. A. Duri, *The Historical Formation of the Arab Nation* (Croom Helm and Centre for Arab Unity Studies, London, 1987), pp. 188–94.
15. A. Hourani, *Arabic Thought in the Liberal Age 1798–1939*, op. cit., pp. 271–3.
16. For more information see M. Abdual Halim, *The Muslim Brotherhood* (in Arabic) (Dar al-Da'wa, Cairo, 1981).
17. See H. al-Banna, *Rasail al-Banna* (in Arabic) (The Islamic Institute, Beirut, no date available).
18. For more information on the Muslim Brotherhood in Jordan see Al-Obedy, *The Muslim Brotherhood in Jordan and Palestine* (in Arabic) (Amman, Jordan, 1991).
19. E. Davis, 'Ideology, Social Class and Islamic Radicalism in Modern Egypt', in Said Amir Arjomand, *From Nationalism to Revolutionary Islam* (Macmillan, London, 1984), pp. 150–1.
20. A. Hourani, *A History of the Arab Peoples*, op. cit., pp. 348–9.
21. H. B. Sharabi, *Nationalism and Revolution in the Arab World*, op. cit., pp. 108–9.
22. C. E. Butterworth, 'Prudence Versus Legitimacy: the Persistent Them in Islamic Political Thought', in A. E. A. Dessouki, *Islamic Resurgence in the Arab World* (Praeger, New York, 1982), p. 97–8.
23. Cited from H. B. Sharabi, *Nationalism and Revolution in the Arab World*, op. cit., p. 110.
24. C. E. Butterworth, 'Prudence Versus Legitimacy: The Presistent Theme in Islamic Political Thought', in A. E. A. Dessouki, *The Islamic Resurgence in the Arab World*, op. cit., p. 99.
25. For more information see S. Qutb, *Al-Adalah Al- Ijtimaiyya Fil-Islam* (Dar al-Sarok, Beirut, 1988).
26. A. Hourani, *A History of the Arab Peoples*, op. cit., pp. 398–9.
27. E. Davis, 'Ideology, Social Class and Islamic Radicalism in Modern Egypt', in Said Amir Arjomand, *From Nationalism to Revolutionary Islam*, op. cit., p. 140–56. The same view has been stressed by the speaker of the Jordanian Parliament Dr Arabyat in an interview conducted by the author in January 1992.
28. See Nazih N. M. Ayubi, 'The Political Revival of Islam: The Case of Egypt', in *International Journal of the Middle East*, December 1980, p. 486.
29. See Nazih N. M. Ayubi, 'The Politics of Militant Islamic Movements in the Middle East', in *Journal of International Affairs*, vol. 36, no. 2, 1982, pp. 282–3.
30. Nazih N. M. Ayubi, 'The Political Revival of Islam: The Case of Egypt', in *International Journal of the Middle East*, op. cit., p. 486–7.
31. For more information on this point see J. Carmichael, *The Shaping of the Arabs A Study in Ethnic Identity* (Macmillan, New York, 1967), pp. 286–97.
32. Abbas Alnasrawi, *Arab Nationalism, Oil, and the Political Economy of Dependency* (Greenwood, London, 1991), pp. 25–7.
33. Bassam Tibi, *Arab Nationalism: A Critical Enquiry* (Macmillan, London, 1990), pp. 107–8.
34. S. N. Fisher, *The Middle East: A History* (Knopf, New York, 1966), p. 353.

35. William Yale, *The Near East: A Modern History* (Michigan State University, East Lansing, 1958), pp. 199.

36. G. Antonius, *The Arab Awakening* (Capricorn, New York, 1965), pp. 106–7.

37. The only exception was Negib Azoury (Christian) in his book *Le Reveil de la nation arabe*, which was published in 1905.

38. For more information see W. R. Polk, *The United States and the Arab World* (Harvard University Press, Cambridge, Mass., 1969), pp. 107–8.

39. See F. J. Khouri, *The Arab–Israeli Dilemma* (Syracuse University Press, 1976), pp. 8–15.

40. J. A. Bill and C. Leiden, *Politics in the Middle East*, 2nd edn (Little, Brown, New York, 1984), p. 308.

41. On this point see S. Neil Macfarlane, *Superpower Rivalry and Third World Radicalism: The Idea of National Liberation* (Croom Helm, London, 1985).

42. See Nasser, *The Philosophy of the Revolution* (Dar al-Macarif, Cairo, 1954).

43. See S. Amin, *The Arab Nation* (Zed Press, London, 1978), pp. 50–8.

44. See M. H. Kerr, *The Arab Cold War* (Oxford University Press, 1971).

45. Abbas Alnasrawi, *Arab Nationalism, Oil, and the Political Economy of Dependency*, op. cit., pp. 34–9.

46. There is a difference between the notion of 'ideology' and that of *al-Din*: ideology connotes much more the efforts of individuals to formulate values with a view to establishing a system, and on the basis of reason unaided by revelation, whereas *al-Din* is a far more comprehensive term denoting the totality of life and implying a primary orientation towards the Divine as the source of final authority. To talk of a 'religious ideology' is thus a fundamental contradiction in terms, and betrays a confusion as to what religion is in its essence: divine revelation.

47. For more detail see, Seyyed Hussein Nasr, *Traditional Islam in the Modern World* (KPI, London and New York, 1987).

8 Egypt, Syria and the Arab State System in the New World Order

Raymond A. Hinnebusch

The Gulf crisis, which exposed and aggravated the bankruptcy of the Arab state 'system', stimulated much discussion of the need for a new Arab order. The most concrete attempt to create one was the Damascus Declaration, in which Egypt and Syria sought to manipulate the opportunities and avoid the threats inherent in the impact of the New World Order (NWO) on the Middle East; its failure leaves the Arab system fragmented and increasingly penetrated. Can Egypt and Syria still provide a pole giving some coherence to an Arab order?

EGYPT, SYRIA AND THE ARAB STATE SYSTEM BEFORE THE GULF WAR

What order the modern Arab world has enjoyed has been imposed by a 'centre' – a leading axis which invariably included Egypt and Syria. These countries occupy the geopolitical centre of the Arab world, historically bridging Maghreb and Mashreq. The two major centres of Arab civilization lacking oil wealth, they have a common stake in a pan-Arabism which entitles them to a share of this resource. They have also been the two major military powers on the front line with Israel. When Egypt and Syria were united they were able to impose a certain cohesion on the Arab states; when they were divided, the Arab world has been fragmented and more vulnerable to external powers.

The Arab state system first emerged as an autonomous entity in the 1950s under Egyptian leadership. Egypt, backed by Syria, sought to expel Western control and impose non-alignment and pan-Arab solidarity on the Arab world.[1] To this Cairo–Damascus axis Egypt contributed its weight as the most populous, militarily strong and culturally advanced of the Arab states; Syria accepted

Egyptian leadership and contributed its intense Arabism and centrality in the Mashreq. Nasser's pan-Arab leadership was built on the combination of his heroic stature in the eyes of the Arab masses with the proselytizing of pan-Arab movements like the Syrian Ba'ath party. It enabled him to impose Arab nationalist standards for the conduct of foreign policy which individual states ignored at their peril. Egypt did not become the Prussia of the Arab world, but the Cairo–Damascus axis played the major role in the rollback of Western hegemony and the birth of a relatively autonomous Arab state system.

The 1967 war destroyed the Egypt-centred Arab system but in the early 1970s a new system which Ajami called the 'Arab Triangle' emerged from the crucible of the 1973 war.[2] Egypt and Syria, driven together by their common need to recapture their territories from Israel, jointly planned and launched the war. They had rebuilt their armies in alliance with the third pole of the triangle, Saudi Arabia, which bankrolled them and orchestrated the oil weapon in support of their postwar diplomacy. The war generated a new consensus among these 'big three' to seek a negotiated peace with Israel in return for the lands captured in 1967. As long as Egypt and Syria stuck together and refused to settle separately, the leverage to achieve such a settlement potentially existed.

This system collapsed when Sadat broke Arab ranks in pursuit of a separate peace with Israel, setting Egypt and Syria at odds. This opened the door to the fragmentation of the Arab world. Syria's Assad, burned by his dependence on Egypt, set out to mobilize the resources to go it alone. He sought military parity with Israel in compensation for the military imbalance resulting from Egypt's defection. He sought an alternative to the Egyptian alliance by imposing Syrian leadership in the Mashreq over Lebanon, Jordan and the PLO, precipitating conflicts and resistance from them. Demonstrating that Syria would have to be satisfied if the 'peace process' was to advance, required delegitimizing Camp David and isolating Egypt from the Arab world. The post-Camp-David front against Egypt rapidly collapsed as the Iran–Iraq war diverted the attention of Saudi Arabia and the Arab Gulf states, while Syria's alliance with Iran isolated it. A centreless Arab world, split, in the first instance, by the Cairo–Damascus rift, was fragmented through much of the 1980s. It was also vulnerable to external power: most notably, the collapse of the Cairo–Damascus axis opened the door to the Israeli invasion of Lebanon.

By 1990, Egypt had used the Iran–Iraq war to re-establish its Arab role, Soviet backing for Syrian military parity had evaporated, and Syria's go-it-alone strategy was exhausted. The weakening of Soviet commitments to Syria led Assad to again explore diplomatic approaches to the Arab–Israeli conflict, and this required concert with Egypt by virtue of its peace with Israel, US relations and its weight in any Arab coalition able to put diplomatic pressure on Israel. The Iraqi victory over Iran, its joining with Egypt and Jordan in the Arab Cooperation Council and its support of General Aoun in Lebanon left Syria isolated and vulnerable. With the Soviet decline and Jewish emigration to Israel, Assad professed to see the Arab world facing great dangers requiring Arab solidarity. In 1990, therefore, after more than a decade of estrangement, Syria and Egypt were reconciled on Egyptian terms. The possibility that this might resurrect the Arab Triangle was cut short by the Iraqi invasion of Kuwait.

THE GULF WAR AND THE CRISIS OF THE ARAB STATE SYSTEM

The second Gulf War grew out of the crisis of the Arab system in the 'centreless' 1980s. Oil and insecurity intensified the particular interests of the separate states and the centrifugal forces pulling them apart. Oil permitted the consolidation of separate state apparatuses. It linked the interests of the Gulf states to the West and separated them from the Arab world. The enormous maldistribution of oil revenues separated Arabs into the enormously wealthy and the poor, who suffered as inter-Arab aid and labour migration declined at the end of the 1980s. Ninety per cent of Arab oil revenues went to states whose populations made up less than 10 per cent of the Arab world, while the most developed, populous, and core states lacked much oil wealth. Egypt, impoverished amid such wealth, and insecure in the face of Israel, sacrificed Arab leadership for a separate peace and total dependency on the United States. Internal fragmentation exposed the Arab world to external penetration and threats. Webs of military and economic dependency tied the Arab states to the

West. Iran threatened from the east, while the isolation of Egypt and the preoccupation of Iraq and Saudi Arabia with Iran allowed the projection of Israeli power in the Arab world with less restraint than ever before. It also made it easier for Israel to maintain its occupation of Arab territory and denial of Palestinian rights, the heart of the Arab cause. The insecurity of the state system was compounded by the enormous power imbalances created by imperial boundary drawing, specifically the contiguous existence of powerful states like Iraq and the weak Gulf mini-states with enormous wealth, small populations and a need for Western protection.

Despite the crisis of the system, the persistence of Arabism prevented the separate states from acquiring the legitimacy which accrues to those corresponding to a unit of distinct nationhood. As state apparatuses solidified, pan-Arabism declined, but mass identification with separate nation-states did not emerge; for the most part, the vacuum was filled instead by 'subnational' sectarian or ethnic loyalties and a 'supranational' Islamic identity. State legitimacy is, however, still intimately linked to Arabism, which, mixed with Islam, remains the strongest component of popular identity.[3] Objectively, in matters of security, transit routes, labour supply, markets, and water supplies, the Arab states are increasingly interdependent.[4] Only in concert were they likely reach an equitable and durable solution to the Arab–Israeli conflict, without which neither the regional system or its individual states can acquire secure nationalist legitimacy. But without a leading state or axis, foreign policies were unconstrained by common Arab interests.

The fragmented Arab system of the 1980s was a power vacuum waiting to be filled: Saddam Hussein's invasion of Kuwait was part of a bid to organize a new Iraq-led system based on a revival of pan-Arab nationalism. Saddam argued that Soviet decline and Jewish migration to Israel threatened the Arabs with American and Israeli dominance; as the main Arab military power, Iraq would lead the Arab world's defence. A US-brokered solution to the Arab–Israeli conflict had failed; Israel would only negotiate when the Arabs combined military power with use of their oil and financial assets as diplomatic weapons. Oil was the common heritage of the Arab world which should be more equitably shared rather than the private patrimony of the oil states. Pro-Western states like Egypt and Saudi Arabia, threatened by this

Iraqi project, rejected it; in taking Kuwait, Saddam hoped to force it on them.

The invasion, however, polarized the Arab states as never before and invited unprecedented Western intervention. Yet even as governments were splitting the Arab world, the Arab nationalism declared dead by many observers was revived at the mass level by the imminent foreign threat and a strong leader who appeared to stand up to it. Saddam's significant success in winning the 'Arab street' mimicked Nasser's ability to mobilize popular discontent with the intolerable gap between pro-Western state behaviour and Arab–Islamic identity. To the West, the threat was that its client regimes had so little nationalist legitimacy they would be swept away if external power enforcing the *status quo* was seen to falter. But, in the Western view, Arabs emboldened by any weakness would submit to overwhelming power and a decisive defeat of Saddam was needed to discredit his confrontational strategy. Historically, imperialism has consistently acted to prevent any local power from organizing the Middle East system through periodic intervention or by playing off the local states.[5]

Some observers expected the cataclysm would precipitate a strengthening of regional institutions and collective security. Members of the Arab League meeting in Cairo shortly after the war, talked of 'a new Arab order built on trust'. In practical terms, the 'Arab Triangle', of Egypt, Syria and Saudi Arabia, seemed poised to construct a new Arab security system. The Gulf War, in demolishing Iraqi power and demonstrating the vulnerability of Saudi Arabia, had left Egypt and Syria as the most credible Arab powers on whom any new Arab security system would need to depend. Egypt and Syria argued that the invasion showed the dangers of too much Western reliance, and that a pan-Arab military force and greater economic integration should be the foundations of Arab security. In the 'Six-Plus-Two' Damascus Declaration, Saudi Arabia and the Arab Gulf states seemed to agree that Egypt and Syria would station 65 000 troops in the Gulf while they provided a $15 billion Arab development fund. But once the Iraqi threat was reduced, the Gulf states' distrust of other Arabs surfaced. While Egypt and Syria wanted to repair relations with the pro-Iraq states, Kuwait remained obsessed with their perfidy.

No new Arab order capable of dealing with the issues of wealth and security emerged. The Damascus Declaration failed, and the

Gulf states chose greater isolation from rather than more integration with the rest of the Arab world. Formerly allergic to an open American military presence, they now opted for US defence pacts. Shocked by the animosity of the Arab masses for them, they expelled large numbers of Arab workers, financially punished poor Arab states which backed Iraq and were 'more concerned with building a fortress against the wrath of poverty than eliminating its cause'.[6] Arab nationalism entered another period of dormancy, the masses disillusioned by Iraq's defeat and the complicity of many Arab leaders in this. But the regional *status quo*, being the product of Arab defeat, lacks legitimacy in the eyes of many Arabs. The precarious stability of the region cannot dispense with the threat of renewed US military intervention. US penetration and Arab dependency have gravely compromised the autonomy of the Arab system. Egypt and Syria nevertheless retain ambitions to play leading roles in this system, and their policies will have a profound impact on it.

EGYPT, THE ARAB SYSTEM, AND THE NEW WORLD ORDER

Egypt's Foreign Policy

Egypt is the largest Arab state, yet the one with perhaps the most distinct identity based on the Nile valley and a history which predates the Arabs. Though few Egyptians deny Egypt is part of the Arab world and, indeed, claim Egypt is its natural leader, most view themselves as Egyptians first. Egypt's Arabism, at least that of the foreign policy establishment, is instrumental – less a commitment for its own sake than a tool in the service of state interests. At least since Nasser, Egypt's geopolitical centrality in the Arab world defined a natural strategy in which Egypt presented itself as the bridge between the international and regional state systems. Balancing between external powers and the Arab world gives it the potential to extract geopolitical 'rent', while protecting its autonomy and security.

Internal legitimacy is intimately connected with success in foreign policy. Nasser made foreign policy an asset: his pan-Arab appeal bolstered his internal legitimacy and allowed him to make the superpowers court Egypt. He played them off in order to both roll back Western dominance in the Middle East and win economic aid from both sides. Until the 1967 war, Nasser was able to combine nationalist achievement and economic benefits, and this set a standard of legitimacy which his successors have been unable to live up to. Sadat opted to extricate Egypt from the consequences of the 1967 war by inviting the Americans back into the Middle East in exchange for massive economic subsidies and a recovery of the Sinai; this sacrificed national autonomy and undermined the regime's legitimacy. In isolating Egypt from the Arab world, Sadat's policies also threatened to reduce the Arab centrality which makes Egypt important to the world powers. Since Sadat, Egypt's foreign policy has chiefly served the mobilization of external economic resources,[7] but at a cost in national autonomy and legitimacy.

Sadat forged a strategic alliance with the US, which still constitutes Egypt's main bridge to the international system. In so far as it remains the hub of the Arab system, Egypt has become a conduit for American influence in the Arab world. It is now a force for stability against anti-Western radicalism, and has played a key role in getting the Arabs to accept Israel. In return, Egypt expects major US economic subsidization, military aid and security coordination, US help in resolving the Arab–Israeli conflict, and acceptance of Egyptian partnership in the workings of the New World Order in the Middle East.

Egypt's strategy was to make itself indispensable to American Middle East interests, and that required a leadership role in the Arab world. But when Egypt's US ally pursued policies damaging to Arab interests, especially its support for Israel so long as the latter refused an equitable peace settlement, Egypt's Arab leadership was undermined. Husni Mubarak, more sensitive than Sadat to the asymmetrical character of the US alliance, tried to enhance Egyptian leverage by manipulating global multipolarity and restoring Egypt's Arab role. But the regime could not do without an international patron and, with the collapse of the Soviet Union, there was no alternative to the US. The American victories in the Cold War and over Iraq brought Arab acquiescence in Egypt's US alliance.

In the Arab arena, Mubarak's main initial aim was to break out of the isolation imposed by Sadat's separate peace with Israel; this had largely succeeded by the late 1980s. Egypt's claim to be indispensable to the Arabs won partial acknowledgement, be-

cause it backed Iraq and the Gulf Arabs against the threat of
Iranian revolutionary Islam. In contrast to Nasser's championing
of revolutionary nationalism, Egypt now promoted itself as
moderator and stabilizer of the Arab world. To this end,
Mubarak established good relations with all Arab regimes: from
the conservative Arab oil states – above all, Saudi Arabia,
which had been the key Egyptian alliance before Camp David –
to Arab nationalist Libya, the PLO, and finally Syria, the
state which had led Egypt's isolation. Egypt promoted its
large army as a deterrent force, part of the Arab balance
of power against potential threats from Israel and Iran,
and, more recently, Iraq. Its US connection was supposed to
deliver pressure on Israel on behalf of the Palestinians. Egypt
expected economic aid from the Arab petro-states in return for
its services. To the extent it secured Arab leadership, Egypt
heightened its importance to the US and shored up internal
legitimacy.

Arab leadership did not come easily to Mubarak's Egypt. To
be credible, it required Egypt to protect Arab national interests.
However, Israeli aggression against Arab states in the 1980s
(against the Iraq reactor, the invasion of Lebanon, the bombing
of PLO headquarters in Tunis), made Egypt look ineffective in its
pretension to guarantee Arab security. When the Israeli threat
was salient and Arab solidarity against it drew Egypt in, Egypt's
Israeli and US relations were strained. When Egyptian leadership
lacked credibility, rival Arab states, notably Syria and Iraq,
challenged its Arab pre-eminence.

Egypt in the Gulf War

Egypt's Gulf war policy was rooted in its attempt to sustain its
economics-driven strategy of bridging between the Arab world
and the West. Under Mubarak a main aim of foreign policy was
to establish national legitimacy for the regime's American alliance
and separate peace with Israel. It saw the road to legitimacy in
establishing itself as the only Arab country, which, having good
relations with Israel, could, in concert with US diplomacy, lead
the Arab world to an honorable peace. Saddam Hussein's bid to
force a new era of confrontation with the US over its support for
Israel threatened Mubarak's strategy; Iraq could have displaced
Cairo as the hub of Arab diplomacy. The Iraqi invasion of

Kuwait showed Egypt to be ineffective as the Arab moderator, since Mubarak had invested his prestige in mediating the Iraq–Kuwait conflict and had obtained a pledge from Saddam not to resort to force. Economics was also determinant in a more immediate sense, because Egypt was on the brink of economic collapse, forced to stop payments on its debt and in danger of becoming a financial pariah. Iraq's challenge to Cairo's bridging strategy threatened the economic subsidies it can purchase, while the invasion was a perfect opportunity to demonstrate Egypt's indispensability to the established order and win increased aid.

Egypt's paramount concern for its bridging strategy can be seen in Mubarak's choices during the crisis. Had Arab autonomy and security been a central concern then he would have sought a diplomatic solution and demurred at the destruction of Iraqi power, which was needed in the balance with Israel and Iran. But Mubarak short-circuited Arab diplomacy in favour of US intervention and sent Egyptian troops to give it legitimizing cover. At the decisive Arab summit on 10 August 1990, where the issue was the Saudi request for US help, Mubarak, as chairman, refused to allow discussion, amendments or votes for alternatives. The evidence is strong that Mubarak subsequently favoured a military solution over a negotiated one. This not only pleased his American patron, but was a bid to fully reestablish the Egypt–Saudi alliance which had been enervated by Camp David. Mubarak also aimed to assume responsibility for postwar Gulf security and to sell the protective services of his large army to the Gulf rulers for petrodollars. In fact, Egypt won massive globally unprecedented debt relief, and a promise of aid from the Gulf, but was rebuffed in its bid to play Gulf gendarme.

In placing Egypt so overtly in the service of an anti-Arab nationalist foreign power, the Mubarak regime risked its legitimacy. Initially, it successfully exploited Egyptians' mistrust of Arab leaders who challenge Egypt's Arab pre-eminence, their resentment of Iraq's maltreatment of Egyptian workers and their disapproval of aggression against Kuwait. But public opinion turned ambivalent as Mubarak's complicity in the US destruction of Iraq became clear. The Left and the Muslim Brotherhood declared that to back a non-Islamic army against Iraq was a worse offence than the original invasion. Indicative of its vulnerability was the regime's repression of dissent and its attempt to disguise its opposition to any compromise that would allow Iraqi power to survive. The war unleashed simmering anti-regime and anti-American feeling in Egypt. Egyptians had no illusions about the self-interested motives of the West: for *whose* New World Order, they asked, was the war waged? Four straight days of clashes between thousands of students and police expressed unprecedented ferment. That such sympathy should be felt for a rival state, and that the nationalist opposition could condemn an attack on Iraq in which Egyptian troops took part, is a symptom of how far even Egypt is from a true nation-state with an identity separate from the Arab world.

Egypt's Post-War Policy

During the war, Egypt expressed ambitions to organize a more secure and coherent Arab system. Putting Egypt at the centre of this new system would give greater leverage over the US and establish Cairo as a partner, rather than a client, in the New World Order. The return of the Arab League to Cairo, from which it had been removed after Sadat's peace with Israel, symbolized Egypt's renewed centrality. The centrepiece of Egypt's bid was the Damascus Declaration. When the Gulf states, led by Kuwait, concluded security agreements with the United States and invited Egyptian and Syrian troops to leave, the postwar vulnerabilities of Egypt's bridging strategy were exposed: the US was now better positioned to bypass Cairo in securing its vital oil interests, and the Gulf states could rely on American guarantees they were previously too timid to openly enlist. As long as the Iraqi threat persisted, they would be totally dependent on the US. The episode was a sign that US and Egyptian interests did not necessarily coincide.

Rebuffed in the Gulf, Egypt aimed, all the more, to capitalize on its supposed indispensability in the peace process, as the only Arab state at peace with Israel. It needed to show the Arabs that it could deliver US pressure on Israel, and to show the US that it could moderate Arab diplomacy, notably that of Syria and the PLO. Egypt played some role in bringing these parties into the peace process, and thereafter played a high-profile role in mediating between the PLO and Israel, especially in attempting to facilitate implementation of the Oslo Agreement. In doing the latter, Mubarak put his stake in demonstrating Egypt's centrality to the peace process ahead of the interest which his new ally, Syria, had in coordinating a common Arab negotiating front with Israel. Moreover, Egypt had no success in delivering US pressure on Israel in these negotiations. And, with direct bilateral peace negotiations on-going between Israel and the Arab parties, and especially after Jordan signed a peace treaty with Israel, Egypt's unique role as Arab–Israeli broker was bound to be gradually eclipsed.

Egypt, Iran and the 'Islamic Threat'

Egypt professed, after the Gulf War, to see Iran as the main threat to its foreign policy. Iran's vision of a pan-Islamic Middle East order contesting Western domination was the main alternative to Egypt's pro-Western state-centric strategy. Iran rejected the concept of an exclusively Arab, Egyptian-led security system in the Gulf, insisting it must be part of Gulf security arrangements. To Egypt, Iran's military buildup was indicative of a larger ambition to project its power into the Arabian and Red Seas. Iranian support for the Islamic regime in the Sudan was seen as threatening Egypt's soft underbelly and its support for Islamic fundamentalism, which bedevilled Egypt itself, a challenge to Egypt's role as regional stabilizer. Cairo saw Iran's denunciation of the Arab–Israeli peace process as threatening to delegitimize Egypt's mediating role in it.

Egypt seemed intent on using the Iranian threat to assert its wider regional importance. Its attempt to use the Iranian seizure of strategic Gulf islands from the UAE to reinsert itself into the Gulf security equation, was not, however, encouraged by the Gulf states. Mubarak depicted Egypt as a bulwark against global Islamic terrorism, supposedly headed by Iran and its Sudanese proxy, which threatened secular Westernized regimes and which could, as the World Trade Center bombing showed, directly threaten the West. This role was, however, undermined by Egypt's own vulnerability to Islamic subversion. After the 1995 assassination attempt on Mubarak by Islamic militants, he blamed the Sudan and used the opportunity to seize the disputed Halaib zone from it. Egypt engaged in joint naval manoeuvres with the US and Britain, accusing Sudan of sponsoring Islamic terrorism.

The Libya Crisis and Egypt's Arab Role in the New World Order

Nevertheless, Egypt could not wholly neglect the Arab leadership on which its importance to the West rested. The crisis precipitated by Western demands for the extradition of Libyans accused of the Pan-Am 103 bombing became a test of Egypt's bridging strategy. Egypt needed to arrange a deal which showed that it could both moderate the behaviour of Gaddafi's radical regime and yet protect Libya, an Arab brother-state, from US punishment. It was bidding to assume responsibility for the impact of the New World Order in the Arab world. Egypt also had an economic stake in Libya, which was an outlet for unemployed labour displaced by the Iraq crisis. Internal legitimacy was at stake because Egyptian public opinion was disillusioned with the double standards by which the Western powers targeted Arab states while ignoring Israeli and Serbian transgressions against Muslims. The initial US insistence on a confrontation, rejecting all compromises offered by Libya, indicated it attached little importance to the vital interests of its Egyptian ally. But the crisis petered out and Egypt claimed credit for shielding Libya from the harsh reach of the New World Order in the Arab world. When the US press later berated Egypt for supposedly breaking UN sanctions against Libya, the Egyptian press reminded the Americans of the services it had rendered: it had rolled back Soviet influence in the area, had started the peace process, had supported Desert Storm and was in the forefront of the struggle against radical Islam which threatened the West.[8]

Increasingly concerned that its role in the peace process was being devalued and overtaken by the creeping normalization of relations between Israel and other Arab countries, Egypt sought other ways to revalidate its Arab leadership role and remind the US that it could not be taken for granted. It distanced itself from the US campaign against Iraq, backed the PLO in its negotiations with Israel and condemned Israel's summer 1993 assault on Lebanon. It sided with Syria in insisting that Arab normalization of relations with Israel be made contingent on actual progress in the peace process. It led a campaign to make Arab support for the indefinite extension of the Nuclear Non-Proliferation Treaty contingent on Israel's commitment to adhere to it. Cairo's eventual submission to US demands it accept NPT extension showed the limits of what the opposition called Mubarak's 'tin cup diplomacy': he could not risk angering his main aid donor. Also indicative of the contradictions in Egypt's policy was its military modernization program, which swallowed up over half of Egypt's US aid. This aimed to counter Israel's strategic superiority as much as such lesser threats as Sudan and Iran. Yet in aiming to wholly Americanize its armed forces, Egypt's military capability and, arguably, its options, were being made totally dependent on Israel's main patron.[9]

Egyptian élites cling to the belief that, however devalued the leverage of the Third World as a whole may be in the new world order, Egypt remains a special case. It detached itself from the Soviet Union long before the collapse of bipolarity and therefore earned a special role as a strategic state able to mediate between north and south, the West and the Islamic world. Even if other Third World regimes go under, the West cannot afford to let this happen to Egypt. While Egypt's élites are prepared for some reduction in the rent they receive as a Western geopolitical surrogate in the region, they expect they will continue to receive enough to defend regime stability.

SYRIA AND THE NEW WORLD ORDER

Syria's Arab Nationalist Role

Syria, unlike Egypt, is an artificial state where, no distinct 'Syrian' nationalism having developed, the dominant identity remains Arab: Syria has seen its role as the most faithful champion of the Arab nationalist cause, notably against Israel. Because it is the main Arab military power confronting Israel, Syria is central to the security of the Arab world and to an Arab–Israeli peace. Its current support, as an Arab nationalist state, for the *status quo*, including the peace process, helps stabilize the region, and its connections to Iran and radical Lebanese and Palestinian factions can potentially curb their revisionism. However, as a militant nationalist state, Syria feels besieged in a US dominated world order, and if its interests are threatened, it can still turn its backing to 'rejectionist' forces.

Syria and the Gulf War

Assad's decision to join the anti-Iraq coalition, a radical depar-
ture from traditional nationalist policy, flowed in part from
tactical opportunities to weaken his Iraqi arch-rival and win
financial subsidies for Syria's faltering economy. But it was
strategically shaped by the breakdown of the bipolar world.
Syrian policy had long aimed to force an Israeli withdrawal from
the Occupied Territories by some combination of Arab solidarity
and the threat of war if a peace settlement was not reached. By
the 1990s the withdrawal of the USSR as a reliable patron–pro-
tector and arms supplier deprived Syria of a war option and
made anti-Israeli brinkmanship too dangerous. Syria could not
realize its goals in opposition to the remaining American superpower. Assad's gamble was that after the Iraqi occupation of
Kuwait was resolved, the US would have to fulfil promises to its
Arab allies and resolve the Israeli occupation of Arab lands in a
comparable way – on the basis of UN resolutions. Syria aimed to
be accepted by the US as the key to peace in the Middle East
whose interests had to be recognized in the peace process. The
war against Iraq demonstrated how little obstacle remained to the
deployment of force and economic isolation against those deemed
by Washington as terrorist or pariah states. Assured there were
no plans for a permanent US presence in the region and that
postwar security would be in the hands of Arab forces, Assad
gambled that participation in the coalition would give Syria a role
in filling the power vacuum once American forces withdrew. In
short, Syria saw the New World Order shaping up and wanted
to influence it rather than be its victim.

Syria's stand damaged its pan-Arab stature and seriously risked
its regime's legitimacy. The Syrian public was divided and
confusion reigned in the regime's very bases of power, the party
and army. Although disapproving of the invasion, Syrians agreed
Kuwait did not deserve to hoard 'Arab' oil wealth and believed
the war against Iraq was on Israel's behalf. The government
justified the dispatch of Syrian troops with the argument that the
Gulf should not be left to foreign forces. While Syrians were
sceptical of Saddam's motives and critical of a reckless strategy
which split the Arabs and put Iraq at risk, they were appalled at
their government's collaboration with the West in the destruction
of an Arab state many regarded as a natural partner; this

sentiment cut across political fault lines, embracing Ba'athists and Islamics, bourgeoisie and peasant. The Iraqi scud attacks on Israel evoked pride in Arab power to inflict hurt on their powerful enemy. Most overt opposition was contained by the repressive apparatus and, in the end, the regime's legitimacy suffered remarkably little. Saddam's defeat cost him much of his appeal. The destruction of Iraq showed what Assad had spared Syria. Syrians grudgingly gave him credit for shrewdly pre-empting plots to make Syria the next victim of the 'New World Order'. Syrians are resigned to this order, but indicative of the little legitimacy they accorded it was their widespread euphoria at the anti-Gorbachev coup which threatened to abort it.

Syria and the Arab–Israeli Peace Process

Assad had long accepted a land-for-peace settlement of the conflict with Israel along the lines of United Nations Security Council Resolution 242. Throughout the 1990s, however, he insisted the strategic imbalance in Israel's favour precluded an honorable settlement, opposed negotiations until Israel committed itself to full withdrawal and sought to obstruct attempts to bypass Syria and broker Israeli deals with Jordan or the Palestinians.

That Assad joined the US-sponsored peace process after the Gulf War was indicative of a radical change in his strategy. The power balance was even more unfavourable than in the 1980s and the proposed negotiations did not meet Syria's traditional procedural conditions, namely, UN sponsorship and a united Arab delegation. Yet Syria accepted direct bilateral negotiations with Israel. Assad's decision protected his investment in joining the anti-Iraq coalition. With no military option left, he could no longer sacrifice diplomatic opportunities which did not meet his full terms for participation. Israel was out to depict Syria as a threat to peace, and the next candidate after Iraq for forced disarming; joining the peace process deflected international pressures from Syria. Assad, however, still aimed to achieve a comprehensive settlement and rebuffed efforts to draw him into a separate agreement divorced from a settlement of the Palestinian issue.

Syria's prospects of achieving a full Israeli withdrawal depended on orchestrating a common Arab front and demonstrating that Israel could not have peace without it. The Gulf crisis allowed a formerly isolated Syria to resituate itself at the Arab centre. Syria's hopes of imposing its strategy in the peace negotiations were dashed, however, as the PLO and Jordan reached separate agreements with Israel while the Gulf Arab states moved toward normalization of relations with it in the absence of a comprehensive peace. The central role of Egypt in brokering Palestinian–Israeli agreements at Syria's expense and Saudi Arabia's sacrifice of Syrian interests to please its American patron's desire for such 'confidence-building measures' as the 'multi-lateral talks' showed the limits of the Cairo–Damascus alignment and marked the reversal of Gulf war tendencies toward resurrection of the 'Arab triangle'. All of this undermined Syria's leverage and confined it, in practical terms, to bilateral negotiations with Israel over the Golan. In these negotiations, Assad still controlled the Lebanese card and could orchestrate rejectionist Palestinians and the Lebanese *hizballah* to stir up trouble in southern Lebanon if Syrian interests were ignored. The US and Israel also appeared convinced no durable regional peace was viable which excluded Syria.

While a comprehensive Israeli withdrawal slipped out of Syria's reach, the bilateral negotiations seemed to gradually close the Syrian–Israeli gap over the Golan. Initially Israel insisted its withdrawal would be merely partial while Syria refused to commit itself to the 'full peace' – normalization of relations – Israel wanted until it committed itself to full withdrawal. By 1994, however, a breakthrough seemed to have been reached whereby both sides tacitly agreed that the depth of withdrawal (full) would correspond to the scope of the peace (full). Negotiations then began over such practical issues as security arrangements and timing, which seemed susceptible to compromise.

Since foreign policy is the key to nationalist legitimacy, the Syrian regime must walk a narrow line between the requisites of peace and domestic opinion. The Alawi-dominated regime has always had to prove its nationalist credentials and the key test was its ability to secure Israel's withdrawal to its pre-1967 borders. Certainly a peace settlement that brought such a withdrawal would have accorded the regime a major legitimacy windfall. But the kind of less-than-comprehensive settlement that appeared likely after Oslo and the prospect of a Syrian peace with Israel while Palestinian national rights remained in good part unsatisfied carried definite domestic risks for Assad. Nevertheless Oslo precipitated a seachange in Syrian opinion. Once the Palestinians – and then Jordan – reached their separate deals with Israel many Syrians became convinced that Syria would have to give priority to its own interest in recovering the Golan. As Assad lamented on Syrian TV: 'What can we do since the others have left us and gone forward?'[10]

Even should a peace agreement be reached, Syria and Israel will remain rivals for influence in the Levant and Syria's position there is threatened by Israel's drive to incorporate the Palestinians and Jordan as virtual political and economic satellites. As against those promoting a Middle East system in which economic ties bridged national cleavages, thereby integrating Israel into the region, Assad rejoined: 'There has been much talk about interests in this historic stage of international development. . . . [But] interests . . . mean . . . not just economic interests, but . . . [national] sentiments and common culture and heritage.'[11]

Syrian Strategy in the Post-Bipolar World

With the disappearance of Soviet support, an exposed Syria scrambled to repair and diversify its connections to other powers. Syria took advantage of the Gulf crisis to show the West it was a factor for stability, and would eschew terrorism and play by Western rules. It re-established its damaged relations with Western Europe, an alternative source of aid to the USSR. American acceptance of Syrian interests in Lebanon, the Gulf war, and the peace process put US-Syrian relations on a better footing.

But Syria remained suspicious of American motives: its attempted blocking of Syrian weapons acquisitions, its failure to remove Syria from the terrorism list, its role in excluding Syria from Gulf security arrangements, its loan guarantees to Israel and its failure to actively broker the peace process, disillusioned Syria that the US would reward it for its Gulf war role and acknowledge its 'strategic weight'.

Despite Syria's inclusion in the Gulf War coalition, Assad perceived the 'New World Order' as largely biased against Arab and Syrian interests. The balance of power, he declared, had been upset – with the collapse of bipolarity – and the 'main winners have been the Arabs' enemies. Perhaps they expect we shall weaken and collapse but we shall not surrender'.[12] A new balance of power would, in time, be established; unfortunately, while other parts of the world were forming regional blocs, the Arab world was going in the opposite direction: 'Some Arabs are absorbed in their own interests or are more at ease with foreigners than brother Arabs and look to them for protection.'[13]

Seeking to shape a more favourable regional power balance, Syria sought alternative arms sources in China and North Korea. Using their desire for debt repayment as leverage, Syria had some success in re-establishing economic and arms relations with Russia and the East bloc, and evidently acquired much high-quality equipment at cut rate prices; interestingly, Gulf aid serviced some of these connections.[14] Perhaps most important, Russia evidently forgave much of Syria's military debt and resumed some arms and spare-parts shipments on a commercial basis, though reputedly deferring to Israeli demands it restrain advanced weapons deliveries.[15] Syria also preserved its Iranian alliance as a counter to US dominance in the Gulf and as a partner in the development of an arms industry.

CONCLUSION

No legitimate, stable Arab order is likely unless the current insecurity, maldistribution of wealth and loss of regional autonomy are effectively addressed. The Gulf crisis aggravated these ills without giving birth to the new regional leadership needed to address them.

For a brief period after the crisis, Syria and Egyptian foreign policies was driven by converging 'pan-Arab' interests, including the containment of Iraq, reversing the disengagement of the Gulf Arabs and Saudi Arabia from the Arab system, and manipulating the US to achieve an acceptable Arab–Israeli peace. Cairo and Damascus needed each other: Syria's preoccupation with Israel required sustained Arab coalition-building; in Egypt the economics-driven bridging strategy requires a leading role in the Arab system. The Damascus declaration joined their interests to those of Saudi Arabi and the Gulf states in a proposed solution to the security, wealth and autonomy issues. It might have generated an expanded 'Arab Triangle' and a foundation for a new Arab order.

The declaration was still born, however, and the Syro-Egyptian alignment was quickly enervated by divergent 'state interests' which expressed the split personality of the Arab world: Egypt expressed the Arab desire to manipulate and profit from incorporation into the New World Order, while Syria expressed lingering nationalist resistance to this as long as Israel refused an equitable peace.

Since separate nation-states have not evolved, there is no obvious alternative to the Arab system, but without its renewal the region is likely to remain vulnerable to Western intervention, incapable of pursuing common interests, deprived of legitimacy, inherently unstable, and vulnerable to Saddam-like challenges.

Alternative scenarios depend on the peace process. If it results in an equitable settlement, Egypt and Syria would share an interest in legitimizing it against potential Iraqi and Iranian rejectionism. Greater legitimacy and security could facilitate inter-Arab and Western aid and investment, economically integrating Egypt and Syria with the Gulf states and into the international market. Only under some such scenario, whereby the 'split personality' of the Arab world could possibly be healed, is Arab membership in the New World Order likely to be legitimized and stable.

NOTES

1. Paul Noble, 'The Arab System: Pressures, Constraints and Opportunities', in Bahgat Korany and Ali E. Hillal Dessouki, *The Foreign Policies of Arab States, Westview Press* (Westview, Boulder, Colo., 1991), pp. 62–5; Bassam Tibi, 'Structural and Ideological Change in the Arab Subsystem Since the Six Day War', in Yehuda Lukas and Abdalla M. Battah, *The Arab-Israeli Conflict: Two Decades of Change* (Westview, Boulder, Colo., 1988), 147–63.
2. Fouad Ajami, 'Stress in the Arab Triangle', *Foreign Policy*, 29 (1977–78), pp. 90–198.
3. Michael Hudson, *Arab Politics: The Search for Legitimacy* (Yale University Press, New Haven, Conn., 1977), pp. 33–55; Eberhard Kienle, *Ba'th vs. Ba'th: The Conflict between Syria and Iraq, 1968–1989* (Tauris, London, 1990), pp. 1–30.
4. Tim Niblock, 'The Need for a New Arab Order', *Middle East International*, 12 October 1990, pp. 17–18.
5. Leon Carl Brown, *International Politics and the Middle East: Old Rules, Dangerous Game* (Princeton University Press, 1982).
6. *Christian Science Monitor*, 4 March 1991, p. 4.

Raymond A. Hinnebusch   181

7. Ali E. Hillal Dessouki, 'The Primacy of Economics. The Foreign Policy of Egypt', in Korany and Dessouki, op. cit., pp. 156–85.
8. *Middle East International*, 16 September 1994.
9. Mohammed Ziarati, 'Egypt's Military Modernization Objectives', *Middle East International*, 23 September 1994, pp. 20–1.
10. *The Middle East*, September 1995, p. 8.
11. *Middle East Mirror*, 10 March 1994, p. 11.
12. *Middle East Mirror*, 1 April 1992, p. 13.
13. BBC *Summary of World Broadcasts*, 14 March 1992.
14. Fred Lawson, 'Domestic Transformation and Foreign Steadfastness in Contemporary Syria', *Middle East Journal*, vol. 48, no. 1, Winter 1994; Israel Shahak, 'Israel and Syria: Peace Through Strategic Parity?', *Middle East International*, 16 December 1994, pp. 18–19.
15. *Middle East Mirror*, 5 May 1994, p. 25.

9 Economic Prospects for Iraq and its Neighbours in the Aftermath of the Gulf War
Rodney Wilson

REALIZATION OF A PEACE DIVIDEND

Only time will tell whether the coming decades in the Middle East will be more peaceful than the last half-century, but there does seem to have been a change in opinions and priorities among both governments and peoples in the region. More attention is being given to economic matters, not least because of the realization that influence and power are more likely to be underpinned in the long term by strong economic performance than through military effort alone. It is not so much a matter of naïvely assuming that the regimes and peoples have turned their back on war, and taken the peace path, although there is a weariness with conflict. It is, rather, the understanding that war has brought few gains for most of the states of the region, and that it is perhaps time to pursue a different course.

In economic terms Middle Eastern states have paid a heavy price for the emphasis on military effort at the expense of civilian developments. During the 1980s and early 1990s per capita gross domestic product growth rates have been less than half those of the states of South East Asia. Perceived political risk has resulted in continuing capital flight, with little offsetting inward investment into the region. Apart from oil-related activity, multinational companies have been reluctant to commit long-term funds in the Middle East. Stock markets are insignificant in the region in comparison with the emerging markets in South East Asia, and the unfavourable investment climate has discouraged entrepreneurial activity.

The speedy conclusion of the Gulf War in 1990, and the peace accords between the Palestinians and Israelis, appear to have marked a turning point for the region, even though the future for Iraq is still unclear, and the negotiations involving Israel and its neighbours have proved as tortuous and difficult as the critics feared. Nevertheless, with the ending of super power rivalries in the Middle East, there has been a the search for new accommodations with the changed world order by the countries of the region. This is evident in the economic sphere as well as the political. Oil continues to account for the major share of Middle East exports, but with the oil price in real terms back to the level of the early 1970s, and with little prospect of significant price rises, the search for alternatives to oil has become more urgent than ever. Turkey, which has become a major exporter of manufactured goods, demonstrates what can be achieved. Although outside the region, Malaysia's economic success also gives hope to other Muslim countries, including those in the Gulf, which have become disillusioned with their northern neighbours, and look increasingly to the wider Islamic world beyond the Arab states and Iran.

Although the Arab–Israeli wars have been much more costly in both financial and human terms than the conflicts in the Gulf, it is perhaps appropriate to focus on the latter, not least because the Gulf War was the first in the post-cold-war period. It provides an interesting case study of the economic costs of conflict management and an illustration of the regional problems resulting from international action in this new context.

THE LESSONS FROM IRAQ'S POST-GULF WAR EXPERIENCE

There is considerable evidence to show that sanctions have little short-term effect, but in the long term the effect can be economically devastating. They have been shown to be an effective tool for political leverage in many parts of the world, and Iraq appears to be no exception. Saddam Hussein may have survived, but he has been rendered powerless as far as regional influence is concerned, indeed he has become virtually a tool of the West, permitted to operate within very tight constraints, as long as his actions do not affect Western interests. His role is to maintain a type of order within Iraq, saving the international community the embarrassment of having to become more directly involved in the country's messy internal politics. Movements of Iraqi troops along the Kuwait border may still capture the headlines, but the reality is that this plays into Western hands, as it only reveals the continued vulnerability of the GCC states, and their need to rely on the West for military protection. Rather than threatening the regimes in the Gulf, Saddam Hussein's remaining actions may actually reinforce the *status quo*, because there is little alternative for these states to Western hegemony.

Iraq's once prosperous economy is now in tatters, with sanctions affecting virtually every sphere of activity. Oil exports fell from an estimated 2.3 million barrels a day in 1989 to 1.6 million barrels a day in 1990, the year of the invasion of Kuwait when sanctions started to bite in the latter part of the year. By 1991 they were down to a mere 39 000 barrels a day, and in 1993 the amount was still only 59 000 barrels a day.[1] New investment has virtually ceased, and although the most seriously war-damaged infrastructure has been repaired, there has been a general rundown of basic facilities. The economy was starting to be liberalized before the invasion of Kuwait, with discussions on privatization as the Ba'athist party moved away from socialist economic policies. This process was abruptly halted, but the economic role of the state has been considerably curtailed as a consequence of the loss of the revenue from oil. Regulation continues, backed by state coercion, but the government has lost most of its power of patronage through its own spending.

In human terms the misery is considerable. Food rations, which provide over a million Iraqis with their basic calorie needs, were cut by half in 1994. As a consequence begging has become widespread, both for food and for money. Even those who had once been relatively well off, including the middle classes, have been reduced to a subsistence, largely vegetarian, diet. An average monthly salary of 5000 dinars would only buy two chickens by 1995, with one egg costing 80 dinars.[2] Inflation has risen to over 100 per cent, with the dinar, which was worth $US3 before the war, trading at 1750 to the dollar by 1995 on the black market.[3] Crime is widespread, in spite of draconian penalties, as the poor and desperate steal merely to survive. The once very adequate health provision is severely stretched, as although essential medical supplies are supposed to be exempt from sanctions, health is not simply a matter of drugs, but also of diet, facilities, personnel and even morale. The infant mortality rate has risen from 25 per 1000 births before the war to 92 per 1000 by 1994 according to UNICEF.[4]

Despite these difficulties, Iraq's economy is basically sound, and could recover quickly if sanctions were lifted. There is a well-educated middle class, and substantial reserves of oil and considerable agricultural potential. Only 43 per cent of available water resources are utilized, compared with 97 per cent in Egypt according to World Bank estimates.[5] Much of the food consumption for the population of 19 million could be locally supplied, and there is scope for increasing exports of dates which were significant in the past. Industries such as cement making have been able to operate in spite of sanctions, and it would be relatively easy to restore manufacturing for the local market. Export-orientated industrialization must inevitably be oil-related, given the country's resource endowment, but the development of petrochemical capacity would bring Iraq into competition with Saudi Arabia and Iran. The restoration of oil exports poses similar problems, with the modest firming of prices in 1995 likely to be undermined if Iraq is permitted to export significant quantities after the lifting of sanctions.

There can of course be endless debate about the economic costs of the Gulf War for Iraq, in terms of what development might have taken place had the invasion of Kuwait not occurred and had the subsequent sanctions not been imposed. Even the narrower estimation of the financial costs is difficult. The calculation of the financial cost of the Gulf War is relatively straightforward conceptually, but in practice is much less simple. As far as the actual conflict was concerned, most of the cost was incurred by Iraq, with the losses in military equipment alone amounting to over $50 billion, though this figure is lower if the second-hand market value of the equipment is counted rather than the cost of purchase when new. Replacement rather than historical cost would of course be higher. The destruction of the Arab world's most expensive, and perhaps most sophisticated, military machine, was only one aspect of the cost. The aerial bombardment of communications infrastructure inflicted damage of an equivalent amount, and the destruction of oil installations and industrial plant may have resulted in damage worth more than $130 billion.

THE FINANCIAL AND ECONOMIC COSTS OF THE GULF WAR FOR KUWAIT

For Kuwait the position was much easier, because although the Iraqis looted movable property, the main infrastructure remained intact, the most expensive damage being to oil installations. The industrial capacity of Kuwait was always limited, as government policy did not encourage local manufacturing because of labour shortages and a limited internal market. Instead, oil revenues were recycled into international financial markets, and it is these investments which sustained the government in exile. As foreign assets worth over $70 billion remained, this was more than adequate to finance the reconstruction required.

Nevertheless, in the postwar period Kuwait has been faced with tough economic realities, with government spending subject to considerable pressures. It has proved difficult to sell oil at more than $13 a barrel, which has limited government revenue. Income from overseas investments has also fallen with assets held in the reserve fund for future generations reduced from $100 billion to $35 billion.[6] At the same time spending demands continue, with citizens accustomed to generous welfare benefits, pressures to spend ever more on defence, and a need for continuing infrastructure investment, including $15 billion if oil production is to be raised from 2 million to 3 million barrels a day, a government objective. As a consequence of these spending pressures and a squeeze on revenues, the government was forced in 1992 to borrow $5.5 billion from international markets. Despite subsequent efforts to control the budget deficit, this still amounted to $4 billion annually by 1995.[7]

It is important to see Kuwait's economic problems in perspective, and not be too gloomy about the deficit figures. With a population of less than one and a half million, reduced by the exodus of Palestinians and other Arabs after the Gulf War, and one of the world's highest per capita GNP figures of over $18 000, the people of the emirate are far from facing hardship. Many of the economic problems are managerial, and can be helped by reorganization. The government's own spending plans remain as vague as ever,[8] with planning hampered by the departure of Palestinian civil servants.[9] The Kuwait Oil Company is far from being efficient, and could be partly or wholly sold off to Western multinationals. This would mean that the multinationals rather than the government could fund the $15 billion investment needed for oil production expansion. Utility prices could be raised further, reducing the needs for government subsidies. Charges could be introduced for some health provision, as most Kuwaitis can afford to pay. The tax net could be extended, although this might result in demands for greater government expenditure accountability.

The major economic uncertainty arises from external security, the continued dependency on Western military underpinning and the perceived threat from Iraq. Although Saddam Hussein has renounced his territorial claim on Kuwait, he is not surprisingly mistrusted, and there can be no guarantee that any successor would not revive the claim. The Gulf War solved none of the basic disputes between Iraq and Kuwait, which could lead to fresh conflict. For the moment Kuwait has the guarantee of Western support, but in the long run its best course of action is to build up its relationship with Iran as a counterbalance to Iraq. The GCC is not an effective counterbalance, as none of the participants has sufficient military strength. It is against these political realities that the economic prospects have to be judged. Kuwait is a low political risk in the short term, which means it can be classified as a prime international borrower, qualifying for low rates. Kuwait equity investors are likely to want to hedge their longer term options, by continuing to acquire assets overseas, and limiting the size of their local portfolios.

SAUDI ARABIA'S POLITICAL ECONOMY

Saudi Arabia has also incurred costs due to the conflict, though physical damage was limited, given the ineffectiveness of the scud missile attacks, the main destruction being to the small border town of Khafji and its refinery. The most costly damage was the environmental disaster caused by the oil slicks, which cost more than $700 million to clean up. The much greater burden was that of contributing financially to the allied military effort for the defence of the kingdom and the liberation of Kuwait. The bill for this exceeded $13.5 billion from the United States alone. There has been much publicity over the Saudi Arabian budget deficit and the borrowing of $4.5 billion from the Euromarkets in London under an arrangement involving Morgan Guaranty.

According to some estimates the total cost of the Gulf War to the kingdom exceeded $60 billion,[10] but this may be an exaggeration. The immediate cost of the war was not a major problem for Saudi Arabia, but the longer-term economic and financial consequences have been more serious. The budget deficit of $10.7 billion for 1994 was high in relation to the GDP figure of $125 billion, and the International Monetary Fund has estimated that the debt to GDP figure could rise to 80 per cent by 1997.[11] However, there is no income tax, but, as in Kuwait, such taxes could be introduced given the political will. Rather than take this action, the government has gone for the easier option of increasing oil production to generate revenue. Saudi Arabia increased its oil production by fifty per cent after the invasion of Kuwait and the imposition of economic sanctions on Iraq to make up for lost production from these countries. The revenue from this increased output made an important contribution to the costs incurred in hosting the allied forces and offering material support. As the kingdom has over a quarter of world petroleum reserves and is the leading exporter, its dominant position in hydrocarbons is assured, as well as its position in OPEC. It has the capacity to export over 13 million barrels a day, but it varies output according to international market conditions, and in 1995 exports amounted to 8.2 million barrels a day.[12]

The Saudi Arabian economy remains vulnerable to oil price developments,[13] and after the post-Gulf War recovery, a slackening in oil prices caused concern in 1993 and 1994. More recently, the firming of oil prices to the $15 to $17 per barrel range has eased financial conditions, and the international borrowing arranged after the Gulf War has been repaid. The trade balance recorded a $10 billion surplus in 1994, and domestic budgetary restraint has reduced the fiscal deficit from $10.7 billion in 1994 to $4 billion in 1995. The rate of inflation was already reduced to a mere 0.6 per cent per annum by 1994, with continuing price stability predicted.[14]

The new development plan for 1995–2000 stresses the role of the private sector in promoting economic growth,[15] a trend that has already been evident since the conclusion of the Gulf War.[16] The commercial banks and private investors are being encouraged to back manufacturing ventures catering for the domestic market, and the state-owned Saudi Arabian Basic Industries Corporation, which is responsible for petrochemical production and exports, has already been partly privatized. With the electricity companies under private ownership, and discussions on the sell-off of other utilities and Saudia, the national airline, the government has considerable scope for raising revenue. The cabinet reshuffle of 1995, in which seven ministers were replaced, including the oil and national economy ministers,[17] was interpreted as enhancing the role of private business in Saudi Arabia and favouring the merchant community more generally. Many Islamists favour these developments and a reduced role for the state in economic activity. The modernization of Saudia's aircraft is to be financed Islamically, with the participation of both Saudi Arabian and foreign commercial banks, but with the whole deal managed without interest borrowings.

IRAN: PERIPHERY OR CENTRE STAGE?

Although on the sidelines of the Gulf War, Iran had a direct interest in the outcome, not least because of its own protracted war with Iraq in the 1980s. GDP growth, which had averaged 8.7 per cent per annum over the period 1965–80, fell to 0.6 per cent between 1980 and 1990,[18] with a decline in both real and nominal terms in the early years of the Iraq–Iran War. This was accompanied by a serious run-down in infrastructure, because there was virtually no finance for the maintenance of existing facilities, and no new investment, because funds were diverted to the military effort. Unfortunately when the war ended, and President Rafsanjani tried to rebuild the economy,[19] low oil prices meant that finance could not easily be found for the reconstruction effort. Iran was forced to borrow almost $30 billion, an estimated $9 billion of which was in the form of short-term trade debt to Western commercial banks. As the Islamic Republic has suffered from a persistent trade deficit with weak oil sales, by 1992 over $3 billion worth of letters of credit had to be rescheduled owing to the country's failure to meet its payments obligations.[20]

This situation was further complicated in 1995 by the effect of United States sanctions imposed by the White House because of Iran's alleged sponsorship of terrorism, and its programme to develop nuclear weapons. Both these allegations have been denied by Tehran, but the United States sanctions introduced in

June 1995 have halted oil sales worth $4 billion annually to American companies.[21] In response Iran has chartered 28 giant oil tankers in an attempt to replace sales to United States companies with increased sales to East Asia and Europe. Oil exports from Iran amounted to 2.5 million barrels a day in 1995, although this was a reduction from the average of 3.4 million barrels a day in 1993. This reduction was caused not only by marketing problems and the effect of sanctions, but by production problems in the oil fields themselves, which are in need of substantial investment.

The five-year development plan for the period 1990–95, like that of Saudi Arabia, aimed to limit the role of the state in the economy, reduce regulation, and promote private business. The economic liberalization measures included unifying and simplifying the exchange rate system with the abolition in 1993 of the preferential rates for so called 'essential imports'. Subsidies were phased out, although this contributed to a substantial rise in inflation. This averaged 22 per cent over the period 1985–93, but by the mid-1990s the rate had risen to over 40 per cent, accentuated by the budget deficit as the taxes collected fell well short of expenditure. With the country's population increasing from 38 to almost 60 million over the period 1979–1994, there were increasing numbers needing schooling and considerable demands on health facilities. Education accounts for almost a quarter of government spending in Iran,[22] one of the highest proportions in the developing world, yet only 45 per cent of women are literate.[23] Despite an increase in health spending the infant mortality rate remains at 41 per 1000 live births, one of the worst figures in the Middle East, and almost 40 per cent of children under five years old are underweight.[24]

Faced with daunting internal economic problems, to a considerable extent the consequence of very rapid population growth since the Islamic revolution, the priorities in Iran are domestic, not international or even regional. The pressing needs are economic, to create employment opportunities for the ever increasing number of school leavers, and raise living standards for the poor who supported the revolution in the first place. The development plan for the 1995–2000 period envisages the creation of 2 million new jobs, with particular emphasis on agriculture and agro-industry.[25] There are some in Iran who continue to be concerned with Shiite interests in the Gulf, but for the government foreign policy is largely motivated by the need to improve relations with the West in order to enhance development prospects. The sanctions imposed by the United States were a setback to the Tehran government. Similarly, any attempt to incite the Shiite populations in Bahrain or Saudi Arabia's Eastern Province which antagonises Riyadh and Washington conflicts with the promotion of Iran's domestic economic interests.[26] Iran is now on the periphery of Middle Eastern politics, not at the centre, its freedom of manoeuvre limited by its own internal economic problems.

JORDAN'S READJUSTMENT TO IRAQ'S DEMISE

As is often the case in regional conflicts, small countries like Jordan have only a limited influence on events, the role of government being primarily that of damage limitation. In the case of Jordan there were two issues, the first being economic relations with Iraq, which was the Hashemite Kingdom's main trading partner. Jordan's small-scale private manufacturing industries exported construction supplies, pharmaceutical products and other goods to Iraq, and in return Jordan received Iraqi petroleum.[27] During the Iraq–Iran War, when the port of Basra was blockaded, much of Iraq's imports passed through Aqaba, which brought Jordanian transportation companies significant transit earnings. As Jordan was forced by the West to comply with the economic sanctions imposed against Iraq in the aftermath of the invasion of Kuwait, this trade came to an end,[28] although some informal dealings continued, constrained mainly by Iraq's lack of foreign exchange, and the rapid depreciation of the Iraqi dinar against the Jordanian dinar.

The second difficulty for Jordan resulting from the Gulf War was the loss of remittances with the expulsion of Palestinians from Kuwait after its liberation, and to a lesser extent other Gulf states, as most of the Palestinians held Jordanian passports and channelled their financial transfers through Amman.[29] Before the war the Palestinians were by far the largest single immigrant group in Kuwait, and many occupied well-paid positions. Their remittances were vital for the economies of the occupied territories and Jordan, and for every salary earner in Kuwait there were several dependants left behind. Not only did the PLO leadership support

Saddam Hussein's position,[30] but individual Palestinians informed on the Kuwaiti resistance, which resulted in torture and executions.

In addition to the loss of remittances, Jordan has been forced to purchase more expensive oil from Syria rather than to obtain favourable barter terms from Iraq. This has added to the country's substantial trade deficit, as even before the Gulf War export receipts were less than a quarter of import payments. Re-exports to Iraq virtually ceased even before the conflict, in spite of Jordanian reluctance to apply United Nations sanctions, severely reducing the country's external receipts.

Even without these difficulties, the economic outlook for Jordan would have been dismal, as aid from Saudi Arabia fell in the mid-1980s following the oil price reductions at that time, and ironically, the need for Riyadh to assist Saddam Hussein financially, in order to support the Iraqi position in the war with Iran. The ending of this earlier conflict and financial wrangling with Baghdad brought an end to this assistance in 1989, but there was no possibility of aid being rerouted to Jordan. In the aftermath of the Gulf War this seemed completely out of the question, given Gulf attitudes to King Hussein because of his stance over Baghdad.

In the past the Jordanian economy has proved to be remarkably resilient, and recovered much faster than most outside observers expected from the 1967 war with Israel and the loss of the West Bank, and then the civil war with the Palestinians. External factors were extremely favourable, however, with inflows of aid and remittances after the 1973–4 oil price rises, and even high prices for phosphates, Jordan's major visible export. After the Gulf War Jordan was in crisis again, but this time the prospects for Gulf assistance were bleak. Living standards in Jordan had already fallen before the Gulf War, but after the pace of decline increased unemployment was an ever more serious problem. Unemployment is estimated to have risen to 30 per cent by 1991, although it has since fallen to 13 per cent.[31] Nevertheless even the educated, including university graduates, cannot easily find work.

This was, however, to provide an opportunity for the United States to step in and provide the aid which helped stimulate Jordan's recovery. The price was the peace treaty with Israel, but this was a price Amman was willing to pay given the lack of other options. The rewards are already starting to become evident, with the average decline of 5.9 per cent per annum in per capita GDP over the period 1985–93 being reversed,[32] and positive growth recorded for the first time in a decade. Jordan has a relatively well educated population, with an adult literacy rate of 82.1 per cent.[33] Given the investment in human capital there has been over the last few decades, aid from the United States to improve the physical capital should bring a substantial payoff, with the tourist industry already growing rapidly now that the border with Israel has been opened.

In the occupied territories the situation was much more desperate, however, as the uprising has undermined the local Palestinian economy much more than the economy of Israel, where it effects have been marginal at best. The complete curfew during the Gulf War meant the population were prisoners in their own homes, and economic activity came to a standstill. Before, but especially during the war and the period since, Arab Palestinian workers in Israel have been replaced by the new flood of Jewish immigrants from the Soviet Union. This has resulted in unemployment becoming a permanent feature of the occupied territories, and a very serious loss of income. The future of the West Bank and Gaza, however, largely depends on the outcome of the peace process with Israel. As far as Palestinians are concerned, developments in the Gulf are less likely to have the impact which they did in the past when more workers from the territories were employed in Kuwait and the other Gulf states.

SYRIA, THE HISTORICAL RIVAL OF IRAQ

In the case of Iraq's final neighbour considered here, the position is even more complicated. For Syria the immediate economic benefits from their support for the allies in the Gulf War were less tangible, but in the longer term these could be substantial, much depending on progress in the peace process with Israel. The Lebanese Christian militia leader, General Aoun, was one of the first casualties of the conflict, as he had been backed militarily by Iraq, and had links with Tariq Aziz, Baghdad's Christian foreign minister. Aoun's demise removed a major source of friction, and helped Syria consolidate its position in Lebanon, with tacit Western approval. President Assad was also concerned about the collapse of the Soviet Union as a superpower, and the state of the Russian economy, as his country's external economic and military relations placed much emphasis on the Treaty of Friendship with the Soviet Union.

Syria has been wanting for some time to improve its relations with the West, and even before the Gulf conflict was rethinking and redesigning its economic policies. The industrialization effort had been based on the establishment and development of state-owned plants, and Soviet planning models. These had proved as unsuccessful in Syria as in the Soviet Union. Although in the 1970s it was usual to blame the state of hostility with Israel for the country's economic difficulties, by the 1980s it was realized that a more realistic approach was needed. In the late 1980s a series of new measures were enacted to encourage foreign investment and stimulate private sector activity. These had not really had time to work when the Gulf crisis erupted. Now, with Lebanon more stable, and the new relationship of Damascus with the West, there are growing hopes of economic recovery and an improvement in living standards. The private sector has finally started to grow, which is encouraging for the future.[34] Most Syrians are tired of austerity and sacrifice for the sake of regional conflicts, and want to see a stronger domestic economy. The Assad government now appears to recognize this, and is rethinking its policies accordingly. This is perhaps one of the most promising changes in the region, from the point of view of future peace and stability.

THE GULF WAR AS AN HISTORICAL TURNING POINT

Clear lessons can be drawn from this survey of economic conditions of Iraq and its neighbours in the period since the Gulf War. First, it is evident that Iraq was not only a military loser, but also an economic loser, and that sanctions have worked. The folly and futility of threatening Western oil interests in the Gulf has been decisively demonstrated, and all Iraqis have been made aware of this in their daily lives. Their government has been humiliated, but it arguably suits Western interests for Saddam Hussein to survive as a spent force. In contrast, Kuwait and Saudi Arabia have been rewarded for their compliance and support for Western action, and their economies have revived remarkably since the War. Democracy remains as distant a goal as ever in these states, and human rights abuses continue, but the Gulf War was about Western oil interests, not questions of liberty or human respect.

Iran continues to be punished for actions which its government can do little about, Rafsanjani's gestures to the United States being rejected, largely because Washington is concerned to keep Tehran weak, both for the sake of its Gulf oil interests and because of Israeli lobbying. There is little real interest in internal political structures in Iran by the West; the policy is simply containment by frustrating Tehran's economic development plans to ensure that the government remains preoccupied with domestic issues. The crude allegations of associations between Islamists and terrorism are a mere pretext for this containment policy, and there is little interest in the subtleties of Iranian politics, or recognition of the extent to which the Islamic revolution was viewed by many in Iran as a force for liberation. Nor is there much mention of the vigour of political debate in the *majlis*, and just how successful the revolution has been in promoting pluralist structures.

Jordan and Syria have always been flexible in adjusting to new political realities. The negotiations with Israel were a direct outcome of the Gulf War. Jordan is already being rewarded for its reconciliation with Israel, and promises are being made to Syria of rewards to come, with the recognition of its hegemony in Lebanon as a first instalment of the payoff. The post-Gulf-War developments demonstrate the weakness of the Middle Eastern states, and how far their economic as well as their political fate is determined by external forces. Internal divisions have reinforced this weakness, with little sign of successful economic renaissance generated from within the region itself, as has been the case in South-East Asia.

NOTES

1. *Country Profile: Iraq, 1995–96* (Economist Intelligence Unit, London, 1995), p. 25.
2. *Country Report: Iraq, 3rd Quarter 1995* (Economist Intelligence Unit, London, 1995), p. 20.

3.   *Financial Times*, 26 July 1995, p. 3.
4.   *Financial Times*, 15 August 1995, p. 3.
5.   *World Bank Atlas* (Washington, 1995), p. 26.
6.   *Financial Times Survey of Kuwait*, 23 May 1995, p. 2.
7.   Ibid., p. 3.
8.   *Country Report: Kuwait, 2nd Quarter 1995* (Economist Intelligence Unit, London, 1995), p. 10.
9.   *Country Profile: Kuwait, 1994–95* (Economist Intelligence Unit, London, 1994), p. 11.
10. *Financial Times*, 3 August 1995, p. 3.
11. *Financial Times Survey of Saudi Arabia*, 22 December 1993, p. 2.
12. *Country Report: Saudi Arabia, 2nd Quarter 1995* (Economist Intelligence Unit, London, 1995), p. 7.
13. Jassin-al-Ali, 'Oil and Investment Policies in the 1990s', in *The Gulf in the 1990s* (Gulf Centre for Strategic Studies, London, 1991), pp. 39–48.
14. *ABECOR Report: Saudi Arabia* (London, July 1995), p. 1.
15. *Country Profile: Saudi Arabia, 1994–95* (Economist Intelligence Unit, London, 1994), p. 13.
16. Caroline Montagu, *The Private Sector of Saudi Arabia* (Committee for Middle East Trade, London, 1994), pp. 60–76.
17. *Financial Times*, 3 August 1995, p. 3.
18. Massoud Karshenas and M. Hashem Pesaran, 'Economic Reform and the Reconstruction of the Iranian Economy', *Middle Eastern Journal*, vol. 49, no. 1, 1995, pp. 89–111.
19. *The Postwar Gulf: New Business Realities in the Middle East*, Economist Intelligence Unit Report 2176 (London, 1991), p. 107.
20. *ABECOR Report: Iran* (London, August 1993), p. 2.
21. *Financial Times*, 26 July 1995, p. 3.
22. *UNDP Human Development Report* (Oxford University Press, 1994), p. 158.
23. Ibid., p. 138.
24. Ibid., p. 136.
25. *Country Profile: Iran, 1995–96* (Economist Intelligence Unit, London), 1995, pp. 18–19.
26. Michael Binyon, 'Five Years After Saddam's Invasion Radical Shias Pose Biggest Threat to Gulf Leaders', *The Times*, 2 August 1995, p. 7.
27. Rodney Wilson (ed.), *Politics and the Economy in Jordan* (Routledge, London, 1991), p. 3.
28. *Country Profile: Jordan, 1995–96* (Economist Intelligence Unit, London, 1995), pp. 13–14.
29. Ibid., p. 4.
30. Philip Mattar, 'The PLO and the Gulf Crisis', *Middle Eastern Journal*, vol. 48, no. 1, 1994, pp. 31–46.
31. *Country Profile: Jordan 1995–96*, p. 17.
32. *World Bank Atlas*, p. 18.
33. *UNDP Human Development Report*, p. 130.
34. *Country Report: Syria, 3rd Quarter 1995* (Economist Intelligence Unit, London), 1995, p. 6.

Bibliography

BOOKS

Ahmed, A., *Postmodernism and Islam: Predicament and Promise* (Routledge, London, 1992).

Al-Baana, H., *Rasail Al-Banna* (in Arabic) (The Islamic Institute, Beirut, no date available).

Al-Hassan, K., *Grasping the Nettle of Peace* (Saqi Books, London, 1992).

Almond, E. and Coleman, J., *The Politics of the Developing Areas* (Princeton University Press, 1960).

Al-Nasrawi, A., *Arab Nationalism, Oil, and the Political Economy of Dependency* (Greenwood Press, London, 1991).

Al-Obedy, *The Muslim Brotherhood in Jordan and Palestine* (in Arabic) (Amman, Jordan, 1991).

Amin, S., *The Arab Nation* (Zed Press, London, 1978).

Antonius, G., *The Arab Awakening* (Capricorn Books, New York, 1965).

Ayalon, A., *Language and Change in the Arab Middle East* (Oxford University Press, 1987).

Ayubi, N., *Political Islam: Religion and Politics in the Arab World* (Routledge, London, 1991).

Barzilai, G., Klieman, A. and Shidlo, G. (eds) *The Gulf Crisis and Its Global Aftermath* (Routledge, London, 1993).

Bickerton, J and Klausner, C.L. *A Concise History of the Arab-Israeli Conflict*, 2nd edn (Prentice-Hall, Englewood Cliffs, N.J., 1995).

Bill, J. and Leiden, C., *Politics in the Middle East* (Little, Brown, 1984).

Brown, L. C., *International Politics and the Middle East: Old Rules, Dangerous Game* (Princeton University Press, 1984).

Burrowes, R., *The Yemen Arab Republic: The Politics of Development, 1962–1986* (Boulder, Westview, Colo., 1987).

Carmichael, J., *The Shaping of the Arabs: A Study in Ethnic Identity* (Macmillan, New York, 1967).

Choudhury, G., *Islam and the Contemporary World* (Thames, London, 1990).

Choueiri, Y. M., *Islamic Fundamentalism* (Pinter, London, 1990).

Cudsi, A. and Dessouki, A., *Islam and Power* (Croom Helm, London, 1981).

Deegan, H., *The Middle East and Problems of Democracy* (Open University Press, Milton Keynes, 1993).

Diamond, L., Linz, J. L., and Lipset, S. M., *Democracy in Developing Countries – Asia* (Adamantino Press, 1989).

Duri, A. A., *The Historical Formation of the Arab Nation* (Croom Helm and Centre for Arab Unity Studies, London, 1987).

Dwyer, K., *Arab Voices: The Human Rights Debate in the Middle East* (Routledge, London, 1991).

EIU, *Oman, Yemen: Country Profile*, 1992–93.

Enayat, H., *Modern Islamic Political Thought* (Macmillan, London, 1991).
Fisher, S. N., *The Middle East: A History* (Alfred A. Knopf, New York, 1966).
Gellner, E., *Nations and Nationalism* (Blackwell, Oxford, 1993).
Graubard, S., *Mr Bush's War* (Tauris, London, 1992).
Haim, S. G., *Arab Nationalism: An Anthology* (University of California Press, 1962).
Halim, M. Abdula, *The Muslim Brotherhood* (in Arabic) (Dar al-Da'wa, Cairo, 1981).
Halliday, F. and Alavi, H., *State and Ideology in the Middle East and Pakistan* (Macmillan, London, 1988).
Hayek, F., *New Studies in Philosophy, Politics, Economics and the History of Ideas* (Routledge and Kegan Paul, London, 1978).
Hobsbawm, E. J., *Nations and Nationalism since 1780: Programme, Myth, Reality* (Cambridge University Press, Cambridge, 1991).
Hourani, A., *A History of the Arab Peoples* (Faber, London, 1991).
Hourani, A., *Arabic Thought in the Liberal Age 1798–1939* (Cambridge University Press, Cambridge, 1983).
Hudson, M., *Arab Politics: The Search for Legitimacy* (New Haven, Yale University Press, 1977).
Kariel, H. (ed.) *Frontiers of Democratic Theory* (Syracus University Press, New York, 1970).
Kedourie, E., *Politics in the Middle East* (Oxford University Press, Oxford, 1992).
Kerr, M. H., *The Arab Cold War* (Oxford University Press, Oxford, 1971).
Khouri, F. J., *The Arab–Israeli Dilemma* (Syracuse University Press, New York, 1976).
Kienle, E., *Ba'ath vs Ba'ath: The Conflict between Syria and Iraq 1968–1989* (Tauris, London, 1990).
Kornhauser, W., *The Politics of Mass Society* (Free Press, New York, 1957).
Landau, J. M., *The Politics of Pan-Islam: Ideology and Organisation* (Oxford University Press, Oxford, 1990).
Luciani, G., *The Arab State* (Routledge, London, 1990).
Macfarlane, N., *Superpower Rivalry and Third World Radicalism: The Idea of National Liberation* (Croom Helm, London, 1985).
McMahon, J., *Reagan and the World* (Pluto Press, London, 1984).
Mill, J. S., *Considerations of Representative Government* (original publication, London, no date available).
Mofid, K., *The Economic Consequences of the Gulf War* (Routledge, London, 1990).
Nasr, S. H., *Traditional Islam in the Modern World* (KPI, London and New York; 1987).
Nasser, G. A., *The Philosophy of the Revolution* (in Arabic) (Dar al-Macarif, Cairo, 1954).
Niblock, T. and Murphy, E. (eds) *Economic and Political Liberalisation in the Middle East* (British Academy Press, London, 1993).
Owen, R., *State, Power and Politics in the Making of the Modern Middle East* (Routledge, London, 1992).
Piscatori, J. P., *Islam in a World of Nation States* (Cambridge University Press, Cambridge, 1986).
Polk, W. R., *The United States and the Arab World* (Harvard University Press, Cambridge, Mass., 1969).
Qutb, S., *Al-Adala al-Ijtimaiyya Fil Islam* (Dar al-Sarok, Beirut, 1988).
Roper, J., *Democracy and its Critics: Anglo-American Thought in the Nineteenth Century* (Unwin-Hyman, London, 1989).

Said, E., *Peace and its Discontents* (Vintage, London, 1995).
Sharabi, H. B., *Nationalism and Revolution in the Arab World* (Van Nostrand Reinhold, London, 1966).
Tibi, B., *Arab Nationalism: A Critical Enquiry* (Macmillan, London, 1990).
Wilson, R., *Politics and Economics in Jordan* (Routledge, London, 1991).
Yale, W., *The Near East: A Modern History* (University of Michigan Press, East Lansing, 1958).
Yemeni Office of Unity Affairs, *Al-Yaman al-Wahid: Silsila Watha'iqya an al-Wahda al-Yamaniya*, 4th edn (Sana'a, 1990).
Zartman, I. W., *Government and Politics in Northern Africa* (Methuen, London, 1963).

CHAPTERS IN BOOKS

Al-Ail, J., 'Oil and Investment Policies in the 1990s', in *The Gulf in the 1990s* (Gulf Centre for Strategic Studies, London, 1991).
Baram, A., 'From Radicalism to Radical Pragmatism: the Shi'ite Fundamentalist Opposition Movements of Iraq', in Piscatori, J., *Islamic Fundamentalism and the Gulf Crisis* (American Academy of Arts and Sciences, Chicago, 1990).
Bessarabski, N., 'Islamisme et arabisme, deux ideologies politiques de reference', in Lacoste, C. and Lacoste, Y., *L'état du Maghreb* (Editions Le Fennec, Casablanca, 1991).
Bessis, S., 'Habib Bourguiba', in Lacoste, C. and Lacoste, Y., *L'État du Maghreb* (Editions Le Fennec, Casablanca, 1991).
Butterworth, C. E., 'Prudence Versus Legitimacy: the Persistent Theme in Islamic Political Thought', in Dessouki, A. E., *Islamic Resurgence in the Arab World* (Praeger, New York, 1982).
Cobban, H., 'The Palestinians and the Iraqi Invasion of Kuwait', in Freedman, R. O. (ed.), *The Middle East After Iraq's Invasion of Kuwait* (University Press of Florida, NJ, 1993).
Davis, E., 'Ideology, Social Class and Islamic Radicalism in Modern Egypt', in Arjomand, S. A., *From Nationalism to Revolutionary Islam* (Macmillan, London, 1984).
Dessoki, A. E., 'The Primacy of Economics: The Foreign Policy of Egypt', in Korany and Dessouki, *The Foreign Policy of Arab States* (Westview Press, Boulder, 1991).
Ehteshami, A., 'The Ingredients of Arms Control and Cooperation in the Gulf and Arabian Peninsula', in Nonneman, G., *The Middle East and Europe: Stability and Integration* (Federal Trust, London, 1993).
Ehteshami, A., 'Palestinian Perspectives on the Gulf Crisis', in Danchev, A., *International Perspectives on the Gulf Crisis* (Macmillan, London, 1994).
Feuerwerger, M., 'Israeli–American Relations in the Second Rabin Era', in Freedman, R. O. (ed.), *Israel Under Rabin* (Westview, Boulder, Co, 1995).
Feuerwerger, M., 'Israel, the Gulf War and its Aftermath', in Freedman, R. O., *The Middle East After Iraq's Ivasion of Kuwait*, (UPF, N.J., 1993).
Garfinkle, A., 'Jordan', in Staloff R. B. (ed.), *The Politics of Change in the Middle East*, (Westview, Boulder, Co, 1993).

Glavanis, K., 'Changing Perceptions and Constant Realities: Palestinian and Israeli Experiences of the Gulf War', in Bresheeth, H. and Yuval-David, N. (eds), *The Gulf War and the New World Order* (Zed Books, London, 1991).

Gunsteren, H. Van, 'Notes on a Theory of Citizenship', in Birnbaum, P., Lively, J., Parry, G, *Democracy, Consensus and Social Contract* (Sage, London, 1978).

Hermassi, E., 'State Building and Regime Performance in the Greater Maghreb', in Salame', G., *The Foundations of the Arab States* (Croom Helm, London, 1987).

Joffé, G., 'A View From the South', in Thomas, C. and Saravanamuttu, P., *Conflict and Consensus in North/South Security* (Cambridge University Press, Cambridge, 1989).

Joffé, G., 'Concepts of Sovereignty and Borders in North Africa', in IBRU, *International Boundaries and Boundary Conflict Resolution* (IBRU, Durham, 1990).

Joffé, G., 'Iran, the Southern Mediterranean and Europe', in Ehteshami, A. and Varasteh, M., *Iran and the International Community* (Routledge, London, 1991).

Joffé, G., 'The Politics of Islamic Reassertion in Algeria', in Nonneman, G., *The Middle East and Europe: An Integrated Communities Approach* (Federal Trust, London, 1992).

Joffé, G., 'The Implications of the New World Order for the Middle East and North Africa', *The Middle East and North Africa* (Europa, London, 1992).

Kuroda, Y., 'Bush's New World Order: A Structural Analysis of Instability and conflict in the Gulf', in Ismael, T. and Ismael, J. (eds), *The Gulf war and the New World Order* (University Press of Florida, Florida, 1994).

Lek Hor Tan, 'Democracy Scores an Own Goal', *Index on Censorship*, 5, 1992.

Magdoff, H., 'Globalisation – To What End'?, in Miliband, R. and Panitch, L. (eds), *New World Order? Socialist Register 1992* (Merlin, London, 1992).

Marks, J., 'Tunisia', in Niblock and Murphy, *Economic and Political Liberalisation in the Middle East* (British Academic Press, London, 1993).

Niblock, T., 'The Gulf Crisis (1990–91) and the Comprehension of Middle Eastern Politics', in Ismael, T. and J., *Politics and Government in the Middle East and North Africa* (Florida International University Press, 1991).

Niblock, T., 'International and Domestic Factors in the Economic Liberalisation Process in the Arab Countries', in Niblock, T., and Murphy, E., *Economic and Political Liberalisation in the Middle East* (British Academic Press, London, 1993).

Noble, P., 'The Arab System: Pressures, Constraints and Opportunities', in Korany, B. and Dessouki, A. E., *Foreign Policies of Arab States* (Westview Press, Boulder, 1991).

Nonneman, G., 'Key Issues in the Yemeni Economy', in Joffe, G. (ed.), *The Unity of Yemen: Crisis and Solutions* (St Malo Press, London, 1996).

Paul Cossali, 'The Arab–Israeli Confrontation 1967–1992', *The Middle East and North Africa 1993* (Europa, London, 1992).

Porat, M., 'Israel and the New World Order', in Ismael, T. and Ismael, J. (eds), *The Gulf War and the New World Order* (University Press of Florida, Florida, 1994).

Rubenberg, C. A., 'The Gulf War, the Palestinians and the New World Order', in Ismael, T. and Ismael J. (eds), *The Gulf War and the New World Order* (University Press of Florida, Florida, 1994).

Russell, S., 'Migration and Political Integration in the Arab World', in Luciani, G., *The Arab State* (Routledge, London, 1990).

Shlaim, A., 'Israel and the Conflict', in Danchev, A. and Keohane, D. (eds), *International Perspectives on the Gulf Conflict 1990–1991* (Macmillan, London, 1994).

Sluglett, M. F. and Sluglett, P., 'The Iraqi Baath Party', in Randall, V., *Political Parties in the Third World* (Sage, London, 1988).

Tibi, B., 'Structural and Ideological Change in the Arab Subsystem since the Six Day War', in Lukas, Y. and Battah Abdalla, M., *The Arab–Israeli Conflict: Two Decades of Change* (Boulder: Westview Press, 1988).

Whitaker, B., 'National Unity and Democracy in Yemen: a Marriage of Inconvenience', in Joffe, G. (ed.), *The Unity of Yemen: Crisis and Solutions* (St Malo Press, London, 1996).

Ziadeh, N., 'Arabism', in Kedouri, E., *Nationalism in Asia and Africa* (Frank Cass, London, 1971).

JOURNAL ARTICLES

Ajami, F., 'Stress in the Arab Triangle', *Foreign Policy*, 29, 1977–78.

Amin, S., 'Fifty Years is Enough', *Monthly Review*, April 1995.

Ayubi, N., 'The Political Revival of Islam: the Case of Egypt', *International Journal of the Middle East*, December 1980.

Ayubi, N., 'The Politics of Militant Islamic Movements in the Middle East', *Journal of International Affairs*, vol. 36, no. 2, 1982.

Boulby, M., 'The Islamic Challenge in Tunisia since Independence', *Third World Quarterly*, 10, 2, April, 1988.

Burrowes, R., 'Prelude to Unification: The Yemen Arab Republic, 1962–1990', *International Journal of Middle East Studies*, vol. 23, 1991.

Carapico, S., 'Elections and Mass Politics in Yemen', *Middle East Report*, November 1993.

Detalle, R., 'The Yemeni Elections Up Close', *Middle East Report*, November 1993.

Dunabar, C., 'The Unification of Yemen: Process, Politics and Prospects', *Middle East Journal*, vol. 46, no. 3, 1992.

Esposito and Piscatori, 'Democratisation and Islam', *Middle East Journal*, vol. 45, no. 3, 1991.

Ghali, B. B., 'Empowering the United Nations', *Foreign Affairs*, vol. 72, no. 5, Winter 1992–93.

Halliday, F., 'Moscow's Crisis Management: the Case of South Yemen', *Middle East Report*, March/April 1988.

Hudson, M., 'After the Gulf War: Prospects for Democratisation in the Arab World', *Middle East Journal*, vol. 45, no. 3, 1991.

Joffé, G., 'The Moroccan Nationalist Movement: Istiqlal, the Sultan and the Country', *Journal of African History*, 26, 1985.

Karshenas, M. and Pesaran, M. H., 'Economic Reform and the Reconstruction of the Iranian Economy', *Middle East Journal*, vol. 49, no. 1, 1995.

Klieman, A., 'New Directions in Israel's Foreign Policy', *Israel Affairs*, vol. 1, no. 1, Autumn 1994.

Lawson, F., 'Domestic Transformation and Foreign Steadfastness in Contemporary Syria', *Middle East Journal*, vol. 48, no. 1, Winter 1994.
Mattar, P., 'The PLO and the Gulf Crisis', *Middle East Journal*, vol. 48, no. 1, 1994.
Moghadam, V., 'Women, Work and Ideology in the Islamic Republic', *International Journal of Middle East Studies*, vol. 20, 1988.
Murphy, E., 'Structural Inhibitions to Economic Liberalisation in Israel', *Middle East Journal*, vol. 48, no. 1, Winter 1994.
Munson, Jr, H., 'Islamic Revivalism in Morocco and Tunisia', *The Muslim World*, 76, 1986.
Muslih, M., 'The Shift in Palestinian Thinking', *Current History*, January 1992.
Roberts, H., 'Radical Islam and the Dilemma of Algerian Nationalism', *Third World Quarterly*, 10, 2 April 1988.
Schmitz, C. 'Civil War in Yemen: The Price of Unity', *Current History*, January 1995.

MONOGRAPH

Murphy, M. *Israel and the Palestinians: The Economic Rewards of Peace, CMEIS*, Occasional Paper no. 47, University of Durham, March 1995.

OFFICIAL DOCUMENTS

International Labour Conference, 80th Session, Report of the Director General, Appendix II.
Prospects for Sustainable Development of the Palestinian Economy in the West Bank and Gaza Strip, UNCTAD/DSD/SEU/2, 27 September 1993, Geneva.
Development Options for Regional Cooperation, Government of Israel, October 1994.
ABECOR Report: Saudi Arabia (London, July 1995).
The Private Sector of Saudi Arabia, Committee for Middle East Trade, London, 1994.
ABECOR Report: Iran (London, August 1993).
UNDP Human Development Report (Oxford University Press, 1994).
World Bank Atlas (Washington, 1995).

PERIODICALS

Al-Ahram: Cairo
Arab Press Service
Challenge
Christian Science Monitor
Economist Intelligence Unit (EIU)
The Financial Times

The Financial Times Survey: Kuwait
The Financial Times Survey: Saudi Arabia
The Guardian
International Financial Statistics, and World Bank Debt Tables
Jerusalem Post International
The Jerusalem Report
MEED
The Middle East
Middle East International
Middle East Mirror
Neue Zürcher Zeitung
New Outlook
The Observer
Reuters
Royal United Services Institution (RUSI), *International Security Review*
Strategic Survey
SWB, Summary of World Broadcasts
The Times
Yemen Times

Index

Page numbers in **bold** denote a major section/chapter on the subject; those followed by *n* indicate note.

204

Index